Stopford Augustus Brooke

Sermons Preached in Saint James's Chapel, York Street, London

Stopford Augustus Brooke

Sermons Preached in Saint James's Chapel, York Street, London

ISBN/EAN: 9783337826901

Printed in Europe, USA, Canada, Australia, Japan

Cover: Foto ©Lupo / pixelio.de

More available books at **www.hansebooks.com**

SERMONS

PREACHED IN ST. JAMES'S CHAPEL

YORK STREET, LONDON

FIRST SERIES

BY THE

Rev. Stopford A. Brooke, M.A.

TWELFTH EDITION

LONDON
KEGAN PAUL, TRENCH, & CO., 1 PATERNOSTER SQUARE
1881

CONTENTS.

SERMON I.

THE VICTORY OF FAITH.

PAGE

1 *John* v. 4, 5.—'For whatsoever is born of God overcometh the world: and this is the victory that overcometh the world, *even* our faith. Who is he that overcometh the world, but he that believeth that Jesus is the Son of God?' 1

SERMON II.

THE DENIAL OF S. PETER.

Luke xxii. 61, 62.—'And the Lord turned, and looked upon Peter. And Peter remembered the word of the Lord, how he had said unto him, Before the cock crow, thou shalt deny me thrice. And Peter went out, and wept bitterly.' 14

SERMON III.

THE LESSONS OF THE CHOLERA.

Amos iii. 6.—'Shall a trumpet be blown in the city, and the people not be afraid? Shall there be evil in a city, and the Lord hath not done *it*?' 27

SERMON IV.

THE NATURALNESS OF GOD'S JUDGMENTS.

Luke xiii. 2-4.—'And Jesus answering said unto them, Suppose ye that these Galilæans were sinners above all the Galilæans, because they suffered such things? I tell you, Nay: but, except ye repent, ye shall all likewise perish. Or those eighteen, upon whom the tower in Siloam fell, and slew them, think ye that they were sinners above all men that dwelt in Jerusalem?' 42

SERMON V.

THE TWENTY-THIRD PSALM.

Psalm xxiii. 1-3.—' The Lord *is* my shepherd; I shall not want. He maketh me to lie down in green pastures: He leadeth me beside the still waters. He restoreth my soul: he leadeth me in the paths of righteousness for his name's sake.' 56

SERMON VI.

THE TWENTY-THIRD PSALM.

Psalm xxiii. 4-6.—' Yea, though I walk through the valley of the shadow of death, I will fear no evil: for thou *art* with me; thy rod and thy staff they comfort me. Thou preparest a table before me in the presence of mine enemies: thou anointest my head with oil; my cup runneth over. Surely goodness and mercy shall follow me all the days of my life: and I will dwell in the house of the Lord for ever.' 71

SERMON VII.

THE VIRGIN'S CHARACTER.

Luke i. 46-55.—' And Mary said, My soul doth magnify the Lord, and my spirit hath rejoiced in God my Saviour. For he hath regarded the low estate of his handmaiden: for, behold, from henceforth all generations shall call me blessed. For he that is mighty hath done to me great things; and holy *is* his name. And his mercy *is* on them that fear him from generation to generation. He hath shewed strength with his arm; he hath scattered the proud in the imagination of their hearts. He hath put down the mighty from *their* seats, and exalted them of low degree. He hath filled the hungry with good things; and the rich he hath sent empty away. He hath holpen his servant Israel, in remembrance of *his* mercy; as he spake to our fathers, to Abraham, and to his seed for ever.' 83

SERMON VIII.

THE DEVELOPMENT OF CHRIST THROUGH THE INFLUENCES OF HOME.

Luke ii. 51.—' And he went down with them, and came to Nazareth, and was subject unto them: but his mother kept all these sayings in her heart.' 95

Contents.

SERMON IX.
THE DEVELOPMENT OF CHRIST THROUGH THE INFLUENCES OF OUTWARD NATURE.

Luke ii. 40.—'And the child grew, and waxed strong in spirit, filled with wisdom: and the grace of God was upon him.' . . . 108

SERMON X.
THE INTELLECTUAL DEVELOPMENT OF CHRIST.

Luke ii. 52.—'And Jesus increased in wisdom and stature, and in favour with God and man.' 124

SERMON XI.
THE SPIRITUAL DEVELOPMENT OF CHRIST.

Luke ii. 49.—'And he said unto them, How is it that ye sought me? Wist ye not that I must be about my Father's business?' . . 136

SERMON XII.
JOHN THE BAPTIST, THE INTERPRETER.

Matt. iii. 1.—'In those days came John the Baptist, preaching in the wilderness of Judæa.' 143

SERMON XIII.
DEVOTION TO THE CONVENTIONAL.

Acts vii. 51-53.—'Ye stiffnecked and uncircumcised in heart and ears, ye do always resist the Holy Ghost: as your fathers *did*, so *do* ye. Which of the prophets have not your fathers persecuted? and they have slain them which shewed before of the coming of the Just One; of whom ye have been now the betrayers and murderers: Who have received the law by the disposition of angels, and have not kept *it*.' 164

SERMON XIV.
DEVOTION TO THE OUTWARD.

John xviii. 36.—'Jesus answered, My kingdom is not of this world: if my kingdom were of this world, then would my servants fight, that I should not be delivered to the Jews: but now is my kingdom not from hence.' 180

SERMON XV.

THE RELIGION OF SIGNS.

PAGE

Luke xi. 29.—'And when the people were gathered thick together, he began to say, This is an evil generation : they seek a sign ; and there shall no sign be given it, but the sign of Jonas the prophet.' . . 192

SERMON XVI.

INDIVIDUALITY.

Luke ix. 24.—'For whosoever will save his life shall lose it : but whosoever will lose his life for my sake, the same shall save it.' . . 207

SERMON XVII.

THE CREATION.

Genesis i. 1.—'In the beginning God created the heaven and the earth.' 222

SERMON XVIII.

THE BAPTISM OF CHRIST.

Matt. iii. 13.—'Then cometh Jesus from Galilee to Jordan unto John, to be baptized of him.' 236

SERMON XIX.

THE FORTY DAYS IN THE WILDERNESS.

Matt. iv. 1.—'Then was Jesus led up of the spirit into the wilderness to be tempted of the devil.' 251

SERMON XX.

THE TRANSFIGURATION.

Luke ix. 28-33.—'And it came to pass about an eight days after these sayings, he took Peter and John and James, and went up into a mountain to pray. And as he prayed, the fashion of his countenance was altered, and his raiment *was* white *and* glistening. And, behold, there talked with him two men, which were Moses and Elias : Who appeared in glory, and spake of his decease which he should accomplish at Jerusalem. But Peter and they that were with him were heavy with sleep: and when they were awake, they saw his glory, and the two men that stood with him. And it came to pass, as they departed from him, Peter said unto Jesus, Master, it is good for us to be here: and let us make three tabernacles; one for thee, and one for Moses, and one for Elias: not knowing what he said.' 262

SERMON XXI.

THE ASCENSION.

John vi. 62.—' *What* and if ye shall see the Son of man ascend up where he was before?' 274

SERMON XXII.

THE FESTIVAL OF ALL SAINTS.

Revelation vii. 9.—' After this I beheld, and, lo, a great multitude, which no man could number, of all nations, and kindreds, and people, and tongues, stood before the throne, and before the Lamb, clothed with white robes, and palms in their hands.' . . . 290

SERMON XXIII.

ANGELIC LIFE AND ITS LESSONS.

Hebrews i. 7.—' And of the angels he saith, Who maketh his angels spirits, and his ministers a flame of fire.' 304

SERMON XXIV.

ANGELIC LIFE IN CONNECTION WITH MAN.

Hebrews i. 14.—' Are they not all ministering spirits, sent forth to minister for them who shall be heirs of salvation?' . . . 318

SERMON XXV.

ISAAC'S CHARACTER.

Genesis xxxv. 27-29.—' And Jacob came unto Isaac his father unto Mamre, unto the city of Arbah, which *is* Hebron, where Abraham and Isaac sojourned. And the days of Isaac were an hundred and fourscore years. And Isaac gave up the ghost, and died, and was gathered unto his people, *being* old and full of days: and his sons Esau and Jacob buried him.' 333

SERMONS.

THE VICTORY OF FAITH.

1 John v. 4, 5.

It would be very interesting if we could have an hour's conversation with an intelligent Pharisee or Sadducee of the time of our Lord, and find out the way in which this religious revival among the poorer Jews appeared to their judgment. There must have been sarcastic Sadducees who had a kind of compassionate admiration mingled with their scorn, for the enthusiasm of the fisher-folk, and who, men of the world, and alive to all the movements of humanity, looked at 'the sect of Jesus' with a slight touch of intellectual interest, as a curious psychological phenomenon.

There must have been some keen political doctors among the Pharisees, zealous, but not too zealous, such as we may infer Gamaliel was, who were interested in all religious movements, and examined them with tolerance and historical curiosity.

We may imagine, without any improbability, that the judgment of both these men would be pretty much the same, though arrived at by different paths. 'This will not last,' they would say; 'enthusiasm so imprudent will burn itself away in contact with the general indifference, or, if it go further, will be burnt up by a vigorous opposition. This man Jesus, if he persists in his denunciations of our parties (and many of them are on the whole deserved), will become a trouble to us, and an object of hatred to our fanatics. We shall get rid of him, and when the head of the movement is gone, it will fall to pieces. It is unfortunate that his death is inevitable, for he is a good man; but what are you to do with an enthusiast, who is so pitifully ignorant of the world?'

So Gamaliel may have spoken, and then, after the Crucifixion, congratulated himself on his knowledge of the world.

For nearly two months not a single event would disturb his intellectual self-confidence. Probably he would hear some rumour of the Resurrection, at which he would smile with scorn; he would hear at least, as a fact, that the disheartened followers of the Crucified had gone back to their usual work in Galilee, and that all had ended quietly. When suddenly the whole matter took a new form. Gamaliel heard that these fishermen and their followers, about a hundred in all, had actually come forward in Jerusalem, more enthusiastic than ever, proclaiming that the man Jesus was the Messiah, that He had risen from the dead, that He was now ascended into heaven, and called by their voice on all men to believe in Him as Lord and Christ; that three thousand had been carried away by the first sermon, that numbers were joining the party every day, and that an absolute wonder had been worked,—the lame man, whom he knew well, into whose hand at the Beautiful gate he had so often dropt an alms, had suddenly been cured in the name of Jesus.

'This is a curious phenomenon,' he would say, 'and worth my study. It does not follow the usual course of religious revivals; its novelty is interesting. But there is nothing to give it endurance if the blind zeal of our religious bigots does not add strength to the movement. It may be pushed by persecution into importance, I shall go to the Sanhedrim and modify their folly.'

So, calling his pupil Saul, in whom he had much confidence, Gamaliel went to the council, and heard with great gravity the examination of Peter and John. When it was over and the council were alone, he made a politic speech, excellent for its end, and interesting to us for the vein of concealed irony against his fellow-counsellors, and the intellectual scorn for the Apostles, with which it was pervaded.

'Ye men of Israel,' he said, 'take heed to yourselves what ye intend to do as touching these men. For before these days rose up Theudas, boasting himself to be somebody; to whom a number of men, about four hundred, joined themselves; who was slain; and all, as many as obeyed him, were scattered, and brought to nought. After this man rose up Judas of Galilee in the days of the taxing, and drew away much people after him: he also perished; and all, even as many as obeyed him, were dispersed. And now I say unto you, Refrain from these men, and let them alone: for if this counsel or this work be of men, it will come to nought: but if it be of God, ye cannot overthrow it; lest haply ye be found even to fight against God.'

Nothing could be happier than this speech, and Gamaliel left the Sanhedrim content with himself. Walking home with Saul, he may have recapitulated it to his pupil. 'There have been,' he would say, 'two revivals already in these times of excitement, and they have both broken down. I see no reason, but the contrary, why this should last longer than the rest. I grant that it is distinct from the others in origin and manner. It is not political, nor does it appeal to popular sympathies, but that only makes it more sure of failure. The only man of real power in it is dead; this resurrection is too absurd even to speak of; the principles on which the movement is founded, such as I heard to-day from those enthusiasts, who spoke surprisingly well, will bring them into opposition with the whole world. They oppose both our parties. The Sadducees will resent the notion of a new religion, and will employ the weapon of contemptuous scorn against their assertion of a resurrection. The fanaticism of our Pharisees, from which I have not been able, Saul, even to set you free, will persecute them from city to city, hating especially that success with the common people, which is so antagonistic to the priestly power for which I do not care. Moreover, if these men be allowed to go on, we shall all be proved to be wrong in permitting the death of Jesus; indeed they stated as much to-day. At present the Roman world does not heed them; but if they should persist in warring against us, they will stir up the Jewish mob against them, riots will take place, and Rome will punish them as disturbers of public order; and once Rome begins, she will make an end of them—the iron nation is not scrupulous.'

So might Gamaliel at that time have spoken, and there are hundreds of political men among us who would have said, in his place, exactly the same things. But that which must have entirely, in his eyes, destroyed the possibility of the success of the Christian movement was the determined attack which, led by his own pupil, it began some years after to make upon the whole fabric of paganism in the country and of paganism and infidelity in the towns of the empire. 'These few wanderers are contending right in the teeth of the genius of the age, right in the teeth of the spirit of the whole world. They intend to prove that Greek, Jew, Roman, Asiatic, Alexandrian, are all wrong. They aver —and this is most ridiculous—that their religion will suit all these diverse nations. Do they imagine that they can revolutionize the whole of society, of thought, of feeling, the habits, manners, and customs of centuries? It is exquisite absurdity.'

Absurd as it seemed, it was the very thing they set themselves to do, not only without a shadow of despair, but with a triumphant security of victory. Nor was it with any blindness of enthusiasm that they began. They were not like men who rush with audacity upon a danger because they are ignorant of it. They had counted the cost, and they went forward fully aware of their work. Their Master had impressed upon their mind that they would be most victorious (and it was an original declaration), when they were apparently most defeated. They quietly accepted this position, and with unexampled hardihood presented a front of a few unlearned men and weak women to the onslaught of the world. Not an eyelid wavered, not a heart sank, as they went to battle, knowingly to die, but in death, they knew, to conquer. Listen to S. John: 'Whatsoever is born of God, overcometh the world.' And the strange thing is that, born of God, they did overcome the world; the whole body of the old society of Judaism and of Heathenism actually crumbled to pieces before these few resolute men.

What was the spell which wrought this wonder? Was it force? They might have had it, like Theudas and Judas, but they would not use it. They remembered their Master's temptation in the wilderness. Their force lay in submission.

Was it cunning diplomacy? Fraud? It is impossible to impute these to the character of any of the Apostles. Imagine S. Peter playing the diplomatist or S. Paul the part of By-ends! They were, on the contrary, extremely imprudent.

Was it intellectual acumen by which they did their work? They did not possess it, and, by itself, they depreciated it. It was by a greater power than any of these—by the power of faith. 'This is the victory that overcometh the world, even our faith.'

Faith, in S. John's idea, is the conquering principle. And this not only in religion, but in common life. For Christian faith is not a thing apart from our nature, and imposed upon it from without; it is the expansion of an original quality; it is the spiritualization of a natural quality; it is the daily faith by which we live brought into contact with the highest possible subject and in the contact with the Divine made divine. So glorified, it overcomes the world. But even unglorified, it has this overcoming power. No one conquers without it.

That is not true, perhaps you say. It is not faith, but prudence and skill and wealth which are victorious. In war, for instance, 'Heaven is on the side of the best artillery.' I reply, first, that prudence is a form of faith; secondly, that I have not said that in such a matter as war faith *alone* conquers; but that faith is necessary for conquest. Take away belief in their cause, or belief in their general, from the soldiers, and all the skill and money and artillery are useless. The men will fight languidly, or run away.

Moreover, a better appointed army, better munitions of war, are in themselves a proof of a higher foregoing faith of the nation, in itself, in its genius, and in the end to be attained.

Nor is it always numbers and the best artillery which conquer. Frederick the Great, with a few intervals, believed in his success, and his soldiers believed in him, and he maintained himself by this faith, almost alone against Europe.

On the whole, the victory falls in the end to those who have the largest amount of faith. In the end, I say, for we must not expect faith always to win at once. It acts on the *spirits* of men—a slow process—and produces chiefly that perseverance which refuses to own itself beaten. It may be overcome again and again, but it finally exhausts the force which has nothing spiritual to back it. Italy had faith in its liberation and unity, but it was crushed in 1848. Of what use was its faith? But look forward twenty years, and see what faith has done, and we have our answer.

In one way or another, all the greatest things are done by it; but whether it be lastingly victorious or not, depends upon the quality of the faith, whether it be in opposition to the spirit of the world, or on the side of the world. If it be the latter, Faith will probably win its victory quickly; if the former, slowly. But the victory of the latter will be short-lived, of the former eternal.

The faith which carried Mahometanism over a fourth part of the globe was a faith which linked itself to the powers of the world—force and fraud. The faith which was victorious in Christianity abjured, in idea at least, the powers of the world, and on the whole continues to abjure them, and the result is that, though not so rapidly successful as Mahometanism, it is growing stronger as Mahometanism grows weaker.

For faith is a noble and spiritual quality, and when it is bound to ignoble and worldly things, it suffers as the living body tied to the dead by the tyrant; it corrupts and dies. Then it is that the powers of the world to which faith gave for a time a semblance of life betray at once, when it is dead, their own innate death.

But the most victorious faith is that which has to do, not with ideas, but with a person, for then the deepest heart-passion comes in to give a living soul to faith. S. Paul saw this truth when he spoke of faith which worketh by love.

But, as above, so in this case also, the lastingness of the victory of faith depends on the nobility of the person believed in. Nothing shatters life so completely, nothing so makes a desert of the world, as the discovery of the meanness or impurity of those in whom we have believed. Nothing makes life so victorious as finding that the object of our faith continues great and good.

Christianity meets both these needs of our nature. It does not say, Believe in ideas, but believe in Christ, and it manifests Christ as the unalterable goodness. Who is he that overcometh? Even he that believeth that Jesus is the Christ.

To believe in Jesus as the Christ, what does it mean? It means to believe in perfect humanity, in God in man.

Most of us believe in exactly the contrary. We believe in roguery, in suspicion, in selfishness, in every man having his price, in the vanity, folly, and sinfulness of humanity. Half our actions—God forbid I should say the whole!—are built upon this miserable faith; and it is nothing more, in spite of its orthodoxy, than a hearty belief in the devil in man.

Now one part of faith in Christ is to deny all that; is to believe that the true humanity is *not that*, but something quite different—the humanity, namely, which was lived out long ago in Palestine.

Such a faith will overcome the world and the worldly

spirit. Believe in the devil in man, and we are slaves of the world, forced to use its powers and its means to live, forced to meet selfishness by selfishness, suspicion by suspicion, lying by lying. Every day we degrade and are degraded.

Believe in Christ, in God in man, and we rise above the world and the use of the world. We meet selfishness by love, suspicion by confidence, lying by truth. We grow better, and we make men better. We have a hope for the race, by which we live ourselves and in which we can live for others. Our eyes are opened to see the goodness in men. The drunken sailors of Columbus saw nothing in the carved wood, and the strange bird, and the floating seaweed, for the tyranny of the present, fear and suspicion, were upon them; but the calm figure watching on the prow saw in them—America.

And he who is drunk with the present, who believes only in the world in the heart of man, sees nothing in the waifs and strays of nobility, self-sacrifice, and endurance which are cast up before him in the lives of even the worst of the race. They are not prophetic to him. But to us who know and believe in the sinless humanity which has been, they speak of the final perfection of the race, of that new world wherein dwelleth righteousness. We have in our faith 'the substance of things hoped for, the evidence of things not seen.'

Again, to believe in Christ is not to believe in ideals, but in ideals realized in a human life. The great philosophers of the ancient world believed in love, truth, justice, and purity. They aspired to reach them and retain them, but they swept away from their embrace like phantom forms of cloud before a rushing wind. For beautiful as their ideal was, it had no heart, no life, no human reality. No human love could be given to it. It was not bound up with social or domestic life. Faith in it produced little, for it was not a faith which worked by human love. Hence the life of the noblest heathen was a desperate effort to realize the mighty dreams and longings of the heart. It was not altogether in vain. God must have satisfied in another world that lofty passion of desire. I have often fancied with delight the rapture of Socrates, Plato, Zeno, when the truth and the light they had been toiling all their lives to find burst upon them in the revelation of the Word made flesh; but here, on earth, there ever came after their brightest vision an encroaching shadow of doubt in which aspiration sank down, trembling with cold and palsy-stricken. They had nothing absolutely perfect in human nature on which to build their faith, no ground for assurance of human attainment in a human life which had attained and triumphed. But *we* have, and it is shame and sorrow if we do not walk worthy of our knowledge.

God has recognized that it was necessary for the victoriousness of faith that the ideals of human nature should be embodied in a perfect personality, capable of being profoundly loved; so He gave us the revelation of a human God, faith in whom is rooted and grounded in love. The difference between our feeling in reading the vague ideality of Shelley's aspirations, and in reading the practical realization of love in the Gospel story, represents almost exactly the difference between the faith of the Greek, who wanted a Divine Person to love, and the faith of the Christian, for whom that want has been satisfied.

Lastly. Faith in Christ overcomes not only the world without, but the spirit of the world within our hearts.

He who believes in perfect love, and loves it in the Saviour, *cannot* live the life of selfishness. He is borne spontaneously above it. He who lives in adoration of an invisible character cannot live in and for the sensual and the visible alone. The love of money and its curse of gnawing restlessness; the love of frivolity and its curse, a vain and petty soul; the love of excitement and its curse, exhausted energies and drear satiety; religious moroseness and its curse, a lonely and hateful life; devotion to the transient and its curse, the grave; over all these the believer in Christ must, he cannot help it, soar triumphant.

For the world overcomes us, or we the world. Here is death come to claim you, and your wealth and position, your work and your enjoyments, all this passing business, to which you gave your whole heart, refuse to have anything to do with your dead body, and naturally have nothing to do with your soul. They come to your bedside to look their last look upon you. They say farewell and go, and you are left alone. In that hour your soul is speechless. In has never learnt anything. The world has overcome you.

But let death come and find you believing in Christ. It is plain that for the loss of all these things you do not specially care, for you have lived above them. You have used them as servants to advance a greater work, as means to realize more fully a glorious world. There is no longer any need of them, for now you enter into the perfect work and the perfect world. They come to your bedside to say farewell. You dismiss them with the smile of a master, and are grateful that you have enjoyed so much. They go to serve another, but you are not alone. You have overcome the world, and another world is yours. You are not leaving home, you are going home. You are not leaving all the charm and movement of society, you are going to live in a more varied and active society than any upon earth. You are not abandoning the masculine pleasure of work and the enthusiasm of production, you are entering into a wider sphere of work with full-grown and creative energies. It is not death but life which is becoming yours; not failure, but victory which sounds its music in your dying ear; the fulness of life, which is love, the fulness of victory, which is the sinless perfection attained in immediate spiritual union with Him through faith in whom on earth you overcame the world.

THE DENIAL OF S. PETER.

S. Luke xxii. 61, 62.

THERE are few histories so touching and so teaching as the history the most striking act of which is narrated in the words which I have read. It has a likeness to an ancient epic, in which the purification of the hero is the goal to which the poem is ever tending.

The story of S. Peter's purification passes through four distinct phases. The first belongs to the night of the last supper. When, on His last evening with the disciples, Judas, the traitor, had left the room, the inner sadness of the soul of Christ came suddenly to the surface. He spoke of His coming departure from them. He told them, deeply moved as they were by His solemnity and sorrow, that they should follow Him afterwards, but not now. It was a moment when quiet listening would have been best; but Peter's impetuous and forward spirit could not be still. He broke in upon the monologue of Christ with eager words: 'Lord, why cannot I follow Thee now? I will lay down my life for Thy sake.'

It had been better had he been silent. The hour was coming when he would want all his force, and he was now expending it in a boast. He had not faced the meaning of his words. True, they were wrung from him by impetuous affection; but what is that affection worth which rises and falls in obedience to the temperature of circumstances? It is not much more than a sentimentalism; the words it utters are a boast, and a boast is not only a proof of weakness of character, but in its expression weakens still more the character. We cannot talk loudly of feeling without exhausting the latent strength of feeling. No man who loves deeply can 'heave his heart into his mouth.' His love is like Cordelia's, 'more richer than his tongue.' Nor can any man boast of his future deeds without endangering his success when the trial comes. 'That a man *well* intends, he'll do it before he speaks.' The boaster has fought a battle against an imaginary foe, and won it, but when the real foe arrives he is surprised at the opposition he encounters. It was easy work in fancy, it is terrible work in reality. The very knowledge that he has boasted confuses him, he is troubled, strikes blindly and flies. So it was with S. Peter. Christ saw the lurking instability, and the Apostle heard amazed the stern rebuke and the prediction: 'Wilt thou lay down thy life for my sake? Before the cock crow, thou shalt deny me thrice.'

The second phase the story passes through is in the garden of Gethsemane.

No doubt S. Peter felt with indignation the reproof of Christ, but he did not believe its bearing. 'Though I die with thee, I will not deny thee.' He seized his sword, and went out into the garden, resolved to prove how much he had been misjudged. All the way there he fought in his fancy for Christ, and delivered Him from His foes. His enthusiasm rose to fever heat.

Then came a pause, during which no circumstance occurred to keep up his excitement. It was night, and the cold chilled the heat of his blood. It was silent among the olive shades, and there seemed no need for all his eagerness. No enemy appeared. He was asked to watch, and not to fight, and being weary, partly through sorrow, partly through excitement, he betrayed his post, and slept, when waking had done more than smiting.

At last the laggard was roused by Christ Himself. 'He that betrayeth me is at hand.' A glare of torches, swords flashing, a mob of men, and Peter's trial came upon him suddenly face to face. He was confused with sleep, he was unprepared to act wisely, he had already broken down. But was all the fine thinking about defence of his Friend to go for nothing? Blindly he raised his sword and struck—impetuously struck, without a moment's thought—struck with a result which, in contrast with the boast and the preparation, was ridiculous.

Again, it had been better had he been still. For resistance was impossible. A blow would do no good, only irritate the men against his Friend. It was constancy, not violence, which was now required. Again, therefore, he earned his Master's quiet rebuke, 'Put up thy sword into its sheath.'

Have you ever seen a man who, having nerved himself for days for some great stroke in life, is suddenly betrayed into striking at the wrong time—too soon for success, or too late for honour? He has put all the concentrated passion of his heart into one blow at the wrong time, and the blow exhausts him utterly. He has no power left. He is thenceforth the prey of circumstances.

Strike as hard as you like at the right time, and everything assists you. The blow, instead of diminishing, redoubles your force; success is parent of success. Strike at the wrong time, or in the wrong manner (and Peter's impetuosity and self-conceit were sure to lead him wrong), and all the virtue goes out of you; you fail, and failure gives birth to failure; your chance is lost, and you become fearful, unbelieving, the victim, for the moment, of any dishonour which may cross your path. So it was with Peter. As high as had been the excitement, so entire now was the exhaustion in the reaction. Fear came in upon him; he turned and fled; and oh! miserable, the brave man became a coward, and the loyal friend a base deserter.

Still Peter did not know his weakness; still did he mistake his impetuosity for power. It may have been an unconscious sense of shame which led him to creep in the distance after his Master. It was more probably conceit of heart. Had he not struck, and struck home, in defence of Christ? He would go and see the end. He did not know that every atom of strength of will had gone, and left him open to any infamy.

We come now to the third phase of this epic—the betrayal and repentance. It took place in the outer court of the high priest's palace.

The Saviour was first brought to the house of Annas, and afterwards sent on to Caiaphas. S. John's account seems to say that S. Peter's first denial took place in the former house. But the 24th verse may be explained as retrospective, and allows us to infer that the first denial, as well as the others, took place in the house of Caiaphas. Into the large open court of the palace Peter was admitted by the influence of S. John. In the midst, as the night was cold, a fire was burning. As the servant opened the door, the light of the lantern fell upon the face of Peter, and the maid seemed to recognize him. When he stood by the fire, she accused him as one of the companions of Christ, and he denied his Lord. He left the betraying light of the fire, and went to the porch. There he was again recognized, and again denied. About an hour afterwards, when the wretched man had returned into the court, another asked him, 'Art thou not also one of them?' and Peter, stung with fear, vehemently denied again, calling God to witness to his lie. At that moment the cock crew, and from one of the chambers which surrounded the inner court and opened into it, through the open door, Peter saw his Master coming forth, who turned and looked upon him. It was too much. All rushed upon him in a moment. He went out, followed by those patient and reproachful eyes—went out and wept bitterly.

It was a cruel sin, and its progress is a type of all sin.

It took its rise from that part of Peter's character which he considered most strong. If in anything he was sure not to fail, it was in passionate constancy to one whom he loved and honoured. If in anything he was confident, it was in his fiery courage. Against all other errors he might watch and pray, but on this side the castle of his soul was inaccessible to evil. So there he left himself unguarded.

Alas! it is up these inaccessible sides of rock that the enemy comes, and, before we are aware, we have admitted the very sin the thought even of which we should have scorned but yesterday. Self enters over the very bulwark of self-devotion. Falsehood comes in over the rampart which truth guards. Sensuality creeps through the postern which pure love has fortified. And once the way is open to one enemy, others come pouring in along with it. The garrison of the soul is taken by surprise. Peter admitted sloth, and after it came dishonour, falsehood to friendship, falsehood to himself, denial of his Master, cowardice, swearing and cursing.

How all that comes home to us! Who has ever boasted and not rued his boast? Who has ever been content with once sinning in a particular way and not gone on, allured by the very horror and danger, as well as by the pleasure and sin, further in the same path? Who has ever admitted one sin and not found himself forced by dire necessity to support that sin by others? A kind of frenzy seems to seize us, and David's adultery is followed by murder, and Saul's jealousy by hatred, and hatred by assassination, and Adam's disobedience by unmanliness and reproach of God, and Demas' love of the world by unfaithfulness to the cause of God. Sin multiplies from itself.

It is trite, but true, 'Avoid the beginnings of evil.' You cannot tell what one hateful thought may end in. Therefore learn this great lesson from S. Peter's guilt —to guard well those avenues of the soul which seem to you the fairest and the nearest passages to God—to be humble, watchful, and prayerful at those very points where you think your character is noblest and your heart most faithful. Hear always in your spirit Christ's words to S. Peter, 'Watch and pray, lest ye enter into temptation.'

Learn this lesson also from the story—that in this world we often stand like Peter in the court, and are called upon to declare our sympathy with our Lord. We despise Peter for his denial. How often have we ourselves acted so, and so denied? You are called upon for your opinion upon a question of principle. You suppress it for fear of men. What is that but saying, 'I know not the man'? You are in a strait between two courses of action; one is right, but it will cause you loss of some dignity or some wealth; one is wrong, wrong *to you*, but it will bring you into Parliament, or give you a fortune. You choose the latter. What is that but the guilt of Peter? You are challenged by men as a believer in Christ, and marked out for ridicule because you will not go with the infidel or the sensualist, and you are silent or deny the accusation. How does that differ from S. Peter's betrayal—'Man, I know not what thou sayest'? There, in the great hall of the world, Christ is being accused and smitten on the face, and we (who in our study, or when danger and difficulty were far away, said to ourselves, 'Though I should die with Thee, I will not deny Thee') now, when we are brought into the open court of life, and, among the crush of scornful men or angry parties, are in fear of losing our prosperity or our social repute—deny Him, abjure Him as our Master! Oh! if it ever should be so with us, and we become so swept away from the region of truth as to deny, in denying Christ, our noble nature, may Christ our Saviour turn and look on us with pitying eyes full of regretful sorrow for our fall, and we go forth and weep bitterly, smitten with the dart of His silent and tender reproach.

We find Peter now convinced of his sin. What were the two outward occurrences which drove home conviction to his heart?

The first was an event which recalled in a moment the prediction of Christ. 'Immediately the cock crew.'

No trumpet of an innocent morn to Peter, but a 'lofty and loud shrilling voice,' which rang 'traitor' in his ear. He had heard the sound a thousand times, and it struck no chord in his heart but one of cheerful life; but now, all came back in a moment—the meeting with the Saviour by the lake, the early friendship so fair and pure, the long discipleship in which he had found himself ennobled, the quiet unwavering love which trained him day by day, the life so holy, harmless, undefiled, yet withal so great in manliness, so bright with courage, the last supper, the talk about betrayal, the eager boast, the sad prediction of denial, the indignant assertion of willingness to die for Christ, the forgetful slumber in the garden, the shameful flight, and now the dark dishonour of a threefold denial of his Master—all, all the past swept in one moment like a storm across his soul. For the first time he saw himself as he was, and shame, burning shame, sorrow, bitter sorrow, invaded his heart all broken with the 'late remorse of love.'

'Immediately the cock crew. *Then* Peter remembered the word of the Lord.'

Make the meaning of this your own. Much of the memory of the past is only waked by coming into contact with those things with which the past has been associated. See once more a river by which you walked in boyhood, hear a song which charmed your youth, and all the past rises from its grave and lives again.

Blessed is he whose life has been pure, on whom the stars smile with the same smile with which they greeted his boyhood, for whom the sea hides no dark memories, in whose ear music is always sweet, who can revisit after years the haunts of the past, and no ghastly phantom come to bring back the exiled memory of guilt to chill his blood and sere his brain.

For there is nothing really dead in this world. You have buried your sin; but it is only buried as the hurried murderer buries the corpse of his victim, with a thin layer of light sand. You pass it by, and inadvertently tread upon the grave. A skeleton arm starts up, and points to heaven and to you.

There is nothing really forgotten. One touch, one sound, one sight, the murmur of a stream, a breaking wave, the sound of a church bell, the barking of a dog heard in the still evening from a hill, a green path in a wood with the sunlight glinting on it, the way of the moon upon the waters, may, at certain moments, turn the heart to stone and fill life with a concentrated agony of remorse. 'Immediately the cock crew. *Then* Peter remembered the word of the Lord; and he went out, and wept bitterly.'

The second circumstance which pierced the heart of Peter was the look of Christ. It is probable that, at the very moment when Peter raised his voice in cursing, Jesus was led out of the hall of Caiaphas and through the court. He heard His disciple's last denial and the crowing of the cock. He turned and looked on Peter.— 'Thou too, who wouldst die with me, thou deniest; thou, the man of rock! my friend, my follower.' The silent glance was vocal with regret and love. And Peter saw the miserable depth of his fall in the look of Christ—saw there not the reproach of anger, but the reproach of tenderness. The arrow of that look went deep. His heart was broken with its pain. He feared no more his enemies, nor danger, nor yet death; for in his own heart he bore a pang deeper than death could give. 'He went out, and wept bitterly.'

Wept bitterly. What were those tears? They were the tears of shame, the tears of the deep remorse of love. How bitter none can tell but those who have denied a love as deep as that of Christ's to Peter; how bitter only those can conceive in degree who have felt, over the death-bed of one who has been neglected while she devoted life to love, that they would give a thousand worlds to hear her voice again and beg of her forgiveness.

Bitter tears they were; but they made him a new man. It was the moment of Peter's true conversion. We have seen him impetuous and brave, but self-conceited and imprudent; we have seen him eager in love and anger, but drifting into neglect of friendship and passing into dishonour. We have seen him as leader of the apostolic group, confessing Christ as the Son of God, and when the hour of trial came, denying Christ as Master and as Friend. We see him now broken in spirit, self-shamed, fallen from his high estate, alone and desolate in heart, leaning against the wall, in the bitter dawn of the spring morning, his whole frame shaken with the weeping of an heroic man. Yes, heroic—for Peter was greater than he had ever been as yet. He passed in those awful tears from the state of childhood to the state of manhood.

It is strange how little we imagine in our youth, when the path of life is woven of the sunbeam and the rainbow, how deeply and bitterly we may yet weep in after life. But till those tears or their equivalent come on us, we are not yet men, but children. Life has not opened to us its terrible but dignifying secrets. We have not yet trodden the inner shrine, the portal of which is kept by sacred sorrow.

This was the hour which had come now to S. Peter. 'A deep distress had humanized his soul.' A deep sorrow had begun within him the formation of the character strong as a rock, on which his brethren and the Church were to repose. A spiritual convulsion had revolutionized his life, and made him into a man.

But such tears may make a hard and bitter man. The tears of remorse may petrify the heart to granite. Manhood comes, but it may be the manhood of contempt of the world, a manhood of scorn and not of tenderness. It was not so with S. Peter. They were not only tears of remorseful love, but tears of penitence. Christ's look was full of sorrow for His Apostle, but full also of ineffable affection. Peter felt he was forgiven, and the bitterness of his tears passed into the indescribable softness of passionate penitence, into the unutterable resolution to be worthy of his Saviour's love. A new life was possible to him, he might yet be counted worthy to die for his Master. And so it was. None was so changed as he. His courage never faltered, his voice never again denied his Lord. His brave words still excite us as we hear them spoken before the Sanhedrim. He testified before kings, he died the martyr of the truth.

O brethren! it should be so with us. When the pain of drear conviction of a lost life or a sinful heart is come upon you, do not go out with Judas into the night of despair; go out with Peter into the chill dawning, with Christ's look of reproachful love within your heart. Learn the meaning of that look, for it means forgiveness. Then remorse will pass into healing penitence. 'A broken and a contrite heart, O God, Thou wilt not despise.' Despise—no! but uplift into power, grace, and holiness. God forgives; and you, touched by the unexpected depth of love into humble but resolute faith, say to your heart, as Peter may have said *after* his tears, My Master, 'though I die for Thee, yet will I never deny Thee.'

The last phase through which this epic passed was by the shores of the lake of Galilee. There the purification of Peter was completed. He had gone back to his old life of fishing with a still heart, full of a noble sorrow. There, where he first had left all to follow the Saviour, he saw Him once again; there, in the dazzling morning light, the well-known figure stood upon the shore. And Peter, impetuous as ever, plunged into the lake to kneel at His sacred feet and worship. There, three times, did Jesus ask him who had denied Him thrice, the question, 'Simon, son of Jonas, lovest thou Me?' and thrice did Peter's heart answer, 'Lord, Thou knowest that I love Thee.' And there the repentance was accepted and secured; thrice did the Saviour by His reply, 'Feed my sheep, feed my lambs,' restore the Apostle to his rank among His followers, and appoint to him his duty.

[Aug. 19, 1866.]

THE LESSONS OF THE CHOLERA.

Amos iii. 5.

THE presence among us of an epidemic as strange as it is deadly, and the special prayer concerning it issued by the order of the Government, make it the duty of the pastors of the Church of England to endeavour, from their pulpits, to divest the mind of the religious public of certain superstitious views which notoriously hinder the labours of men of science to get rid of the plague. For there is no doubt that in all ages there has been as much evil done and as much good prevented during epidemics, by certain theological theories on what are rightly called God's judgments, as there has been good done and evil overcome by the self-denying devotion of those who hold these theories.

In fact, the good they do is less than the evil. Devotion to the sick relieves a few individuals; a superstitious idea leads astray all the souls of a nation for centuries, and retards the salutary work of science.

It is very hard on scientific men that their conscientious obstructors in every age have been those religious men who, from want of faith in a God of order and truth, and from blind cleaving to blind opinions, have opposed instead of assisting those whose objects were the welfare of the race through the discovery of truth.

It is almost too strange to think that the spirit of the inquisitors who condemned Galileo has not yet died out. There are not a few teachers now who excommunicate in thought those who say that the cholera is subject to laws; that the best way to put an end to it is to find out those laws and range ourselves upon their side; and that this investigation and effort are the true prayer to God, and the true way of meeting the judgment of God in pestilence. It is incumbent on every clergyman now to free himself from this party of retrogression, and to endeavour to free his flock from its superstition. We will try, with God's help, to do so to-day.

I speak, first, of the cholera as a judgment.

The home of this dreadful disease is in India. It never, for example, altogether abandons Calcutta. But from thence, and from India in general, it now and then, at varying periods, proceeds westward; sometimes loitering on its course, sometimes turning backwards for a time, but always marching on, till, crossing the Atlantic, it seems to die out in America.

For many years the most remarkable ignorance prevailed about it, and even now we have no accurate acquaintance with its ways. We have no *real* knowledge of how it originates, of the cause of its curious periodicity, of the means whereby it is propagated. Different theories account for different outbreaks, but none are sufficient to explain all the outbreaks which have taken place. Nor have we any knowledge how to cure it.

The medicine which relieves one patient seems to increase the disease of another. Nor can we predict the mode in which the cholera will kill or will affect a patient; nothing, apparently, is so capricious. Some are ill for days, others for a few hours only; some have died, it is said, in incredibly short spaces of time. Some have acute pain, others have very little. Some wrestle out of life, others drift quietly into death. It seems as if death were the result of some subtle poison received in smaller or larger doses, and having the peculiar property of changing its mode of operation in accordance with the particular constitution it attacks.

Now put yourselves back into old Athenian times, and ask what would be the result on the people of such a new phenomenon—of the cause, the cure, and the mode of operation of which they were entirely ignorant. They could refer it to no law; they saw no reason for it or in it. It was so *strange* that it could not be the work of any of their common gods. At once they leaped to the conclusion that it was the doing of some unknown god, whom, in some way or other, they had offended, who had got into a passion with them and was resolved to have his revenge. Hence they strove to propitiate him by sacrifice and prayer. The story goes that, at least once, they let loose some sheep from the Areopagus and wherever the wandering animals lay down, built an altar to the unknown deity and sacrificed them to appease his wrath. One thing they did *not* do. They did not try to investigate the causes of the disease; they did not collect facts about it. They assumed it was supernatural, instead of assuming it was natural.

Such was the style of thought and theology in vogue among the heathen.

Ours, of course, is entirely different from that of these 'benighted idolaters.' We, who know God as the unalterable, the uncapricious, whose unchangeable love constitutes unchangeable law, we do not impute this plague of which we know nothing, and the strangeness of which seems to separate it from other diseases, to a caprice on the part of God which He will remove on our imploring Him to let us off.

Yet, wonderful to say, if we do not do that exactly, we do something so very like it that I have no hesitation in saying that, considering our additional light, a part of our religious world is guilty, with regard to the cholera, of grosser superstition than the Athenians.

Ignorant of how it comes, looking at its suddenness of slaughter, its curious partiality, its horrible strangeness, we separate it from other diseases which we are content to consider natural, and refer it to a supernatural origin. We talk, and pray, and teach, as if it had no natural cause, obeyed no natural laws. We call it, theologically, not religiously, a judgment of God, and we use the term with a supernatural meaning attached to it. We called the small-pox a judgment of God in this supernatural sense till we found out vaccination. We called the famine in Ireland a judgment of God in this supernatural sense till we arrived by investigation at its real causes. A boat goes out from a seaport town on Sunday; it is overturned, and the crew are drowned. Next Sunday the pulpit tells you it was a judgment of God on the men for breaking the Sabbath, and though a hundred other boats have gone and returned in safety, the preachers repudiate the notion that the boat went down because the men were careless or because it was struck by a squall. It is astonishing to think how widely English theological thought is leavened with this superstition. Surely, surely, Christian men might have learned enough from the words of Christ and from science as the interpreter of His will, to have passed beyond Jewish and heathen thought and to have attained a higher region.

We judge, and judge rightly, a mode of thinking by its results. What are the results of this superstition?

According to its theory, the cholera is supernatural. 'Nothing will stop it, then, but prayer; for we cannot by natural means attack the supernatural.' So, as history has often shown us, all energy is diminished, all effort against the evil is crushed. Fortunately, though the supernatural theory is taught, it is not generally acted upon. It is good for exciting fear, religious excitement, and for hiding from men's eyes the real evils which the cholera points out to us as deserving of God's anger. It is good for nothing else. Indeed it is good for nothing. It creates a miserable fear and terror. No one knows that he may not have committed the unknown sin which is the cause of the cholera; and every sect according to its hatreds, and every one according to his prejudices, lays down a different sin as that cause. Men are thrown into a state of vague dread and confusion of mind. Some become abject and fly; others become reckless and licentious—eat and drink, for to-morrow they die. Their religion is a religion of fear and ignorance—the true definition of superstition. God is regarded as a foe who is to be bought off or coaxed by prayer to give up His wrath. He is spoken to as if He were liable to sudden incursions of anger, subject to our passions and our weakness, as if He were the God of disorder and not of order, of special providences and not of law.

These are the evil results, on life, action, and theology, which have in all ages flowed from this superstition and which condemn it; and though they do not present themselves now in the same strongly outlined aspect (a result we owe to scientific men), yet they still exist and their source exists.

Is there no truth, then, in the phrase, 'A judgment of God'? Yes; plenty of truth.

These things—famine, pestilence, revolution, war—*are* judgments of the Ruler of the world. What sort of a Ruler, we ask, is He? The answer to that question will determine the true sense of the term, a judgment of God. The heathen saw Him as a passionate, capricious, changeable Being, who could be angered and appeased by men. The Jewish prophets saw Him as a God whose ways were equal, who was unchangeable, whose decrees were perpetual, who was not to be bought off by sacrifices but pleased by righteous dealing, and who would remove the punishment when the causes which brought it on were taken away: in their own words, when men repented, God would repent. That does not mean that He changed His laws to relieve them of their suffering, but that they changed their relationship to His laws, so that, to them thus changed, God *seemed* to change. A boat rows against the stream; the current punishes it. So is a nation violating a law of God; it is subject to a judgment. The boat turns and goes with the stream; the current assists it. So is a nation which has repented and put itself into harmony with God's law; it is subject to a blessing. But the current is the same; it has not changed, only the boat has changed its relationship to the current. Neither does God change—we change; and the same law which executed itself in punishment now expresses itself in reward.

Such a God as this, so represented by the Jewish prophets, must rule the world in an orderly manner. His judgments could not be arbitrary. Each judgment was connected with its proper cause, and was the result of the violation of a particular law or set of laws. In its execution God pointed out the causes which had brought it on, and said, Change those causes; repent of those transgressions of my laws. Find out my laws and accord with them your action, and my judgment will become to you not punishment but blessing.

Now all this, long ago manifested in the prophetical teaching, is the very thing which science teaches. Take the case of an epidemic. The scientific man says, ' It has its own causes and its own conditions. Remove the causes, change the conditions, and you will destroy the epidemic. All that is wanted is investigation, questioning of the facts. The existence of the disease is a proof of the existence of some evil which ought to be rooted out.'

So said the scientific man, unconsciously teaching us,

when we had nigh forgotten it, that God is a God of order and love. But sometimes enamoured of his laws and his results, he refused to see God at all in the universe; and, going as far in his incredulity as the theologian in his superstition, smiled at the declaration of a pestilence being a judgment of God. It is nothing, he said, nothing but natural laws working out their results.

Brethren, the Christian believes it to be much more. He says to the physician, 'You speak truth so far as you go. I accept your teaching, with all its results. But there is something more. These natural laws, these series of causes and effects, are ordered by a Divine intelligence and a moral will. Their violation is a transgression, but the moment man becomes aware that evil follows on their violation, it is not only a transgression but a sin. Moral guilt attends the nation which refuses to take measures for the extinguishing of disease. It is not only, then, the sense of physical disorder, but also the conscience, which these judgments appeal to. We find ourselves not only in the presence of mere law, we are brought into the presence of God. The materialist, in calling on us to remedy these national evils, can only appeal to one part of our nature, that part which loves comfort or dreads death, or is pained by the suffering of others. We can take up the materialist's position, and appeal to something further—to the profound sense of right or wrong in man, and to that spiritual motive which is born of desire to obey a loving Father. Hence we are anxious to say, These judgments are *God's* judgments. He is displaying His justice in punishment;

but the very punishment itself is a proof of His love. For the disease does not only punish evils, it points them out; it discloses to us the evils we were ignorant of, in order that we may remedy them. This is God's love in judgment.

Let me apply these principles to the cholera. Science would not accept the superstitious teaching of the theologian. It set itself to work on the facts of the cholera. It learnt something of its mode of propagation; it discovered some of the conditions which either increase or diminish its virulence. And as this knowledge developed itself, we saw that the cholera *was* a judgment of God. We saw that the conditions in which it developed itself were national sins. It laid its finger on the disgrace of England, the canker which eats into the heart of our nation—the neglected state of our poor. It said to us, Look *there*, and repent, and do works meet for repentance. For where does the cholera take its dreadful march most unresisted, and do its dreadful work most easily? Not among the rich, the well-housed, and the comfortable, but in places where our sinful neglect has left the poor crowded together like negroes in the Middle Passage; where the commonest sanitary arrangements are so passed over, that the air is a mist of foul and pestilential vapour; where the water is all tainted with unspeakable filth; where to relieve thirst with water is to produce disease or death by poison (when we complain of the drunkenness of the lower classes, we ought first to examine the water they have to drink); where the dust-heaps remain for weeks piled up against the windows; where the cholera finds weakened bodies, starved frames, ignorant, fear-enslaved minds on which to work its will. It is here that the plague revels. These are the conditions of its virulence; and the existence of these things is the national sin which God is judging, and of which He is warning us now and has warned us again and again.

And what have we been doing in obedience to this warning? We have been expelling the poor to build houses of justice, and to make city improvements. We give £2 compensation to enable them to pay their rent for six weeks, and then we leave them to find a place to live in, in courts where already families of six and eight are crushed into a single room. The lawyers have not air enough in Westminster Hall, but we think the poor have air enough in a house where forty people live in eight lumber rooms. We compensate the farmers for the loss of their cattle lest our great landowners should be forced to reduce the rent, but no one dreams of compensating the poor for the loss of the roof which covers them. The boards, vestries, and other dead bodies in whose hands such matters lay are incompetent to meet the difficulties which overwhelm them. It is time that Parliament should interfere and do the work they cannot do. The new Sanitary Act makes overcrowding a nuisance; but till we force railway companies, city mprovers, and Government works to build houses for those whom they dispossess—till we really face the fact that there is not room for our poor in London; and build for them—that part of the Act can never be enforced.

Again. It has been proved over and over again that it is want of a continual supply of pure water which is the fruitful cause not only of cholera but of half the diseases which decimate the poor. Many of the courts in London have no water laid on, and the inhabitants are forced to drink of pestilential wells, or from cisterns so foul that they are centres of disease. There is a general wish to remedy this, but no real vigorous interest is taken in the question. We can only hope it may be settled in the time of our grandchildren.

'Shall not I visit for these things? saith the Lord.' Yes; He is visiting us, and He will visit us again and again with cholera, till we learn what it means and do the necessary work of repentance. We keep the conditions of disease close at hand, we actually increase them. We keep up with insane selfishness our nurseries of cholera, typhus, and consumption, and then, when cholera comes, we institute a day of special prayer, and go off to our country-houses contentedly. That is not religion, but a mockery of God; for a national prayer without national exertion to remedy national evils is simply a national insult to God. There is much of individual self-devotion, of individual liberality, but we want more than that. Individual effort is nothing against our enormous evils, aggravated by an enormous population; it is the stroke of a reed against the shield of a giant. God calls upon us to repair our national wrongs by a national effort. That is the great religious lesson of the cholera; not at all to repent of our peculiar sins, of our neglect of God—that is quite true in its place; but *the* religious lesson of the cholera is that we and our representatives should rouse from our stupor upon these things, and legislate for the remedy of evils which are at once the curse and the weakness of the nation.

I trust—I trust we shall do this, and not go on sinning, and talking repentance to God in national prayers, with words which mean nothing while .we do nothing. It is astonishing that our prayer takes no notice of these things, that it does not ask God—since it is a special prayer for special gifts, of use under our special circumstances—to open the minds of men to see the evils which are corroding the bones of the nation, to put it into the hearts of men of mark to speak in Parliament of these evils, to give us wisdom and power to legislate wisely, to give us large ideas and energy to carry them out, to give us that power of organization, the want of which is our great failing; to inspire the scientific men of the nation with keener intellect and insight to discover the remedy of the disease, and to enable us all to see the causes of the cholera and to stamp them out.

I believe cholera could be diminished in the same proportion as small-pox has been, by destroying the conditions in which it becomes deadly to life. Years ago, in Cheshire, some new plants, quite unknown beforehand to the country, sprang up beside the canals by which the salt was carried and in the pools around the salt-works. The people did not know what to make of this phenomenon. At last, some one who had lived by the seaside recognized the plants as the very ones which haunt the ledges of the rocks just above the flow of the tide, but within the wash of the spray. Then the thing was clear. The germs of the plants had been from year to year borne by the wind or carried by birds to that place, but the conditions under which they could grow had not arisen. At last the same conditions which prevailed on the sea-coast were fulfilled, and the germs which formerly had died took root and grew. Remove those conditions, and though the germs are brought there at intervals, they will not develope into life. Just so it seems to be with cholera. The poisonous germ is in the air, but it is innocuous, does not grow into actual disease unless certain local conditions are satisfied. Of course, once begun thus, it is propagated by contagion to the stomach. But it could not have *begun* at all if the conditions were not ready for its reception; and if we remove these conditions, it will not, unless we are shamefully careless, develope itself at all.

But this is the very thing we will not do; instead thereof, we keep the causes of the development of disease on hand, ready to co-operate with any atmospheric poison there may exist, and then, with an exquisite unconscious irony, we pray that the cholera may be kept far from our borders.

I have said that that sort of prayer, while we do not act against the great evils I have mentioned, is nothing less then an insult to God, and God will not, nay, He cannot, hear our prayer. Prayer of that kind is not the slightest good.

Moreover, it would be a positive evil if God were to take us at our word; for then we should be freed from that judgment which points out the diseased spots in our social organization, as pain points out the spot in our body where disease is settling. Who would ask that pain should not come, and prefer that he should have no warning of the disease which is about to kill him? And yet we have been asking God to leave us in ignorant carelessness and without warning of our national diseases. Better far to ask for the cholera to come (if we only could save some of the thousands who must be sacrificed to teach us our duty—a dreadful thought, which should make us easy-going people shudder and tremble when we think of the reckoning God will require at our hands for all these lives), better far to ask that the cholera should come, than that we should remain as we are. Better far to have the cholera, if it produces action against our wrong-doing and our neglect, than not to have it. For what is it which has roused us to do what we have done, little as it is? What is it that has been the cause of our efforts to improve the condition of the poor? Why, God's judgments—cholera, typhus, diphtheria, which are not quite content with feeding on the wretched, but come and knock at our fine houses, and wake us with death's cry to our duty. By the lessons which every visitation of cholera has taught us, the death-rate has been permanently diminished—but oh! by how much less than it might—from year to year. And now it has come again. It has *not* been kept far from our borders. God is calling us to awake to work, and warning us how little we have done. His judgment touches our evils in the clearest manner. We cannot be blind unless we blind ourselves by selfishness and want of thought. I do trust not a year will pass by without some effort on the part of Government to call the nation to the only repentance worth having—a united effort to remedy the condition of the poor. If not, we shall have the cholera again, and we shall deserve it, and all the prayers in the world will not guard our shores against it.

One word more. We have neglected our duties as a nation; do not let us neglect them as individuals. Let us labour to spread true views of this subject, labour to overcome ignorance and stupidity. Let us give largely to help the exertions of overworked physicians. Let us give largely to succour the poor, the bereaved, the weakened convalescent. Above all, let us do all in our power to prevent this sanitary excitement, usually so miserably short-lived, from dying out when the danger has passed by. So shall we, at least, have learnt what a judgment of God means—learnt something of the blessed truth hidden in that strange but deep utterance of the old prophet—' Shall there be evil in a city, and the Lord hath not done it ?'

[Dec. 1, 1867.]

THE NATURALNESS OF GOD'S JUDGMENTS.

Luke xiii. 2—4.

LAST year, during the prevalence of the cholera, we spoke of it from this place, and of the lessons which it taught us. We then laid down the principle that all the so-called judgments of God were the natural results of violation of laws, and as such always unarbitrary.

The principle is a common one, but it requires to be stated and restated continually, and especially so from the pulpit. First, because it is explicitly or implicitly denied by a large number of religious persons, to the great detriment, I believe, of religion; and secondly, because in establishing it firmly we get rid of nearly all that sets scientific men in opposition to religious men.

Now the principle that every judgment of God is connected, in the way of ordinary cause and effect, with the sin or error therein condemned, destroys at once the notion that plague or famine are judgments upon us for infidelity, or rationalism, or sabbath-breaking, or our private sins, for there is plainly no natural connection between the alleged sin and the alleged punishment. For example, the town which takes due sanitary precautions may refuse to give one penny to missions, but it will not be visited by a virulent outbreak of cholera.

The town which takes no sanitary precautions, but gives £10,000 a-year to missions, will, in spite of its Christian generosity, become a victim to the epidemic. The lightning will strike the ship of the good man who chooses to sail without a lightning-conductor, it will spare the ship of the atheist and the blasphemer who provides himself with the protecting rod. The cattle plague will not touch the cattle of the most active Roman Catholic in England if his quarantine is exclusive enough, while it will destroy all the cows of the best Protestant in the country if he be careless of their isolation. We may sin as much as we please in our own persons, but we shall escape cholera as much as we shall escape famine if we discover the source of contagion and guard against it.

There is, then, always a natural connection between the sin and the punishment, and the punishment points out its own cause. To follow the guiding of its finger is to discover the evil, and, when discovered, to rectify it. But we assume a supernatural cause and the evil remains hidden from us. There is no hope of success till we act upon the principle which is here laid down.

It is my intention this morning to show the truth of this principle in other spheres than that of epidemic disease. If we can manifest its universality, we go far to prove its truth. Take as the first illustration the case of the Moral Law.

The ten commandments appear at first sight to be arbitrary rules of conduct. Why should we not kill a man when he has injured us? Why should we not steal when we are in want? Many a savage community has argued in this way, and we do not want for isolated instances of the same feeling in civilized societies. But as civilization increased, the commands of the Decalogue were felt to be right, not only because they were re-echoed by an inward voice, but also because they were proved to be necessary for the progress of humanity. They were commanded, then, not only because of their agreement to eternal right, but also because of their necessity. Some of them were in very early times clearly seen as needful—the sacredness of an oath, the sacredness of human life, the sacredness of property; on the other hand, it has taken centuries to show that polytheism is a destructive element to national greatness. Others were not so clearly seen to be just. 'Thou shalt not covet' seemed to make a great deal out of nothing; but experience taught men, though slowly, that inordinate desire for the goods of another was the most fruitful source of violation of social rights. Again, to reconcile the fourth commandment with a natural feeling of right has been a puzzle to many. But men saw, as the labour of the world increased, the naturalness of a day of rest and its necessity for human nature. It was seen to be commanded not of caprice on the part of God, but because it was needful for humanity. The commandments have force, therefore, not because they are commanded by a God of power, but because they are either needful for, or natural to, human nature.

Nor is the judgment which follows on their violation any more arbitrary than the laws themselves. As they have their root in our nature so they have their punishment in our nature. Violate a moral law and our

God's Judgments. 45

constitution protests through our conscience. Sorrow awakes, remorse follows, and remorse is felt in itself to be the mark of separation from God. The punishment is not arbitrary, but natural. Moreover, each particular violation of the moral law has its own proper judgment. The man who is dishonest in one branch of his life soon feels dishonesty—not impurity, not anything else but dishonesty—creep through his whole life and enter into all his actions. Impurity has its own punishment, and that is increasing corruption of heart. Each sin has its own judgment and not another's, and the judgment is so naturally linked to the sin that it points out unmistakably what the particular sin is which is punished. The moral pain calls attention to the moral disease. It is the voice of God saying ' *There*, in that thing you are wrong, my child ; do not do it again, do the very opposite.'

Take, again, the intellectual part of man. The necessities for intellectual progress are attention, perseverance, practice. Refuse to submit to these laws and you are punished by loss of memory or inactivity of memory, by failure in your work or by inability to think and act quickly at the proper moment. The intellectual punishments follow as naturally upon violation of the laws of the intellect as sickness does on violation of the laws of health, and they point out as clearly their causes as trembling nerves point out their cause in the indulgence of the drunkard.

Again, take what may be called national laws. These have been, as it were, codified by the Jewish prophets. They were men whose holiness brought them near to God and gave them insight into the diseases of nations. They saw clearly the natural result of these diseases and they proclaimed it to the world. They looked on Samaria, and saw there a corrupt aristocracy, failing patriotism, oppression of the poor, falsification of justice, and they said, God will judge this city, and it shall be overthrown by Assyria. Well, was that an arbitrary judgment? It was of God; but given a powerful neighbour, and a divided people in which the real fighting and working class has been crushed, enslaved, and unjustly treated—and an enervated, lazy, pleasure-consumed upper class, and what is the natural result? Why, that very thing which the prophets called God's judgment. God's judgment was the natural result of the violation of the first of national laws — even-handed justice to all parties in the State. The same principle is true in a thousand instances in history; the national judgments of war, revolution, pestilence, famine, are the direct results of the violation by nations of certain plain laws which have become clear by experience. Unfortunately, men took them to mean a supernatural expression of God's anger, instead of looking for their natural causes. It is this notion of God not being a God of order but a God who interferes capriciously with the course of society, which has made the advance of the world so slow and made so many of His judgments useless. For these judgments come to teach nations what is wrong in them, and the judgments must come again and again while the wrong thing is there. It is slow work teaching blind men, but God does not spare trouble, and the laws of the universe cannot be bought off by prayer. There is but one way of making them kind, and that is by getting on their side. We find them out by punishment, as a child finds out that he must not touch fire by being burnt. Look at slavery. It was not plainly forbidden, but no nation practised it without paying dearly for it. It devoured, like a slow disease, national prosperity and uprightness. It was not so deadly to the earlier nations as it has been to the Southern States, but then ancient slavery was not so bad as American slavery. Ancient slavery had no vast breeding system. Its oppression was more cruel, but it was not 'so degrading, so systematic, and so unrelenting.' The slave had hope, had a chance of liberty, could hold some property, could receive some education: none of these things alleviated slavery in America. Wherever it has prevailed in modern times it has corroded family life, degraded national honour, and reduced flourishing lands to wildernesses. The Southern States would not learn that lesson from history. They were judged and sentenced by God. But their defeat was the natural result of their clinging to slavery. They were destitute of men and of means to fight the North. They had no middle class, no working-men class, they had no manufactories, scarcely any of the natural wealth of their States was worked, vast tracts of once productive land were exhausted. How could the Southerners succeed when all the vast resources of the North, supported by a spiritual idea, were brought to bear upon them? The result could not be doubted for a moment. It was God's judgment, but it was naturally worked out.

The conclusion I draw from this is, that all *national judgments of God come about naturally*.

But there are certain judgments mentioned in the Bible which seem to be supernatural—the destruction of Sodom, of Sennacherib's army, of the Egyptians in the Red Sea, the plagues sent upon the Israelites, and others. These are the difficulty. How shall we explain them? or shall we seek to explain them at all? First, we must remember that the writers had not the knowledge capable of explaining them; that nature to them was an insoluble mystery. They naturally, then, referred these things to a direct action of God, or rather, because they were out of the common, to an interference of God with nature. They were right in referring them to God, but it is possible that, owing to their ignorance of nature, they were wrong in their way of explaining them. If they had seen clearly, they would have seen sufficient reason for them in ordinary causes. We accept their teaching as far as it is connected with the spiritual world; we cannot accept it as far as it is concerned with the physical world, for they knew nothing about it.

Secondly. There is a thought which goes far, if it be true, to explain these things—it is that the course of human history may be so arranged, that, at times, healing or destructive natural occurrences coincide with crises in the history of a nation. For example, we might say that the sins of Sodom had reached their height at the very period when the elastic forces which were swelling beneath the plain of the Dead Sea had reached their last possible expansion. Or that the army of Sennacherib lay encamped in the way of the pestilential wind, which would have blown over the spot whether they had been there or not.

Thirdly. Whatever difficulty these things present to us in the Bible, the same difficulty occurs in what is profanely called profane history. There is not the slightest doubt that had the Carthaginians been Jews, the earthquake at Thrasimene would have been represented as a miraculous interference of God. There is not the slightest doubt, were our English history written by a Hebrew of the time of the kings, that the eclipse and the thunderstorm at Creçi, and that the storms which broke the Armada on the rocks of England and Scotland, would have been imputed to a miraculous interference by God with the course of nature. We do not believe these to have been miraculous; but we do believe them, with the Jew, to be of God. But we must also believe that they are contained in the order of the world—not disorderly elements arbitrarily introduced. That is, while believing in God as the Director and Ruler of human affairs, we must also believe in Him as the Director and Ruler of the course of nature. While we believe revelation, we must not disbelieve God's other revelation in science. One is as necessary to believe in as the other.

We see in all things this law holding good—that God's judgments are natural. In these apparently supernatural judgments it would also hold good if we knew all; and our attitude towards science, therefore, should not be an attitude of attack, or even an attitude of defence, but an attitude of ready assistance and inquiry.

We should endeavour, as religious men, not to attack scientific men because they endeavour to discover truth, but to assist them with all our power, knowing that the more we do in this way, the better chance there is of getting at the truth which will reconcile the teaching of science with the teaching of revelation. At present we force on them the attitude of opposition, we call them names, we ourselves are frightened out of our senses at every new discovery—we are faithless men. Necessarily, men of science attack us with contempt for our unbelief, and they are right; though it is curious to watch how Pharisaism and Priestcraft are creeping upon them, and how their hierarchy are reproducing in intolerance and ignorance of our position the very sins and mistakes of which they accuse us. It would be worth while if we were both to try the other mode of action, and see if truth would not better come out of union than out of disunion.

There is another class of occurrences which have been called judgments of God, but to which the term judgment is inapplicable. The circumstance mentioned in the text is an example of these, and the violent destruction of human life by the late hurricane of Tortola is another of the same type. About the latter, I wish, in conclusion, to say a few words.

There are even now some who say that the sufferers under these blows of nature suffer because they are under the special wrath of God.

What does Christ say to that? He bluntly contradicts it! 'I tell you nay'—it is not so. There are not a few who still blindly think that suffering proves God's anger. Has the Cross taught us nothing better than that, revealed to us no hidden secret?—not the explanation given by a fierce theology, that there we see God's necessary anger expended on a surety, but the healing truth that there God's Love died for the sake of man, and that the self-sacrifice did not expiate wrath, but manifest eternal Life—was necessarily the salvation of man from death. The instant we realize this our view of suffering is changed. We see it always, not as the misery-making, but as the redemptive power in the world. There is no pain, mental or physical, which is not a part of God's continual self-sacrifice in us, and which, were we united to life and not to death, we should not see as joy. Who regrets that the martyrs perished so cruelly? Not they themselves, not the Church whose foundations they cemented with their blood? Sympathy we can give, but regret? To regret their death is to dishonour them. Who can say that the death and pain of thousands in America for a great cause is matter of indignant sorrow? They died—half a million of them—to establish a principle, and so to redeem from curse and degradation, for all the future, millions of their countrymen; and they suffered devotedly, and died well. And those young hearts in Italy who fell on the vine-slopes of Mentana, fighting to the last, were they fools or redeemers? Redeemers, if the Cross be true. Every man who dies for Italy adds to Italy a new element of salvation, and makes it more impossible that she should much longer exist either as the slave of tyrants or the dupe of kings. It is an eternal law—if you wish to save a thing die for it; if you wish to redeem a man, suffer for him. And when God lets men suffer and gives them to pain and death, it is not the worst or the guiltiest but the best and the purest, whom He often chooses for His work, for they will do it best. Men wring their hands, and weep and wonder; but the sufferers themselves accept the pain in the joy of doing redemptive work, and pass out of the region of complaint into that of the nobler spirit which rejoices that it is counted worthy to die for men.

But, say others, God is cruel to permit such loss. Three thousand souls have perished in this hurricane. Is this your God of love?

But look at the history of the hurricane. A mass of heated air ascends along a line of heated water. Two currents dash in right and left to fill the space; they clash, and a whirlwind, rotating on a vast scale, sweeps along the line. It is the only way in which the equilibrium of the air can be restored. Those who object to this arrangement will perhaps prefer that the air should be left quiet, in order to protect their notion of a God of love! Well, what is the result? Instead of 3,000 by a hurricane, 30,000 perish by a pestilence.

'But why restore it so violently? Could not God arrange to have a uniform climate over all the earth?' We are spiritually puzzled, and, to arrange our doubts, God must make another world! We know not what we ask. A uniform climate over all the earth means simply the death of all living beings. It is the tropic heat and the polar cold which cause the currents of the ocean and the air and keep them fresh and pure. A stagnant atmosphere, a rotting sea, that is what we

God's Judgments.

ask for. It is well God does not take us at our word. When we wish the hurricane away, we wish away the tropic heats in the West Indies and along the whole equator. What do we do then? We wish away the Gulf Stream and annihilate England. How long would our national greatness last if we had here the climate of Labrador?

More than half of the solemn folly which is talked about a God of love not permitting these physical calamities is due to pure ignorance—is due to sceptical persons never reading God's revealed book of nature. A mere smattering of meteorology would answer all spiritual doubts, of this kind, of God's tenderness.

Because a few perish, is God to throw the whole world into confusion? The few must be sometimes sacrificed to the many. But they are not sacrificed without due warning. In this case God tells us plainly in His book of nature, that He wants to keep His air and His seas fresh and clean for his children to breathe and sail upon. The West Indies is the place where this work is done for the North Atlantic and its borders, and unless the whole constitution of the world be entirely changed, that work must be done by tornadoes. God has made that plain to us; and to all sailing and living about warm currents like the Gulf Stream it is as if God said, 'Expect my hurricanes; they must come. You will have to face danger and death, and it is my law that you should face it everywhere in spiritual as well as physical life; and to call Me unloving because I impose this on you, is to mistake the true ideal of your humanity. I mean to make you active men, not slothful dreamers. I will not make the world too easy for my children. I want veteran men, not untried soldiers; men of endurance, foresight, strength and skill for my work, and I set before you the battle. You must face manfully those forces which you call destructive, but which are in reality reparative. In the struggle, all that belongs to your intellect—invention, activity, imagination, forethought, combination—will be enkindled and developed; and all the nobler qualities of the spirit—love to Me and man, faith in Me and man, sympathy with the race, tender guardianship, the purity of life which is born of activity of charity—will enter into you and mould you into my likeness.'

Brethren, we cannot complain of the destructive forces of nature. We should have been still savages had we not to contend against them. But oh! we might bitterly complain of the ruin wrought by them if the souls who perish in the contest died for evermore.

What happened when the 'Rhone,' in mid-day midnight, went down with all its souls on board? Was it only the descent of a few bodies of men and women into the silence of an ocean death, or not rather the ascension of a number of emancipated spirits into life? When the hungry sea had swallowed all, and the loud waves rolled onwards unconcerned, where were the dead? We know not where; but this we do believe, they were better off than they had been alive—the good in that they had entered into their rest, the evil in that God had taken in hand more sharply to consume their evil. For He will not let us go, evil or good, till He has brought us all to His perfection. It matters little whether we die by hurricane on the sleepless sea, or quietly by disease in the sleeping city; the result is the same—we go to a Father who is educating us, we fall into the hands of Eternal Justice.

[March 10, 1867.]

THE TWENTY-THIRD PSALM.

Psalm xxiii. 1—3.

THE great characteristic of the Psalms of David is a swelling rush of overwhelming joy, or grief, or triumph, on which he is borne along as upon a torrent of feeling. In almost every psalm he seems to speak after long repression, to break suddenly into spontaneous song.

This psalm is almost the only instance in which softness and sweetness are pre-eminent, in which we find that musical, river-like gentleness of diction and thought which belongs to some of the other psalmists. These qualities, however, exist in perfection in this shepherd song.

Even in the garb of another language it seems to lose nothing but its rhythm. The shepherd, the confiding sheep, the green pastures, the waters of quietness, the paths of straightness, suggest a restfulness of peace in outward scenery which is perfectly attuned to the thoughts with which it is connected and of which it is the symbol. We cannot read the first verses, steeped as they are in the depths of patient trust, without an indefinite sensation of blissful rest.

Towards the close of the psalm, there breaks in a different picture. We see rising before us the rocky sides of a gloomy valley shrouded in the horror of death. The contrast of this scenery throws out into fuller relief the tenderness of the pastures and the sweetness of the waters, and while it deepens our conception of the faith which would follow the shepherd as fearlessly in darkness as in sunshine, adds force to the triumphant joy with which the psalm concludes.

A poem so finished we might impute to laborious art, but this was not the genesis of the psalm. It is a work of genius; it sprang forth almost unconsciously out of the depths of a child-like heart. David sang it because he could not help it. His feelings flowed to his lips in song with the same spontaneous gush as the waters of a mountain spring.

Now add to that power of genius a heart full of the sense of God's presence, deeply loving God as the kingly promoter of good and the kingly destroyer of evil, and we approach, at least, to the true idea of scriptural inspiration as far as the Psalms are concerned.

Before we explain the psalm, it is well, if possible, to ascertain the time at which it was written. We have supposed it to be one of David's Psalms. The great German critic denies this for two reasons: first, on account of its softness and sweetness, so different from the striking and overmastering force of David's style; and secondly, on account of the reference to the Temple in the last verse. But these reasons do not seem to be sufficient to deny the old tradition of its authorship. The house of the Lord may mean the tabernacle, and the tender quality of the psalm comes naturally out of the time at which I shall suppose it to be written.

Others refer its composition—and the idea lies upon the surface—to the time when David lived the life of a shepherd. The extreme simplicity of the language would also seem to carry us back to the early period of his life. But the religious depth and the whole drift of the psalm tend to make this view untenable. Again, the whole sentiment and scenery of the poem seem to prove, by accumulative evidence, that it was written at the time when the forty-second Psalm was written, when David had taken refuge from Absalom among the wide uplands which lie around the city of Mahanaim.

This is the view we shall endeavour to develope.

Meantime one critical remark will lead us to the spiritual exposition of the psalm. It is demanded of a lyric poem that it should be a united whole. Every part must have an influence on the whole impression, and be itself bound to every other part. There may be marked transitions of thought, abrupt changes in the scenery, as in this psalm; but overmastering these separate impressions, there must remain at the end of a perusal a single great impression. Now we find this poem impregnated with one feeling, the feeling of trust in God. This enters into all the images and their ideas. This it is which harmonizes all its contrasts, mellows all its changes, and unites into one whole the quiet contemplation of the first verses, the gloom of the fourth, the triumph of the fifth, and the combined retrospect and prophecy of the last; David's spirit of trust in God pervades the whole.

The Twenty-third Psalm.   59

The illustration of this trust is taken from pastoral life. The faithful care of the Oriental shepherd and the trustfulness of the sheep, furnish a symbol to David of the mutual relations between himself and God. On this account the psalm has been referred to his shepherd life. But let us see if these images were not suggested to him in the country over the Jordan. He had crossed the river and ascended the slopes till he came to Mahanaim. All round about the city lay the great pastoral land of Palestine. Wide-rolling downs, cut by deep gorges where Jabbok and his brethren had cleft their paths to the Jordan; great patches of forest where the vast herds of cattle wandered at will, made it a country of 'enormous parks.'

With Moab, Bashan, and Reuben, it was the great sheep-farm of the East. And it requires no imagination to picture David looking forth in melancholy thought from the terraced wall of Mahanaim upon the uplands, and seeing, as the traveller may see now, the shepherd bringing the flocks at noontide beneath the shadow of the trees to the greenest and tenderest pasture, and, as evening fell, leading them down to the springs of quiet waters to slake their thirst.

Picture to yourself the mournful king watching that landscape in his solitude, and then, as darkness suddenly fell, and the outward images became ideas in the brain, you will feel how natural it was that this psalm should well upwards from his heart. We can almost hear the quick, spontaneous words which rushed to his lips as he retired to rest—' The Lord is my shepherd, I shall not want '

Here, in this first verse, we find two of the activities of faith. *First*, it appropriates God. 'The Lord is *my* shepherd.'

There is a lifeless faith which believes in God as an Omnipotent Being, far away in the heavens, or as Eternal law, or as a metaphysical abstraction of our own ideas— a belief in a God external to us. This is belief in the worst and grossest idol which the heart of man has ever worshipped. From it no noble act, no spiritual power has ever flowed.

There is a living faith by which a man realizes God as the King of his innermost heart, as the Presence and Spirit who moves in all his action and all his suffering, as the Father, loving, good, and just, who is educating him hour by hour, day by day, into perfection. This is the ennobling faith of life. It is the origin of the highest aspiration, self-devotion, and strength. Out of it have arisen the noblest human lives. It is the power of appropriating God. It was the faith of David—'*My* shepherd.'

The second way in which faith displays itself in these verses is as the power of seeing the invisible in the visible. For other men, the scenery and life which moved round Mahanaim was merely scenery and life and no more; to David, the whole was a parable of which God was the interpretation. The waving terebinths, the blowing grass, the tender curving of the downs, the deep shadows, the musical waters, and the wandering sheep, spoke to him in a spiritual language and made him partaker of the deeper secret. The veil of the phænomenal was lifted up and he beheld the spiritual. God is here—*my* God; it is He who *is* all that I behold. This is to see what men have called the 'open secret.'

Now David did not think this out. It can never be thought; it must be felt, as he felt it, in a high poetical moment of inspiration. But it is the only truth worth grasping with our most passionate strength in our relation to the world of Nature.

It was seized by David; his activity of faith beheld beneath the seen, the glory of the unseen.

And, brethren, to go through this world of God's, seeing beneath the material the realities of the immaterial, gaining confidence in the immortal from the vision of the mortal, beholding in the manifold life of Nature revelations of the manifold life of God—no flowing mountain curve, no sound of wood or water, no delicately tinted cloud, no march of stars nor order of the seasons, which does not speak to us of Him—no horror of gloom and ruin of earthquake, no death, no apparently merciless destruction, which does not shake us to our centre with a passionate desire to prove Him right—this is to make life beautiful and awful, dramatic, awake, alive, a thing of high passion and of deep communion with the Greatest Mind.

To live with the invisible, and in it, to make our dull common life, and the pictorial show which doth encompass it, the image of the character of God, the picture of His work in us and on the world, that was David's power in this hour of sorrow, and is for ever one of the noblest exercises of Christian faith.

Again, we find in this psalm the child-like simplicity of faith.

Some, as I have said, have argued, from the simplicity of the diction, that it was written in David's youth. But its simplicity may be otherwise accounted for. David was, when he fled from Absalom, a partaker of very bitter sorrow.

Now one of the most remarkable effects of intense grief is that it brings back to us the simplicity of childhood. We do not argue about our sorrow when it is an overwhelming sorrow. We are blinded, speechless, conscious of a deep darkness and of nothing more. The feelings, then, are not manifold, not influenced by our subtle peculiarities of temperament, but simple. We hear, not the peculiar minor of our own character, but the great common chords of the universal sorrow of humanity. By a sorrow such as this, David had been made in feeling a child again. So it happened that the expression of his grief was soft and sweet rather than sublime. Quiet, deep words, freed from all self-consciousness, all metaphysical thought, all delicate shades of sadness, tell us here of his profound and simple pain. I have been through the valley of the shadow of death, yet the Lord is my shepherd. That was all—child-like sorrow, child-like trust.

How often, oh! how often, do we desire *that* in pain. When our sorrow has swept over us like a torrent and left the plains of the heart like the wilderness of stones and desolation which an Alpine inundation leaves behind it, who has not felt the intensity of desire to get rid of the imaginative thought which wearies life, the imaginative feeling so torturing to the heart, the vividness of memories which will invade the soul, the reiterated self-consciousness and the mysteries of doubt which, suggested by grief, come crowding in upon the intellect—and to return to the simple passion of sorrow which belongs to the heart of a child?

And if our sorrow be deep enough and be not connected with mental doubt, this *is* what takes place. Our grief becomes almost infantine in feeling. We only feel, 'I am miserable,' and no more. Sometimes with that there comes 'the passion of death,' but oftener (for the heart, even in its agony, is elastic), there is the craving, intensely strong, of throwing our whole being, with all its unbearable burden, upon another heart. The usual haughty isolation, the customary reserve, is lost in the longing for sympathy. Nature conquers conventionality; we become the natural child again.

But the craving does not die; it increases till we find its deeper meaning. It dimly points to a diviner Friend than any one on earth. It can only find its full satisfaction in the realized sympathy of God our Father. 'The Lord is my shepherd.'

Brethren, in the eternal love of God in Christ find your refuge from hopelessness. Let the child-like depth of sorrow bring about the child-like depth of trust in Him. Your pain is His. He is sacrificing Himself for the world in your agony. Realize that your sorrow is His love working in you for the blessing of the race. Throw yourself into that thought, and trust in Him. And there will be with you then the peace which believes, the peace which makes you content to sacrifice yourself as the instrument of love, the peace of being loved and of loving. You shall lie down in tender pastures of God's calm, and be led beside the quietness of His waters of refreshment.

We can account still further for the simplicity of this psalm, because David had really returned, through the power of association, to his childhood. As he looked forth upon the grassy country covered with the feeding sheep and saw them led by the shepherd, his thoughts were swept back to Bethlehem and he breathed the atmosphere of his childhood. He became a youth again. In his exile, once more he saw, 'flashing upon his inward eye,' the wild ridges eastward of Bethlehem, where he had shepherded his flocks upon the pastures over which centuries afterwards a greater than David was sung by the heavenly host. Again he saw himself leading his sheep with staff and rod through the gloomy gorges of the hills to shelter them at noon and water them at even: and now, with the faith of the man and child combined, he represented to himself in simple words a like relation between himself and God. 'The Lord is my Shepherd. My care for my sheep of old is a faint image of His care for me.'

There is something wonderfully touching in this simple faith in God. What would not some of us give if we could free ourselves from our passionate questionings of the love of God, from the torture of feeling that this world is an accursed place, where God cannot be, and gain this unquestioning tenderness of quiet faith? It is so hard a battle against doubt and fear and coldness of heart, harder the more we know and the more finely we feel, that to win that faith seems almost the most beautiful possession possible to man. And yet David was not one of those apathetic characters to whom we usually attribute such a faith. He had passed through nearly every phase of life and been great in each—had been shepherd, hunter, warrior, musician, poet, the people's idol, the exile, the freebooter, the chivalrous companion, the general, the king. He had felt nearly every phase of feeling and that with peculiar depth, pure love and impure, patriotism, friendship, sorrow in all its forms, joy and triumph in varied circumstance: almost every feeling in relation to God, as Lord of Nature, Director of life, ideal Perfection to be thirsted after, the Punisher and Forgiver of sin.

This was no dull unimpassioned spirit, and yet here we find the many-sided, deep-souled man speaking like the simplest child. It is a deep, deep lesson. What it means cannot be put in words. Those who can read it true will feel it better for the silence.

But when the impulse derived from association was over and David began to realize that he was no longer the youth of Bethlehem, still he looked back upon his life with the same thought in his mind and felt that through all Jehovah had been his Shepherd. Out of a thousand dangers rescued, out of deep guilt restored, in times which needed wary walking directed, there had been ever with him an invisible Guide and Friend. Thinking on this, David's faith would take to itself additional force. For the strength of faith is the product of experience. In the past I see now He has been with me, therefore in the present He will still be true.

Therefore, Christian men, when the gloom round your path is deep and incomprehensible, then it is wise sometimes to look back; not to add to your darkness by regret for vanished joy, but to see what God has done for you. We cannot understand any portion of our life when we are involved in it. We see it too closely and too passionately. Much, as long as we are here, we shall never comprehend, but some things we may. Look back on yourself many years ago, hovering on the brink of some terrible temptation, and you will see now, in some slight occurrence which scarcely struck you then, the hand of God which drew you back from the precipice. Look back upon yourself when you were enslaved by some guilty passion, or losing your true life in fashion or in gain, and now, in some dim impulse which came, you know not how, you will recognize the voice of the Spirit of God which drove you forth from ruin. Look back upon yourself when your grief was deep and your trial too bitter for your heart, and you were tempted to drown memory in excitement or to harden your heart to rock that you might feel no more, and you will now see how some fresh interest, or some friend, or some new sympathy, reconciled you to life and made your heart beat with added tenderness. You will now feel that these were the messengers of an ever-watchful God, and faith in God in the gloomy present will be born, like David's, afresh from the knowledge of His presence with you in past experience. The Lord *has been* my Shepherd, therefore He *is* my Shepherd.

Then it is that we are enabled through this retrospective faith to see, even in the darkness of the present, not all, but something of God's love. David learnt three things. He learnt that the intervals of rest in trial are the kindness of God. There is nothing without its compensation in this world. Some are happy all their lives. Set over against that, that they never know what exquisite, passionate joy may be. Others are, like David, tried continually; but in the intervals of trial, how deep is the relief and how intense the joy! No one who has not suffered great physical pain can know the indescribable repose of freedom from it. No one who has not endured a long illness can understand the fine and delicate delight which is given to a slow convalescence. Never can a man forget what then he felt and saw and heard. The voice of one he loved, the sympathy of a friend, the care of a mother, brought with them then a marvellous thrill and quivering of heart unknown before. How every sense was quickened, and with what a subtle rapture did floating cloud and flowing water, the whispering talk of the trees, the fresh breath of the pure air, allure the ear and charm the eye, and drop upon the heart the dew of a second life.

So it is in trial when God gives an interval of rest. 'He maketh me to lie down in green pastures, He leadeth me beside the still waters.' These are the simple expressions of the serene joy of David in the moment when God had lifted him above his sorrow into the region of pure trust. It is thus that God concentrates joy for the weary of heart. That which is spread for the happy over a large surface is poured by God in its quintessence into a day or an hour for the suffering.

But it is not only keen joy which God gives us in trial, but also strength. 'He restoreth my soul;' i.e. He gives me back my vitality, my force of life. He does not remove at once our suffering—that would ruin our character; He does not *only* give us comfort — that would weaken character. He gives us power; for the true comforter is the strengthener in pain, not the remover of pain.

So we are restored through trial to the force of character which we had lost in ease; we are fitted for our toil on earth and in heaven as the mountain pine is fitted for its work, by the tempests which sway into strength of soft iron the folded fibres of its trunk, and cause its roots to clasp with a giant's grip the rocks and earth beneath. There is much for us to do here, there is infinitely more for us to do beyond the grave; we need to be prepared, and God prepares us by resistance in difficulty, by endurance in pain.

Lastly. God is teaching us in trial to walk after Him in a straighter path. David saw the shepherd going before the sheep and, by his straightness of walk, keeping them from wandering, and he made the picture spiritual. In my sorrow, by my sorrow, He is leading me into paths of righteousness. 'Before I was chastened I went wrong, but now have I kept Thy word.'

When all is most happy, then are we in most danger. Not on the rocky ridge of difficulty, but in the ease of a summer life, are our feet most doomed to slip. Excitement passes into folly, and folly into sin. We enervate ourselves in the oasis, till we have no strength to combat with the desert.

But when God burns up our conventional life, we dread for ever afterward our comfort and our ease. We contrast, then, the fever of passions which youth has almost consecrated with its own brightness with the lasting enthusiasm of the higher love. We contrast the excitement of the earth with the still joy of union with the truth; the vain show in which we have walked, and its disquietude, with the deep realities and deeper peace of the eternal life with God. The visions of this world are seen worn and faded in the glow of the Sun of Righteousness. It is in the hour of that stern revelation, when our old life is shrivelled like a scroll, that we are thrown upon the Shepherd and Bishop of our souls. He goes before us, and we know His voice. Straight as an arrow He leads us on in righteousness, day by day we follow Him more truly. Before us shines the goal, and subdued and strengthened by our trial, we turn aside no longer, but in the midst of a wavering and evil world run home.

This was the vision of experience which David had in the hour of his suffering. God, the giver of great joy; God, the strength of his heart; God, the guide into righteousness; in one word, God, the Shepherd of his life.

There is but one organ whereby we may see the same. It is faith exhibited as trust. Without it, this world is still that ancient, terrible mystery, deepening into deeper gloom as sorrow deepens in us and around us, and rolling in upon the heart ever colder and lonelier waters as life grows darker to its close. With it, the darkness is uplifted. We see the other world of life and love beneath.

We behold God as He is—the Father of the race, the Lover of our souls, the Educator of humanity. Life leaps out of trial, joy out of pain, at this vision. It *is* true, we cry; God has not forgotten me, nor my brothers. The Lord is my Shepherd, the Lord is our Shepherd; we shall not want for evermore.

[March 17, 1867.]

THE TWENTY-THIRD PSALM.

Psalm xxiii. 4—6.

THE essential value of the Bible as the book of books is its union of the universal and the particular. Its grand subjects are the history of God's education of the race of man and the history of the heart of man in its relations to God. As such it speaks of feelings common to all men and of principles which are true for all men. This is its universal interest. But it has also a *particular* interest. It was written by men, but these men were Hebrews. The mode, then, in which these universal truths were given was Hebrew; they were clothed with images taken from Hebrew scenery and Hebrew life, they were connected with Hebrew history, they were inwoven with the lives of particular Hebrew men. The Bible, then, is not only divine but human, and not only human and divine but Hebrew.

Now when the two former ideas, which are universal because they are spiritual, are alone dwelt on, the Bible is in danger of becoming unreal. We see ourselves, our own trials, our own opinions, our favourite doctrines, in the Old Testament history. We become fond, like the Greek boy, of the reflection, and we can see nothing but ourselves. This tendency has expended itself upon the Psalms. They have been so robbed of personality, so exclusively, some of them, applied as Messianic prophecies, so exclusively, others of them, seen as mystical expressions of spiritual feeling, that all sense of their historical reality has perished in the minds of many. They are a source of comfort and help to especially religious men, they have but little interest to the generality. They have been removed into a sphere of thought into which many no more enter than they do into the writings of the mystics of the middle ages.

Therefore, if we wish to re-awaken interest in the Psalms, we should try to add to that which is universal in them that which is particular. We should dwell upon the Hebrew element in them, connect them with the lives and passions of the Hebrew writers, and show how their imagery grew as naturally out of the scenery of Palestine as their modes of expression were coloured by the every-day life of its people.

On the other hand, when we have thus clearly found out what is Hebrew and temporary in them, we are for the first time in the position to find out clearly what is universal in them. Knowing the particular, we can abstract it and leave the universal. Without the knowledge which can make this distinction, we are in danger of making Hebrew modes of thought and action the measures of the thought and the models of the action of the present day. The whole of the history of the Christian Church, from the very earliest period, is rife with examples of this tendency. Men imputed to that which was Hebrew, human, and temporary in the Old Testament, the same divine authority and infallibility which belong only to that which is universal in the Bible. It is here, therefore, that the usefulness of accurate knowledge and criticism appears most clearly as a balance to ignorant but well-meaning spiritual enthusiasm.

Our object this morning is to show the particular in this Psalm by connecting the last three verses with the history of David when he fled to Mahanaim, and to bring out that which is universal in it—the pervading idea of faith in God.

We begin, then, with the fourth verse.

The image of David's great distress, 'the valley,' or ravine, 'of the shadow of death,' or, as it may be translated, 'of deep shades,' can, without any fancifulness, be connected with the scenery through which he passed in his flight. He must, after crossing Olivet, have descended to the fords of the Jordan by one of the rocky passes which lead from the table-land of Jerusalem. These deep ravines are full of ghastly shadows, and David passed down one of them as the evening had begun to fall, and waited by the ford of Jordan till midnight. It is not improbable that we have here the source of the image in this verse. Such a march must have impressed itself strongly on his imagination. The weird and fierce character of the desolate ravine, the long and deathly shadows which chilled him as the sun sank, the fierce curses of Shimei, the fear behind him, the agony in his own heart repeating the impression of the landscape, fastened the image of it in his memory for ever. He has thrown it into poetry in this verse. For, now, when he mused upon his trial, he transferred to the present feelings of his heart at Mahanaim the agony of that terrible day, but added to it the declaration of the faith in God which his deliverance had made strong within him.

And his words have become since then the expression of the feelings of all men in intensity of trial. They are generally applied to that time when the last great struggle is approaching, when the soul, entering on the border land of the unknown, shudders in the chill shadows of coming death. No man can say that that sharp severance from all that is customary, and that first moment of a strange life, is not a time of awe and trial; but oh! God knows that there are valleys of the shadow of death in life itself which are worse than death a thousand times. It is enough to make a grave man smile to hear death spoken of as *the* evil of evils. Why, thousands, every year, even of those who have no hope in the future, welcome death as the releaser, the friend. It is more tolerable than life.

There are times when a man feels that all real life is over for ever, when he has seen every costly argosy of hope sink like lead in the dark waters of the past, when the future stretches before him a barren plain of dreary sea, on which a fiery sun is burning.

There are times when another has at last felt that all the past has been unutterable folly and darker sin. He looks back upon his youth, and knows that never, never more 'the freshness of his early inspiration' can return. The pure breeze of an innocent morning was once about his way, he hides his head now from the fiery simoom of remorse in the desert of his guilty life. It is the conscience's valley of the shadow of death.

The Twenty-third Psalm.

There are times, too, even in youth, when, by a single blow, all the odour and colour have been taken out of living, when the treachery of lover or friend has made everything in existence taste badly afterwards, and we, tortured and wrung with the bitterest of bitternesses, say in our blindness that all is evil and not good. It is the heart's valley of the shadow of death.

And there are times, even in the truest Christian life, when all faith is blotted out and God seems to become a phantom, an impersonal fate, careless of the lives of men, or exacting a blind vengeance; leaving us here to struggle for our life as a man struggles in a stormy sea; so unsustained and so abandoned that we cry out in despair, 'There is no Father in heaven, no goodness ruling all.' Our prayer, wild in its fervour as the Syro-Phœnician woman's, has the same reply—'He answered her never a word.' It is the spirit's valley of the shadow of death.

Now what was David's refuge in one of these awful hours? It was faith in God, the Ever-Near. David had entered the valley of the shadow of death of the heart; he had been betrayed, insulted, exiled by the one whom he had loved best. It was enough to make him disbelieve in divine goodness and human tenderness, enough to harden his heart into steel against God, into cruelty against man. In noble faith he escaped from that ruin of the soul, and threw himself upon God—'I will fear no evil, for thou art with me.'

Brethren, who have suffered from the disappointments of the heart, from human treachery when the traitor has been most dear to you, the only refuge of your soul is to believe in a living Person, who through the gloom, with undying love, is guiding your blind steps as a shepherd with his rod and staff; for *that*, if it cannot yet be comfort, is at least the source of endurance, the means of avoiding hardness of heart or recklessness of life, the one thing which keeps alive the old tenderness of feeling. For life and death, cling to the love of God. Have faith in God, the Educator of human souls.

It is the same remedy when you despair of the past or of the future. 'It is well,' you say, 'to speak of faith to me. I *cannot* believe.' Yes, you *can*; for in your case it is not the feeling of faith which is wanted, but the action of faith. 'All has been failure,' you say. 'I had rather die than endure the future.'

It is faith in God, then, to try again; to cast that thought of death away and go forth into the wilderness to bear your cross in solitude, till God bring to your heart the virtue of Christ's conquest in the desert, and the angel of strength send you forth again to lead a tenderer and an intenser life.

And if it is not so much the horror of the future as the recollection of sin in the past which makes memory a curse and a fire within you, then God does not demand of you a high-wrought feeling of faith and trust. The faith He asks then is only enough faith *not* to despair, *not* to sin the sin of Judas, only sufficient faith to strive to do better for the future. The *effort itself* is faith in Him. And if God be true, there is a blessed redemption which has been wrought for you. God's love in Christ forgets and forgives the past, and opens to you a new life. Remorse is slain by belief in love.

The spirit of Christ's sacrifice becomes in you a power of resistance against evil, and a life which kindles in you a progressive righteousness. Following Him with faltering steps, you will pass out of the valley of the shadow of death in sin.

And if there be one among you who has entered that awful shadow of doubt, which is sometimes the fate of the truest follower of Christ, to him we do not say 'Believe,' for belief is the very point attacked, but we do say 'Do not despair.' There is a faith even in doubt, and it consists in striving to be true to goodness and truth, even though you cannot believe in God the good or in God the true. It consists in feeling that doubt is, though sometimes necessary, not the healthy condition of the soul. It consists in determining to realize and know clearly what your doubts are, that you may contend, not with a shadowy enemy, but with a well-defined enemy. It consists in resolution not to be satisfied with your condition, but to press forward to something higher, for doubt is often as lazy as religious assurance tends to be, and as productive of the same kind of spiritual pride and isolation. To act on these principles in the deepest darkness of the spirit is still possible, and it is a germ of faith in God which will grow into the perfect flower of a bright belief. For God's presence with you is not destroyed by your doubt. You are still His child. No feeling of yours can alter that divine fact. He is too persistently your Father to permit your cry of unbelief to become the cry of your whole life. Out of the gloom of outer darkness He is at this very moment leading you like a shepherd.

These are some of the spiritual applications of this verse. It sprang from the heart of a Hebrew king. It has found an echo in the heart of all humanity.

The next verse—on the supposition that the psalm was written at the time when David was at Mahanaim, is at once comprehensible. It is a thanksgiving to God for the blessings of friendship which were given him in his exile.*

Far away in the Eastern city there came consolation to the wearied man. New friends sprang up out of his misfortune, old friends were proved in his misfortune. Food, comfort, sympathizers were given to him, till at last his heart expressed its gratitude in this psalm—'Thou preparest a table for me,' &c.

One of the sad comforts of trial is this, that it is the touchstone of friendship. We realize then who are true gold. One of its deepest blessings is that then friendship, by its expansion, by its abandonment of reserve, by the pleasure of giving and of receiving, is deepened into an abiding power. We often lose in trial what is calculable, we oftener gain what is incalculable.

Precisely the same principle holds good in the spiritual world. The blessing of all trial is that it disperses the vain shows of life on which we rested, and makes Christ, the Eternal Certainty, more deeply known, more deeply ours as the Friend who loveth at all times. This is one of the true points of view from which to look upon the sufferings of life—they are leading us to know Christ better.

But how? How do we know another? Only by

* 2 Sam. xvii. 27—29.

entering into his spirit, by sharing in his life. There is a broad distinction between an acquaintance and a friend. We may see an acquaintance every day, but we never see his heart. We hover with him over the surfaces of things, touching, it may be, now and then the real inward life as a swallow touches a stream in its flight, but we never dwell with him within the temple of inward thought or enter with him into the inner shrine of feeling.

A friend—how different! one to whom your heart has opened itself as freely as a flower to the sun, to receive from whom is pleasure, for whom to sacrifice yourself is the purest joy, the secret springs of whose life you have stood beside with awe and love, whose silence is as vocal to you as speech, whose passing expressions of countenance convey histories, whose being has passed into yours, and yours into his, each complementing and exalting each, with whom you have shared existence and all its passions, whose sorrow and whose joy move you as the coming spring moves the woodland, who has received as much from you as you from him. This is true friendship, and its peculiar mark is that through participation in the life and feelings of your friend you have become at home in his nature.

So is it with Christ and the Christian man. You ask to be the friend of Christ. You cannot be that without partaking in some degree of His life. You ask to be glorified with Him. You must first drink the cup He drank, be baptized with His baptism. The great law of His life must embrace us also—the law of sacrifice. We should not grieve too sorely when we pass through the valley of pain, for in that God is accepting us as His sons. When the sacrifice is accomplished, we shall find that we have made centuries of progress in the knowledge of our Saviour and our Father. We shall know that we have entered into their life; that conformity to their sacrifices has been indeed the gate to their marvellous friendship. Our cup will run over with joy—the joy of willing love.

Finally, the last verse combines the retrospect and the prospect of faith. David glances back over his whole life, and declares that it has been very good. 'Surely goodness and mercy have followed me all the days of my life.' That is the expression, not of a youthful shepherd's, but of a man's experience, and it is an expression of triumphant faith.

It was not every one who in David's place would have said so *then*. Who was it, we ask, who spoke these words? Was it one who had been a child of good fortune from his youth? No; it was one who had held his life in his hand for years, whose life as king had been one of sore trial and of constant war, who had borne the toil of forming a wild people and of weighty cares of State, whose spiritual trials had been deep as his own passionate character; one who even now as he spoke these words was under the thundercloud of an awful sorrow. His dearest had deceived his heart. On one all the affection of David's princely, sensitive spirit had been lavished, and it was that very son who now repaid him by rebellion, by dark ingratitude, by insults darker still. Add to this, that David must have felt that this was the foretold punishment of his worst and blackest guilt. This man, then, driven out an exile, a prey to such a vulture pain in his heart of sorrow and of sin, how do we find him? Crying out against God with unmanly railing, miserable retrospective weeping, hopelessness for the future? Anything but that. Resolute, cheerful, victorious over himself and circumstances, triumphant in faith in God, looking back on his life as if it were one scene of blessing, looking forward with radiant hope to dwelling in the house of the Lord for ever.

It does the spirit good, and makes the blood run quicker, and kindles in our faithless sentimental hearts some fire of manly and Christian strength, to read this.

This is the victory of faith in God—in the midst of bitter sorrow and outward gloom—thanksgiving for the past, joyful hope for the future.

O brethren, who are mourning, or despairing, or sleeping in the sloth of trouble, you who have higher teaching and a nobler example than David had, awake out of your dreamy, self-conscious, self-torturing life, and go forth like men who know what Christ Jesus was, to meet the solemnities and to conquer the trials of existence, believing in a Shepherd of your souls. Then faith in Him will support you in duty; and duty firmly done will strengthen faith, till at last, when all is over here, and the noise and strife of the earthly battle fades upon your dying ear, and you hear, instead thereof, the deep and musical sound of the ocean of eternity, and see the lights of heaven shining on its waters, still and fair in their radiant rest, your faith will raise the song of conquest, and in its retrospect of the life which has ended, and its forward glance upon the life to come, take up the poetic inspiration of the Hebrew king, 'Surely goodness and mercy have followed me all the days of my life, and I will dwell in the house of the Lord for ever.'

[March 31, 1867.]

THE VIRGIN'S CHARACTER.

Luke i. 46—55.

In the course of last week, the Church celebrated the Annunciation of the Blessed Virgin. Lady Day, as we call it in common talk, is the day on which the history of Christianity begins, and the collect which is read in the course of the appointed service supposes this by speaking of the Incarnation.

It is impossible, in treating of the beginnings of Christianity, to pass over without a word the life of one whose image has dwelt so long and so purely in the heart of Christendom, whose worship has moulded so deeply the movements of history, and so civilized and softened the character of nations; whose tender womanhood as maiden and mother has so supremely influenced art, and so widely modified by its ideal the literature of Europe.

She probably passed her early life in the village of Nazareth. The village lay surrounded by its curving hills, hidden, like a cluster of stamens in the cup of a flower, from the gaze of men, most like in its lowly and concealed position to the character of 'the handmaid of the Lord.' The grassy slope on which it stands is still more haunted by flowers than any other spot in Palestine, and it is not without an inherent fitness that the Roman Church has ever connected the Virgin with all the unconscious loveliness, with all the freshness, delicacy, and carelessness of ostentation which mark the life of flowers. It was a still and beautiful quiet among the hills. Remote, unknown, far from the bustle and confusion of politics and parties in Palestine, it was, though inhabited by a wild and rough population, a fitting home for the young girl who was destined to be the mother of Him who was to contend in the power of lowliness for the salvation of the world.

Pure in heart, she could have no fear of the lawless men who surrounded her; rather we may suppose that a rude homage was paid to the gentle maidenhood which walked among them. Humble in heart, she drew into herself, by the very receptiveness of her humility, all the loveliness of the flowers and hills. All the silent sympathy of nature, and the 'vital feelings of delight,' which flow into us from the beauty of the world, went to form her character and purify and refine her heart. Lowly in rank, she never dreamed of the blessedness which should overshadow her, or of the honour she should hold within the world. She grew serene and pure, in the liberty of humility, in the dignity of secluded gentleness, into her perfect womanhood.

And here, observe, we have a type of that character in which Christ is for ever being born. To the pure, the humble, and the unselfish, the Blessedness of blessedness was given. The Saviour of the world was born in her. It is no solitary instance when we transfer it from the world of reality to the world of spirit. That which took place once in the outward history of our race takes place continually in the inward history of the human heart. The miracle of the Incarnation is renewed again and again in another form. Wherever the pure heart, the humble spirit, the seeking and receptive soul are found, there Christ is born. To all who live in the clear air of truth, in the gentleness of charity, in unconsciousness of self, the Holy Spirit comes. These are the rare angel souls whom the power of the Highest overshadows, and in whom the Saviour is reborn for men.

And Mary felt this. God had not chosen her for her dignity, her wealth, her power. He had regarded the low estate of His handmaiden.

One morning, according to the old legend, 'as she went to draw water from the spring or well in the green open space at the north-west extremity of the town,' the angel met her with the salutation. And Mary was troubled at the tidings and the praise. It was the trouble of a beautiful unconsciousness. She had never thought of herself, never asked herself whether she were pure or lovely, did not care what people thought of her, made no effort to appear to the little world of Nazareth other than she was.

A rare excellence in man or woman, this fair unconsciousness!—rarer than ever now. Our miscalled education, which looks chiefly to this, how a young girl may make a good figure in society, destroys often from the earliest years the beauty of unconsciousness of self. There are many who have never had a real childhood, never been unconscious, who possess already the thoughts and airs of womanhood, and who are applauded as objects to admire, instead of being pitied as victims of an unnatural training. Their manners, their conversation, their attitudes, are the result of art. Already they tremble, as we do, for the verdict of the world. They grow up and enter into society, and there is either a violent reaction against conventionality, or there is a paralyzing sensitiveness to opinion, or there is a dull repose of character and manner which is all but equivalent to stagnation. We see many who are afraid of saying openly what they think or feel, if it be in opposition to the accredited opinions of the world; we see others who rejoice in shocking opinion for the sake of making themselves remarkable—perhaps the basest form of social vanity, for it gives pain and does not spring from conviction. Both forms arise from the education which makes the child self-conscious. It is miserable to see how we actually take pains to root out of our children the beauty of the Virgin's early life, the beauty of a more divine life in Christ—the beauty of unconsciousness of self. We take away all the charm of freshness and Christian grace of childhood, and we replace it by the insertion into the child's mind of that degrading question which must preface act and speech, 'What will people say of me?'

For, to make your children live only by the opinions of others, to train them not to influence but to submit to the world, is to educate them to think only of themselves, is to train them up to inward falseness, is to destroy all eternal distinctions between right and wrong, is to reduce them to that dead level of uneducated un-

The Virgin's Character. 87

originality which is the most melancholy feature in the young society of London. Let them grow naturally, spontaneously, and keep them unconscious of themselves: and, for the sake of the world, which, in the midst of all its conventional dulness, longs for something fresh and true, if not for the sake of God, do not press upon them the belief that the voice of society is the measure of what is right or wrong, beautiful or unbeautiful, fitting or unfitting for them to do. The unconscious life of Mary—what a charm those who possessed it might exercise upon the world!

2. Look next at the Virgin's quiet acceptance of greatness.

Nothing impresses us more than the calmness with which, after the first trouble was past, the Virgin received the message of the angel. She was not dazzled nor excited by her glorious future. She was not touched by any vanity. 'Behold the handmaid of the Lord.' In nothing more than in this is the simple greatness of her character displayed. What was the reason of this? It was that the thought of God's presence with her destroyed all thought of self. She could not think of her greatness otherwise than as bestowed by God. 'He that is mighty hath magnified me.' She could not feel the flutter of vanity. It died in the thought of the glorious salvation which was coming to her country and the world. 'My soul doth magnify the Lord, my spirit hath rejoiced in God my Saviour.' She was nothing; God was all.

Do you want a cure for that false humility, that mock modesty, which says, 'I am not worthy,' and trumpets its denial till all the world knows that an honour has been offered; which, while it says with the lips, 'It is too great for me,' feels all the time in the heart that self-consciousness of merit which betrays itself in the affected walk and the showy humility? Would you be free from this folly? Learn Mary's secret. Feel that God is all; that, whether He makes you great or leaves you unknown, it is the best for you, because it is His work. 'Behold the handmaid of the Lord. Let Him do unto me as it seemeth Him good.'

Do you want a cure for that unhappy restless vanity, ever afraid, yet ever seeking to push itself forward; ever shy, yet ever trembling on the verge of impertinence; which shows itself to inferiors in rank in a bustling assumption of superiority which suspects it is not superior, and to superiors in rank by an inquietude, an ignorance of when to speak and when to be silent, sometimes by a fawning submission, sometimes by an intrusive self-assertion? Learn Mary's secret. Feel that you are the child of God, not the servant or the master of any man, but the servant of Christ, who was the servant of all. Vain! What have any of us to be vain of? Rank? wealth? beauty? pomp of household? dress? splendour of appearance? A few years, and we are lying in the chill earth of the churchyard; our eye dead to admiration, our ear to praise; and the world—whose smile we forfeited eternal life to court—regrets us for an hour and then forgets. And *that* is human life! No; it is the most miserable travesty of it. We stand in the presence of God. What are all the adventitious advantages of rank or wealth to Him, or to us in Him? Only the tarnished spangles, the tinsel crowns, the false diamonds, which are the properties of this petty theatre which we call the world. Once be able to say in your heart, 'Behold the handmaid of the Lord; be it unto me as He will,' and vanity and all its foolish fluttering tribe of small victories over others, of pushing meannesses, of restless desires, of little ostentations, will abandon your hearts for ever. The true greatness, wealth, nobility, is to be at one in character with the everlasting goodness, truth, and love of God; to be great with the magnanimity of Christ, to be rich in all the eternal virtues, to be noble among the aristocracy of the best men. He who possesses these can never be vain, and the way to possess them is the Virgin's way—to be the servant of God, to do His will.

The journey to Judah followed on the Annunciation. Mary had heard that her cousin Elizabeth had attained the dearest wish of a Jewish woman—she was to have a son. So the Virgin, full of the thoughts which thrilled her as she pondered the angel's message, full of the sympathy of eager friendship, rose and went into the hill country to see her cousin. As she entered the house, Elizabeth, full of the Holy Ghost, saluted her almost in the same words as the angel.

What a moment was that for Mary! For the first time since the Annunciation the tidings of the angel were confirmed by a human voice. That which she had hidden in the silence of her heart, that which she had believed but half feared to realize, was spoken out to her and made real by another.

And then how natural that Mary's heart, so long quiet,

so long filled with the marvellous thought to which she had given the full force of that meditative spirit which was so fully developed in her after life, so long repressed —should have stirred at the touch of human and womanly sympathy and burst out into the song of joy and exultation, 'My soul doth magnify the Lord,' &c.!

This, brethren, is unaffected truth to nature.

In this unpremeditated song of the Virgin's, we find some further points of her character as the type of noble womanhood.

First, her idea of fame—'All generations shall call me blessed.'

A true woman's thought! For so far as a woman is sincere to the nature God has given her, her aspiration is not so much that the world should ring with her fame, or society quote her as a leader of fashion, but that she should bless, and be blessed in blessing. It is not that she should not wish for power, but that she should wish for a noble, not an ignoble power. It is not that she should not wish to queen it in this world, but that she should wish to queen it, not by ostentation of dress or life, nor by eclipsing others, but by manifestation of love, by nobility of gentle service, by unconscious revelation in her life and conscious maintenance in others by her influence, of all things true and pure, of stainless honour in life, of chivalrous aspiration in the soul. At home or in the wider sphere of social action her truest fame is this, that the world should call her *blessed*. The music of that thought sounds through every line of the Virgin's psalm.

And there is no sadder or uglier sight in this world than to see the women of a land grasping at the ignoble honour and rejecting the noble; leading the men, whom they should guide into high thought and active sacrifice, into petty slander of gossip in conversation, and into discussion of dangerous and unhealthy feeling; becoming in this degradation of their directing power the curse and not the blessing of social intercourse—becoming what men in frivolous moments wish them to be, instead of making men what men should be; abdicating their true throne over the heart to grasp at the kingdom over fashion; ceasing to protest against impurity and unbelief, and giving them an underhand encouragement; turning away from their mission to bless, to exalt, and to console, that they may struggle through a thousand meannesses into a higher position, and waste their divine energy to win precedence over their rival; expending all the force which their more excitable nature gives them, in false and sometimes base excitements day after day, with an awful blindness and a pitiable degradation; exhausting life in amusements which fritter away, or in amusements which debase, their character; possessing great wealth, and expending it only on self, and show, and shadows; content to be lapped in the folds of a silken and easy life, and not thinking, or thinking only to the amount of half-a-dozen charitable subscriptions — a drop in the waters of their expenditure—not thinking that without 'their closed sanctuary of luxurious peace,' thousands of their sisters are weeping in the night for hunger and for misery of heart, and men and children are being trampled down into the bloody dust of this city, the cry of whose agony and neglected lives goes up in wrath to the ears of God. This is not our work, you say, this is the work of men. Be it so if you like. Let them be the hands to do it; but who, if not women, are to be the hearts of the redemption of the poor from social wrong? As long as the women of England refuse to guide and to inspire, as long as they forget their nature, and think of pleasure instead of blessing, as long as they shut their ears to the agony of the cities of this land, that they may not be disturbed in their luxury, and literature, and art, so long men will, as they have ever done, take the impulse of their lives from them and do nothing chivalrous, nothing really self-sacrificing, nothing very noble and persistent for the blessing of the world. The regeneration of society is in the power of the woman, and she turns away from it. All future English generations might call her blessed, and she prefers to be called fashionable. The hearts of men, the lives of men, are in their hands. How do they use their power?

It seems unnecessary to say that this is but a one-sided representation. But it *is* one side, and a side necessary to dwell on. There is no fear of the other being forgotten.

That womanhood will not rise to the height of her true vocation, as the saving, exalting, and blessing element in society, is sad and pitiable, beyond all human sadness and pity, to every one who loves and honours England.

This large conception of womanly duty, this which is the patriotism of the woman, was not absent from the Virgin's character. She rejoiced in being the means of her country's blessing. 'He hath holpen His servant Israel, in remembrance of His mercy, as He spake to our

The Virgin's Character.

fathers, to Abraham and his seed for ever.' It might be imagined that thoughts like these would be too universal for a simple Jewish maiden. But remember she was espoused to one in whose veins ran the blood of Abraham, whose fathers had been kings in Jerusalem. Joseph was a Hebrew of the Hebrews, and in him she was linked to all the glorious past of her nation. From the hill-top, too, of Nazareth she saw daily the peaks of Hermon, Tabor, and Carmel, and the mist above the distant sea. `So wide a prospect is scarcely seen in Palestine. And as the woman walked at eventide, the beauty and glory of her land must have grown deeply into her heart, till love of country was mingled with the life-blood in her veins. And now, inspired with the thought of the blessedness coming on her nation, the whole past and future of her race, from the tents of the wandering patriarch to the church of the Messiah to come, lay before her patriotic eyes, as blessed at last through Him who should be born of her.

The heart of the Virgin broke into a song of joy. She forgot her own honour in God who gave, she forgot herself in her country.

And this is that which we want in England—women who will understand and feel what love of country means and act upon it; who will lose thought of themselves and their finery and their pleasure in a passionate effort to heal the sorrow and to destroy the dishonour, dishonesty, and vice of England; to realize that as mothers, maidens, wives, and sisters, they have but to bid the men of this country to be true, brave, loving, just, honourable, and wise; and they will become so, as they will become frivolous, base, unloving, ashamed of truth and righteousness, if women are so; to be not content to live only for their own circles, and to be self-sacrificing and tender there, but to take upon their hearts the burden of the poor, the neglected, and the sinful, for whom many of the most influential now exercise a dainty distant pity and no more. This is the woman's patriotism, and the first note of its mighty music—a music which might take into itself and harmonize the discords of English society—was struck more than eighteen hundred years ago in the song of the Virgin Mary.

[January 20, 1867.]

THE DEVELOPMENT OF CHRIST THROUGH THE INFLUENCES OF HOME.

Luke ii. 51.

OF the childhood of the Regenerator of the world we possess, strange to say, scarcely any record. A few mysterious and tender pictures, coloured with the grace of unconsciousness and touched in with the tenderness of a pure woman, meet us in the Gospels. Their most marked characteristic is their simplicity. The stories could not be told in shorter words. There is no parade of wonders. If they are, here and there, supernatural, it is the most natural supernaturalism in the world. There is no exaltation of one fact above another. The commonest occurrence is told with the same quietude as the most uncommon, as if in the presence of the Holy Child all things became equally wonderful. The adoration of the wise men is narrated with no more emphasis than the circumcision of Christ. The revelation to the shepherds is told in the same unassuming strain as the speech of Simeon in the Temple.

Pass on to His boyhood, and the same reticence and simplicity prevail. It is almost as if the compilers of the Gospels wished to answer by anticipation the mythical theory. Jesus is not represented as a youthful prodigy.

There are no accounts of His wonderful acuteness at school, His more than human wisdom, His miraculous power. There is no mist of ornament around Him, no glitter, no enthusiasm, no fantastic marvels; He rose into manhood, like the Temple of Solomon, in solemn noiselessness.

Again. Observe that all these stories are joined to natural events and to common life. Now there was and is still a tendency in Christian theology to idealize Christ's childhood and His life, to seek for the supernatural in it, to multiply miracles, to dwell upon His divinity to the detriment of His humanity; in fact, to do that very thing which the destructive criticism declares the Christians did unconsciously after the death of Christ, to make a picture of His human life in accordance with their conception of His divinity, instead of forming a conception of His divinity from the picture presented in the Gospels of His humanity. To speak of the development of Jesus, of His growth in wisdom and in moral power, is, in spite of the text which states these facts, considered inconsistent with the honour due to Him. To say that He exhibited anything so human as wonder, that He was ignorant of some things, is denounced as heretical, in spite of the assertions of the Evangelists that He marvelled at the centurion's faith, of His own assertion that He did not know the hour of the day of judgment, and of the story that He came to the fig-tree expecting to find fruit thereon, and finding none. To say that Christ, being the reputed son of a village carpenter, probably pursued his father's trade, to speak of Him as entering into the sports of childhood, or sharing in the every-day life of the Nazarenes, is irreverent to these delicate theological susceptibilities.

They all share in the same miserable mistake, the same false conception of an aristocratic Christianity.

I thank God that all these stories are linked to common, every-day life, are bound up in our thoughts with simple childhood, with homely feelings, with quiet village existence, with manual labour, with the belief in a Divine Son of man, who was not 'too bright and good for human nature's daily food.' For next to the blessedness of feeling that in Christ our spiritual being is made alive, is the blessedness of knowing that every phase of pure human life is dignified and beautified in Him.

It lies in the very depth of the idea of Christianity that it is the Eternal Word made flesh. The ancient philosophers were, and we ourselves, in the unconscious philosophy of the heart, are crushed too often with the thought that we can never make the miserable details of a common life agree with the high ideals of the soul. But Christianity (and in this it is essentially a new principle) declares in the life of Christ the actual union of pure Divinity with ordinary human life. Those who, in well-meaning efforts to keep up the dignity of Christ, practically deny this, deny the very deepest thing in Christianity, and deprive it of its greatest power over men. They lose the real in clinging to the ideal; they forget that if they wish to gain the ideal they must pass to it through the real—must, as the Saviour first taught, win the perfect life of Spirit by serene and resolute accomplishing of every stage, of every duty, of every phase of the imperfect life of man.

He traversed all—childhood, boyhood, youth, and manhood; he touched all that was universally common to pure humanity in each, and from henceforth there is no life, even to the very lowest, in which the real may not become what it is in its purity—the ideal; no office, no work, which, done in His spirit, the making of a book or the digging of a garden, may not accord with the highest imagination of your spirit, and chime in with your most poetical vision of perfection.

It is now the time of the Christian year when the childhood and youth of Jesus Christ are brought before our minds. This morning we trace rapidly the influence of His home life upon the character of Christ.

1. It established His love of man upon a sure foundation.

There are dangers in mere philanthropy, or the love of men in the mass. It often sacrifices the individual in its eagerness for the good of the generality. You can never tell what a philanthropist of this kind may become. Robespierre was one, and he decimated France to attain a perfect republic.

Again, in creating large duties abroad, he often neglects small ones at home. The man most benevolent on a large scale may be thoughtless of the peace and comfort of a few workmen personally dependent on himself. Pity and active relief of those in visible and dreadful distress, such as the prisoners in the jails last century, may co-exist with a virulent temper and a cruel tongue. Philanthropy not based on natural affection, not developed naturally from the beginning, has often in practice a tendency to cruelty.

Again, the philanthropist often busies himself about schemes, not persons. His tendency then is to fall in love with his own schemes, and to forget the persons. In this way he sometimes arrives at a curious goal; either at coldness of heart, or at that obstinate rigidity of plan which has in charitable schemes produced greater suffering than that which they were intended to alleviate. If his schemes fail, we see plainly the want of love at the root of his character. He becomes the harsh satirist, and the harsher judge of those men who refused to be benefited by entering into his view of the universe. His pride is hurt, he coils himself up in his own moroseness. That is the inward result of his philanthropy.

Again, philanthropy sometimes degenerates into injurious extravagance. The desire of giving away to others is often nothing more than the mere gratification of an instinct. It produces almost a sensual pleasure in some men, and is a kind of disease. Such a man is the victim of flatterers, and the 'friends' who receive his gifts are worthless. The commonness of his generosity destroys all gratitude, as the commonness of a miracle destroys belief in the supernatural. He is the unintentional enemy of a true society, and when he discovers that he has wasted all on a heartless world, the reaction is terrible. He goes forth from Athens, the misanthrope, hurling imprecations on the society which has disappointed him, to make his solitary grave 'upon the beachèd verge of his salt flood.'

These results are only avoided by beginning from the beginning, from the broad foundation of home affection. We are insensibly taught in the circle of home some useful lessons—taught not to expect too much; taught how necessary flexibility is to love; taught to mould the means of love to the end of love; taught to apply different methods to different characters; taught that delicate economy of affection which restrains the extravagant impulses of affection that it may have more to give. We gain a resting-place of love, whither we may retire with a certainty of finding healing when we are disappointed. We gain a security against moroseness, harshness, and misanthropy. Above all we so root love within our hearts by slow and natural growth that nothing afterwards can eradicate it. We develope our charity in the natural order. First, love of parents, love of family, love of friends; then we are ready to love our country well, to become the wise philanthropist, and finally to concentrate this tried and well-grounded love in one great volume upon God. First, the natural, then the social, then the spiritual.

That was the way of Christ. He grew naturally in love. It was a normal, slow development of the affection which was to die for the world. His love for the mass of men was laid on the foundation of the home life at Nazareth. And afterwards, when He embraced the human race in His infinite charity, the immensity of His view did not destroy His tender sense of the dearness of still domestic life. It is most touching to watch Him, as He drew near to the time when the sacrifice of His life for the world was to be consummated, returning every night over the silent paths of Olivet to seek the same repose and love which he had once enjoyed at Nazareth, in the village home of Bethany. It is the profound lesson of His life that that philanthropy is only true, lasting, and fruitful which has its root in the sanctities of home; that there is one sense in which the proverb, 'Charity begins at home,' is as entirely just as in another it is unjust.

From this love of home life was developed, in the mind of Christ, His deep sense of the worthiness of domestic and social relations.

There are those who do not agree with Him — men who think that in separation from all domestic and social ties they can live more purely and worship God with a more entire devotion; that a systematic contempt for all the bonds which bind mother to son, and wife to husband, is a proof of the highest spirituality; whose spiritual religion consists in a denial of the natural piety of the heart, and whose efforts for a reformation of human nature are founded on a denial of human nature.

This was not the feeling of the Perfect Man; He had learnt other lessons from his Heavenly Father's teaching given through the blessed influences of home. He sanctified the marriage tie by His first public miracle. He sanctified the social meetings of the world by the same miracle. He came to men, not fasting and living apart like the ascetic John, but eating and drinking; and hallowing the life of business and of daily work by walking continually among the throng of men in active labour and in social communion. He met once a widow weeping over the dead body of her only son. Did He meet her with a stern and harsh reproof, or with a recommendation to a conventual life? 'And when the Lord saw her, He had compassion on her.' He stood by the grave of His friend, and heard the sister of Lazarus weeping. Did He check the tears, and denounce the love of nature? 'Jesus wept.' He hung in dying agony upon the Cross, and beneath Him stood the friend of His manhood and the Mother of His youth. Did He unbind the band of sorrow which united them? In words crowded with the brief eloquence of death, He bore a dying witness to His sense of the blessedness of the domestic ties, and to His own remembrance of their power. 'Woman, behold thy son.' Friend, 'behold thy mother.'

In this development of love in the heart of Christ there were two other conditions of affection which arose directly out of His home life. These were *friendship* and *patriotism*. The necessity in his heart for friendship, i.e. for affection for distinct persons, as distinguished from the general love of the race, was developed by the home life at Nazareth. Supposing it possible to conceive of Christ as the mere philanthropist who sacrifices particular friendships to universal love, how much had been lost to us for ever! For we stand in wonder and in awe before the love which died to save the world; but when we are left desolate in life, and no human voice can give to us either power of will or resignation of heart—then we turn for personal consolation to Him who loved John with the distinguishing love of friendship, for sympathy to Him who felt alike with the impetuous repentance of

Peter and the silent tears of Mary for the brother she had lost.

Not only friendship but also patriotism. The source of the tears which the Saviour wept over Jerusalem arose, humanly speaking, in the heart of His Mother. From her lips he learnt to love His country. The last thought of the Virgin's hymn of joy shows how the young girl of Nazareth loved her fatherland. Her soul magnified the Lord, because He, remembering His mercy, had holpen His servant Israel, as He promised to our forefathers, to Abraham and his seed for ever. Patriotism passed from the mother into the son. Once aroused within His heart, it rose far beyond her teaching, expanding to meet the infinite proportions of His Being, but its germ was stirred to life by the influences of home.

And here we meet not only the general influence of home life, but a particular influence which bore upon His childhood and His youth—the influence of His mother's character. It has been said 'that it is almost unnatural to ask, to whom we are indebted for the information respecting the childhood of Jesus; that as it is mothers who supply the stories of their children's history, so the source of the early history of Jesus was undoubtedly Mary.' It is probable that she is referred to as the authority, when we are told in my text that Mary 'kept all these things, and pondered them in her heart.' Indeed the colouring is altogether feminine. The memories are those of a woman; and besides this there is in all these stories such an unapproachable gracefulness, quiet loveableness, and holy solemnity, that we refer them at once to the Virgin who sang the hymn of joy, to the Mother whose heart a sword had pierced.

How else, then, but in patriotism did Mary's character influence the development of Christ? First, through her reverence for the mind of her Child. When He came home from that scene in the Temple, so strange to the curious love of a Mother who had lived a peaceful village life, we gather from the text that she did not force her way with curiosity into the holy of holies of a human soul. 'She kept all these things, and pondered them in her heart.' But the reverence was not all on one side. We are told that the Saviour 'was subject to' His parents. There was, then, a mutual respect. This it was which made love so lasting. For there is no permanency of love but that which is based on mutual reverence. That affection is the highest 'which is mingled of two feelings—love which attracts, veneration which repels.' Mary respected the reserve of her Child; made no demand on the mysteries of His heart, used no authority to force Him to disclose His thoughts, and in so doing stirred to life in His heart the seeds which produced in His manhood reverence for the souls of others. For if there is one thing more than another which marks the ministry of Christ among men, it is this—reverence for the human soul. Startlingly different in this from the teaching of many of our modern doctors, He seems never to have believed in the entire wickedness of any one, except perhaps in that of the religious bigot who condemned others bitterly because of his own hypocrisy. The doctrine of 'total depravity' was unknown to Christ. Everywhere He believed not in the vileness, but in the greatness of the human soul; and He called forth in men, by this trust in them, a conviction of their immortality, a longing for a nobler life, a sense of their degradation and death as long as they sinned, a conviction of the glory and beauty of holiness. He saw in the publican whom all men shunned the germ of an honest life. He believed in it, and it grew and bloomed into spiritual beauty. He saw in the fallen woman, whom the proud Pharisee thought had defiled his house, a spark of the Divine love. He believed in it, and it was quickened into a holy flame. In the most ignorant and lost He saw the children of His Father, the citizens of heaven. As the artist's shaping imagination beholds within the unhewn block of moss-stained marble the form and loveliness of the statue he has already created, and will now embody, so Christ saw in the most degraded soul a 'temple of the Holy Ghost' with capacities for infinite progress, with powers for noble work, with possibilities for perfect holiness. Reverencing, then, the human soul above all things, it mattered little to Him whether He dined with the rich Pharisee, or entered the cottage of the outcast. The immortal dweller in the body was the object of His love, and it was nothing to Him whether it dwelt in prince or working man, in the moral Pharisee or the immoral harlot; wherever it was, it was worthy of His reverence, and the object of His work. He devoted Himself to its deliverance from those who usurped within it the righteous rule of God. In deep veneration for the image of God which it presented to His eyes, He restored it to its ancient beauty.

Lastly. The meditative character of Mary influenced

the character of Christ. That is, her character did not create this faculty in His mind, but brought it forth into distinctness, aided in its development. 'She kept all these things, and *pondered* them in her heart,' till the time for action and for speech had come. It was long, long before she revealed to any one the message of the angel. Her silence is, next to that of Christ's, the most remarkable thing in this history. She was a woman of quiet thought, of solitary prayer, of tacit power. It is impossible to get rid of the belief that this had its natural influence on the development of the human nature of Christ. We see at least that in the highest and noblest way our Saviour's life embodied this strength of waiting, this silence of growth, this love of lonely meditation. Those thirty years of hidden stillness, those forty days of solitary thought within the wilderness, what lessons do they not both contain!

When the turmoil of conflicting parties, the noise of controversy, and the babble of slander had wearied His sacred heart, He went away into the mountain solitudes to God, and on the rocks of Hermon, or in the deserts of Perea, or on the waves and shores of the Sea of Galilee, entered into the silence of deep communion with His Father. Even in the midst of active life there seems ever to have been within Him a second inward life of meditation. The awful sorrow of the world, the vast extent of His work, the illimitable results which were to flow from it, were with Him ceaselessly as thoughts. 'I have a baptism to be baptized with; how am I straitened till it be accomplished!' 'The work which my Father hath given me to do, shall I not do it?' 'Other sheep I

Influences of Home.

have, which are not of this fold; them also I must bring.' These and many other expressions which seem to come almost involuntarily from His lips are hints by which we may comprehend what was passing in His secret soul. We think too exclusively of His life as a life of action; we should more and more try to realize it as a life of thought.

From all this learn some large lessons. Seek to develope yourselves slowly, steadily, believing that God has given you a work to do in the world. Do not be in a hurry to seize on life. The man who believes in God and in himself does not make haste. Do not rush rashly out of the Nazareth in which you may be placed, even though thirty years may pass by unoccupied. The time of action will come at last, and your seeming inaction is necessary for right action.

Be not impatient of obedience. It is the parent of the power of governing, it is the parent of true self-liberty. Freedom can only develope itself within the circle of law.

And when you are called upon to issue from your time of quiet training into actual life, forget not these two last lessons—one for your private life, one for your public life.

Remember that some hours of quietude are necessary as a support of energy—that thought is the only true support of action.

Remember that reverence for the souls and thoughts of men whom you meet is not only the way to redeem them, but the way to conquer them.

To suspect every one is the maxim of the world; to reverence every one is the principle of Christ.

[February 2, 1867.]

THE DEVELOPMENT OF CHRIST THROUGH THE INFLUENCES OF OUTWARD NATURE.

Luke ii. 40.

IN the history of the early Church we meet with a sect the members of which were called Ebionites, who thought the natural humanity of the Saviour's early life unworthy of a Divine Person, and who necessarily denied His essential divinity. Hence to them Christ was, till His baptism, a common man. It was at His baptism that He received from God, as an external gift, the consciousness of His divine mission and special powers for it.

This opinion, which arose from the idea that human nature is in its essence antagonistic to the Divine nature, appears under various forms in the present day: in the extreme doctrine of the corruption of human nature, in the offence which is taken when Christ is said to have been a working man, in the horror which is expressed when Christ's knowledge of the heart and His predictive power are referred rather to His perfect humanity than to His divinity. So far as this tendency prevails in the Church, it is the tendency to deny the humanity of Christ; and such a denial is the worst of heresies if we measure the evil of a heresy by the evil results which it produces. If we were *forced* to choose between two half-truths, between believing only in the divinity or only in the humanity of Christ, there is no doubt that to believe only in His humanity would be less destructive to Christian life and to Christianity than to believe only in His divinity.

But we are not driven into that dilemma. We do not hold the necessary unworthiness of human nature as a habitation of the Divine. We hold, with the old writer, that man is 'the image of God;' that humanity in its purity is divine, and that as such, and in proportion to its purity, it has always been the chosen organ whereby God has manifested Himself in time. Through a long line of patriarchs, kings, and prophets among the Jews, through thousands of noble creatures among the heathen nations, God at sundry times, and in divers manners, has declared Himself partially to man. Partially and imperfectly, because all these were partial and imperfect men. At last the fulness of time came, and with it came the archetypal Man ; and in Him God spoke unto us Himself as He was in His essential life. 'The Word was made flesh.' The organ was perfect, and the Divine nature found itself perfectly at home. In Christ these two natures, originally one, but separated in us, re-united, interpenetrated one another, and found themselves One.. This union of two natures was not then, as has been too much conceived, a thing entirely new, a new order of life, it was the re-establishment of the old and perfect order.

Hence, instead of looking upon Christ's youth and childhood, and His common life, as derogatory to His glory, we see in them the glorification of all human thought and action in every stage of life, in every kind of labour. The whole of humanity is penetrated by the Divine. This is the foundation-stone of the Gospel of Christ. On it rest all the great doctrines of Christianity, on it reposes all the noble practice of Christian men, and we call it—the Incarnation.

But this re-uniting of the divinity and humanity took place in time, and under the limitations which are now imposed upon humanity. The Divine Word was self-limited on its entrance into our nature, in some such sense as our spirit and our thought are limited by union with body. Consequently, we should argue that there was a gradual development of the person of Christ; and this conclusion, which we come to *à priori*, is supported by the narrative in the Gospels. We are told that Jesus 'increased in wisdom,' that He 'waxed strong in spirit,' that He 'learned obedience,' that He was 'made perfect through suffering.'

This is our subject—the development of Christ. And first, we are met with a difficulty. The idea of development seems to imply imperfection passing into perfection—seems to exclude the idea of original perfection.

But there are two conceivable kinds of development; one, development through antagonism, through error, from stage to stage of less and less deficiency. This is our development; but it is such because evil has gained a lodgment in our nature, and we can only attain perfection through contest with it. But there is another kind of development conceivable, the development of a *perfect* nature limited by time. Such a nature will always be potentially that which it will become; i.e. everything which it will be is already there, but the development of it is successive, according to time; perfect at each several stage, but each stage more finished than the last. The plant is perfect as the green shoot above the earth, it is *all* it can be then; it is more perfect as the creature adorned with leaves and branches, and it is *all* it can be then; it reaches its full perfection when the blossom breaks into flower. But it has been as perfect as it can be at every stage of its existence; it has had no struggle, no retrogression; it has realized in an entirely normal and natural way, at each successive step of its life, exactly and fully that which a plant should be.

Such was the development of Christ. He was the perfect child, the perfect boy, the perfect youth, the perfect flower of manhood. Every stage of human life was lived in finished purity, and yet no stage was abnormally developed; there was nothing out of character in His life. He did not think the thoughts of a youth when a child, nor feel the feelings of a man when a youth; but He grew freely, nobly, naturally, unfolding all His powers without a struggle, in a completely healthy progress.

A second illustration may make the matter clearer. The work of an inferior artist arrives at a certain amount of perfection through a series of failures, which teach him where he is wrong. By slow correction of error he is enabled to produce a tolerable picture. Such is our development.

The work of a man of genius is very different. He has *seen*, before he touches pencil, the finished picture.

His first sketch contains the germ of all. The picture is there; but the first sketch is inferior in finish to the next stage, and that to the completed picture. But his work is perfect in its several stages; not a line needs erasure, not a thought correction; it developes into its last and noblest form without a single error. Such was Christ's development—an orderly, faultless, unbroken development, in which humanity, freed from its unnatural companion, .evil, went forward according to its real nature. It was the restoration of humanity to its original integrity, to itself, as it existed in the idea of God.

Having thus freed our subject from a natural objection, we proceed to speak of the development of the human character of the Saviour. First, think to-day of His development through the influence of outward nature.

The scenery of Nazareth is known, or ought to be well known, to you all. I will not describe it. It is sufficient to say that from the summit of the hill in whose bosom Nazareth lay, there sweeps one of the widest and most varied landscapes to be seen in Palestine. It is impossible to over-estimate the influence which this changing scene of beauty had upon the mind of the Saviour as a child.

The Hebrew feeling for nature was deep and extended. Nations have generally many words for that which interests them the most, and, to take one example which is only a type of all, the Hebrew language has more than ten different words for different kinds of rain.

By race, then, alone the Child Jesus was prepared to

Influences of Outward Nature. 113

feel the most delicate shades of change in the aspect of outward nature. But as He was not only Hebrew but the type of pure humanity, we may, without attributing to Him anything unnatural to childhood, impute to Him the subtler feelings which are stirred in the western and northern races by the modes of natural beauty.

Childhood is the seed-time of the soul, and the great sower of seed in the child's heart is nature. Now that time and rough contact with the world have worn out our early impressions, now that the light of common day glares upon us so fiercely, we can scarcely recall our childhood's sensations or see our childhood's visions. But whatever we then felt, whatever we then beheld when, left alone, we saw the 'visions of the hills,' and felt the 'souls of lonely places,' and received from them high impulses which in maturer years germinated into action—or deep emotions which stirred the heart unconsciously with passions and with hopes which became in after time one of the sources of our belief in immortality—whatever, then, our childhood half perceived and half created, was seen and felt by Christ. Whatever noble intercourse we have had in our far-off childhood with the enduring beauty of the world, that beauty, in its recurring freshness so young, in its inconceivable age so dignified, and which, as such, comes 'to purify the elements of feeling and of thought,' Christ in His childhood also possessed, and loved to possess. Whatever of 'those hallowed and pure motions of the sense, which seem, in their simplicity, to own an intellectual charm,' we have ever in our youth received—whatever 'gleams like the flashing of a shield' have come upon us of things mysterious and beautiful, not of earth, but of a higher region in which the spirit lives and loves— were received and felt profoundly by Christ our Saviour as a child.

But there must have been this difference. To us they are mysterious, inexplicable, attended with the phantom, Fear; to *Him* they came as guests, as natural ministers, attended by the consciousness of love and fatherhood. They stirred, they woke, they fostered His early feelings and His childish thought. WE are conscious of our homelessness in contact with these deep impressions. HE, while receiving the same impressions, was conscious of being at home in a Father's world.

Again. The feeling of our childhood is that nature is alive. We tread lightly through the forest, for we feel there is a 'spirit in the woods.' 'The trees nod to us, and we to them.' The sea sympathizes with our passion and our calm. The brook, over its pebbles, sings to us a loving song. Our childhood is all Greek. Every fountain has its indweller, every mountain is alive with living creatures, every oak whispers through its leaves of a living soul within, and the breaking music of the wave upon the beach is the laughter of the daughters of the sea.

But as we grow older, we unlearn the faith of childhood; and as science gives to us its teaching, we find that we can only explain phenomena on the supposition that nature is not living, but dead.

But the fact is that our childhood is really right in principle, though wrong in its application of the principle. Nature is living, though not in the way we then imagine. We fancy that we are moving, the only living things, in a dead world; the fact is we are moving, the only dead things, in a living world. And there are moments, even now, 'when years have brought the inevitable yoke,' that we catch some glimpses of the truth; when we are freed from this incubus of a dead world, and realize the living world; when the old stars of our childhood reappear, and we learn a deeper lesson from them than childhood could receive; when the trees talk to one another in the wood, and we hear and understand their speech; when we listen to the voice of the great deep with the same awful joy as the child, but with a completer comprehension; when the mountains, watched by us at night, are not dead forms, but gray-haired sages, who sit in silence waiting for the dawn. These do not speak to us then of the old Greek humanities, but of *God*. We stand in His presence, and the trees and sea, the stars and mountains, whisper to us that it is not they which exist, but that invisible world of which they and their relations to each other are at once both form and symbol—the spiritual world of God's eternal love, enduring sacrifice, ever-moving progress, the calm of his order, the rest of His unopposed activity, ' His righteousness like the great mountains, His judgments like the deep.'

Falling back to common life from such a momentary revelation, we feel that we are dead, that we are not at one with the living Spirit who represents Himself to us in the universe, that there is a secret there we have not wit to penetrate, a life there we have not power to share. But miserable as is the reaction from such a revelation of the living God, there is left behind within our hearts a light of hope. We should not be able to enter thus, even for a moment, behind the veil, were not God resolved to make us fully capable of doing so. This 'muddy vesture of decay' shall fall away for ever, and we shall pass from death to life. We shall behold for ever what we have seen in moments. We shall live in the spiritual world of which the physical is the appearance, and see and feel and move in that which is not lifeless but alive.

In such a world, while here on earth, we reverentially conjecture that the Saviour moved. He learned to see, in childhood, the spiritual world beneath the physical. The phenomena of nature and their relations awoke in His heart the germs of those spiritual realities of which they are the symbols. They impressed His senses with their beauty; but they also made His spirit conscious of the divine principles of Being. Hence He gradually became at home with the spirit of the universe, and knew that it was living. That which comes to us at instants only was His daily life. Listen to His conversation, mark His parables. Do not we hear in phrases like these, 'I am the true vine,' 'Consider the lilies of the field,' &c., and in parables like that of the sower; the kingdom of heaven like the mustard-seed; like the seed sown in the earth which grew up, no man knew how; in the likeness of Himself to the dying seed, which died to produce life; the note of some concealed harmony, the possession of some deeper secret, which made the outward world to Him the image of a living spiritual world?

Influences of Outward Nature. 117

Yes; He possessed the life in which we are defective. He grew up from childhood seeing the invisible, hearing the unheard, feeling the inconceivable. The life of God in nature awoke into conscious being the life of God which was within Him. The truths of God were borne in upon His childhood through the influence of nature, and they found in Him not opposition as they find in us, not a darkness which cannot comprehend them. They found *themselves* in germ, they touched these germs, and at the touch the seeds awoke to life, grew into ideas, and became consciously the property of the child. So swiftly did they develope their being, that, waxing strong in spirit, He could at twelve years old realize His mission and His work, and wonder that others were astonished that He should be about His Father's business.

This is something, as I conceive it, of the development of Christ through the influence of nature.

On all this, one inference. We have supposed in what we have said that Christ in the humanity of childhood became conscious, through nature, of what we call natural religion. The very shock which this phrase of mine will give to some in this congregation, and the instinctive feeling of reluctance with which I speak it, lead me to the thing I wish to say. Some things shock us because we have been educated to think otherwise. Some things shock us because they injure the moral sense. It is custom only which is shocked in this case.

I believe that in our ardour for spiritual religion we have neglected too much the religion which springs from nature. Spiritual religion alone, leaves part of our nature unsatisfied—all that large region of imagination and feelings which are kindled into awe and joy by the influences of natural beauty, by the activity and change, by the passion and calm of nature. The poets have seized on this region and made it their own, and it might be called the region of natural poetry. It has lost its true name, which is the region of the religion of nature. It is considered as the realm in which beauty, and sublimity, and a hundred other abstractions are revealed; it has ceased, practically, to be considered as the realm in which God is revealed. We confine the revelation of God to the spiritual truths disclosed in Christianity. It is not too much to say that that is a great practical mistake. There are two books of revelation—the book of nature and the book of God's speech to man's spirit. When the latter succeeded the former, it did not intend to push the religion derived from nature away for ever, but to supplement it. Both were to be retained by us, only one naturally was to be higher than the other. But the overwhelming importance given to spiritual religion has removed out of the sphere of our religious thought the religion of nature.

Consequently, the study of nature by scientific men, and the contemplation of nature by poetic men, have both become irreligious. There is no living God within the world to many scientific men. They see only a rigid chain of antecedents and sequences. And the poet, and those who live in the poetic atmosphere, shudder at the thought of the dead world which the exclusive insistance on spiritual religion has forced them to contemplate, and sometimes, carried away by their passion, wish, for the moment, that they were once more at home in that old Greek religion where the world was a living world. There are times when we cannot but sympathize with Schiller's passionate cry in his hymn to the gods of Greece. And who has not felt what Wordsworth meant (and he cannot be accused of want of Christianity), when, rather than be so out of tune with nature, he wished to be

> A Pagan suckled in a creed outworn;
> So might I, standing on this pleasant lea,
> Have glimpses that might make me less forlorn.

What does this mean? Surely we are to find the answer, not in the destructive influence of Christianity on the imagination, but rather in our neglect of that religion of nature which Christianity was to take into itself, and not to overthrow. The tendency for centuries, I repeat, both of science and of spiritual religion, *exclusively* insisted on, has been to make nature godless, to take away the light and joy, the beauty and the harmony of our life with nature.

Brethren, it should not be so. While clinging fast to Christianity as the life of the spirit, we should recover the ancient natural religion which saw in mountains and forests, in the changing beauty of the heavens above, and in the varied loveliness of the earth below, the revelation of the movement and life and beauty of the living God.

There is no need of a return to Greek conceptions, but there is much need among us of a return to the old

Jewish conceptions which we have forgotten. The Psalmists were not Greeks, and yet we never find them use the mournful cry of modern poetry.

To them nature was not dead, but peopled with the life of Deity. The light was the garment of the living God, the clouds were His chariot. The wind was winged, and in its swift approach there walked Jehovah. He caused the grass to grow upon the mountains. He planted the cedars of Libanus. The deep places of the earth were in His hand, the sea sang His praise, the floods clapped their hands, and the hills were joyful together before the Lord. The heavens declared His glory, and the voice of the thunder was the voice of the Lord.

It is exquisitely sad to think how much we have lost of this. Science comes and gives us an explanation which kills the livingness in the wind and the joy in the sea; and, worse far than this, 'the world is too much with us,' and, 'getting and spending, we lay waste our powers.' We are groping in the dust of the exchange or wearying our imagination for new pleasures. The season is coming on, and, driven by energies and aspirations, the true end of which we blind our hearts to, we shall exhaust enthusiasm and spend our noblest passions in things and scenes which, to say the least of them, are utterly divided from all natural existence, and out of it all, at the end, we shall come jaded and worn, with energies exhausted and feelings ragged with weariness, and go off to recruit in the country; as if, in *that* condition, the country had anything to say to us. For who sees God in the stars, or hears His voice in the wind, in the full rush of a

London season? We are killing in us all the religion of nature.

He does the same evil to himself—I speak without fear of being misunderstood—who shuts himself up in the dreary kingdom of a dry theology, or who morbidly broods upon his own spiritual state, or who reads of his God *only* in the pages of a printed book. We are not all spirit; we are heart, imagination, feelings, and these demand their food.

O brethren! add to the spiritual revelation of God in Christ the Man, the revelation of God in Nature. Let the living Being who speaks in the universe share in your development. Open your heart to the ceaseless tide of influence which streams in upon it from the world of nature; and believe me, if you are a child of science, your scientific acumen will be none the worse for feeling that there is another world in nature than that which your methods reveal to you—a world which appeals not to the intellect, but to the heart and the spirit, the world in which the ancient Jew saw God, and wherein we may see, if we have eyes, the Lord God walking in the garden in the cool of the day. If with one part of my nature I have measured the speed and the orbit of a comet, am I the worse if with another I see in the wanderer of space the mystery of God's nature and the wonder of His order? If with my intellect I analyze the light, am I the worse if with my heart I behold in it the Light of the character of God?

I am the better, on the contrary, inasmuch as I have got a more varied and a larger view. I allot to each conception its own sphere, but I *maim* my nature if I allow one sphere to eclipse the other. Keep your scientific conceptions clear, keep them apart from all confusion with the feelings of religion, or with the play of the imagination, but do not forget to feed your imagination and to feed your spirit with their natural food, for it is this forgetfulness which tends to make scientific men what they sometimes are, monsters of abnormal intellectual development.

Once more, let not the spiritual man despise or ignore this religion derived from nature. We have shown what evil this has done. It has left the world of nature without a God, it has made it lifeless—in modern poetry especially, only the reflex of our humanity; in science, only a circle of continuous force, for ever returning upon itself. We are bound to restore God to our conception of nature. We are bound to make use of all the feelings which are kindled by beauty of sight or beauty of sound, to teach our children those great fundamental conceptions of God which the fathers of the world possessed, and which the ancient heathen asserted under the false forms of polytheism. This religion of nature preceded spiritual religion, and was its preparation. It is unwise to destroy the stage by which we were fitted to enter on the higher stage. It is unwise, in the education of our children, to neglect the historical order. God educated the childhood of the world through the religion of nature; if what we have said be true, Christ passed through the same training. We ought to educate our children at first in natural religion; they will then gradually and naturally pass on with us to the loftier region.

And we ourselves, looking back from our spiritual realm of thought, and with its added knowledge, will be able to gain new thoughts and exalting feelings from our contemplation of the outward world of God—feelings which will supplement and fill up that which is deficient in our spiritual experience, thoughts which will add force and reality to our spiritual principles. For having gained the Spirit of Christ through the higher revelation, we shall have our eyes opened to see His Spirit also in the revelation of creation. We shall see in the involuntary death of things to produce new forms of life, His spirit of sacrifice, who died for us that we might live; in Nature's quiet order, His rest upon His Father's fidelity; in Nature's uncomplaining labour, which ceases not for ever, His Spirit whose meat and drink it was to do His Father's will and to finish His work; in all the principles of Nature's life the principles of the life of Christ.

Thus, finally, in our daily existence these two great religions, each appealing to two portions of our nature, will be interwoven together into an harmonious whole, each supplementing and strengthening the other, till under their teaching we develope ourselves and our children in a manner more closely in union with the development of the Perfect Man.

[Feb. 9, 1867.]

THE INTELLECTUAL DEVELOPMENT OF CHRIST.

Luke ii. 52.

THE subject on which we are employed is the development of Christ. Seeing that the term is challengeable, I attempted to explain last Sunday, when treating of the Saviour's development in childhood through the influence of outward nature, the meaning which I attached to it in reference to Him. Before I proceed to speak of His intellectual development, which is our subject for this morning, I repeat in other words the distinction I made between our development and His. We, being defective in nature, are developed through error. By slow correction of mistakes, we arrive at intellectual, by slow correction of faults at moral, excellence. But it is quite possible to conceive the entirely natural development of Christ's perfect nature, limited by time; the development, as it were, of a fountain into a river, perfect as the fountain, but not more than the fountain as a child; perfect as the rivulet, but not more than the rivulet as a boy; perfect as the stream, but not more than the stream as a youth; and perfect as the majestic river as a man. At each stage greater than at the last, more developed, but as perfect as possible to nature at each; and as the water of the fountain, rivulet, stream, and river is the same throughout, self-supplied, perennial in its source and flowing, so was it with the nature of Christ, and with His growth.

The intellectual development of Christ is then our subject. We derive the term from the words, 'He increased in wisdom.' But before we begin, I must ask you to bear in mind throughout this principle—All outward influences did not *give* anything to Christ; they awoke and presented to His consciousness that which was already there in germ.

The first hint which we receive of this intellectual development is the story of His journey to Jerusalem. We find Him in the Temple listening and asking questions of the doctors; or, in other words, exhibiting Himself as possessed of the two first necessities for intellectual development—engrossed attention and eager curiosity.

Now what were the steps by which we may reverently conjecture the Divine Child had arrived at this kindling of the intellect, and how did these several steps affect His character?

Last Sunday we endeavoured to represent Him as stirred by the outward scenery of nature to recognize what was within Himself, and as recognizing in nature not the dead and lifeless world, as we conceive it, but a living world, beneath whose outward forms lay spiritual realities.

Now communion with nature intensifies the desire of communion with man. And it seems to me impossible to deny that He who afterwards, even in His most solemn hours, on the mount of Transfiguration and in the garden of Gethsemane, sought and surrounded Himself with the sympathy of His three favourite disciples, did not also as a child seek for human sympathy to share with Him His childhood's delight in the beauty and solemnity of nature. Hence there was strengthened in Him love of man arising from love of nature; there was quickened in Him desire of social communion, desire of seeing His own thought reflected by other minds, desire of knowing what other beings than Himself both knew and thought and did in the world.

There was not much to gratify these desires in Nazareth. We know the character of the place, and the Holy Child must even then have felt the first keen stings of that agony for the sin of the world which made Him as man die to redeem the world. Moreover, a remote and petty village could supply but little food to His awakened and craving intellect. He had soon assimilated all He could find there of the elements necessary to develope His mental powers. I can conceive Him, I trust without irreverence, eagerly looking forward to the day when He should accompany His parents to Jerusalem; not unduly excited, not impatient, but nobly curious to see human life concentrated in one of its great centres, to watch the movement and the variety of the crowd of many nations who poured into Jerusalem at the Feast of the Passover.

At last the hour came, and with the 'quiet independence of heart' which He had secured through still communion with nature, with the deep desire of knowing men, and with a deep sense of child-like repose on

The Intellectual Development of Christ.

God, the Boy, Christ Jesus, set forth with His company from Nazareth. No doubt, according to pious Jewish practice, He had been instructed in the history of His people, and now, what thoughts were His as for the first time He saw the interior of Palestine, the Jordan rolling deep between its banks, the savage landscape of the eastern desert! There was not a spot along the route which was not dignified by some association, or hallowed by some great name.

Whatever we in youth have felt—for life wears out the keenness of receptiveness—when we have stood upon some spot made glorious in our country's history, whatever thrill of high emotion or rush of noble impulse has then come upon us, and swept us out of our narrow sphere of childish interests into the wide region of interests which cluster round the words 'our country and its heroes,' came then, we may be sure, upon the Child. A larger horizon of thought opened before Him. The heroic past of Israel became a reality. The sight of places where noble deeds were done made the deeds themselves real. And not only the deeds, but also the *men*; for in the years gone by Hebrew men had here done and suffered greatly. Here was their theatre; this was Jordan; there was Jericho; there David had passed by; there Jacob had set up his rugged pillow. At once, localized, impersonated by the landscape, the men of Israel became real living personages, the past was crowded with moving forms, and History was born in the intellect of Christ. The impression must have deepened in Him as He entered Jerusalem. He must have felt in heart and soul the shock of the great town's first presence. He could not walk unmoved among the streets, so vocal with the fame of Solomon, the patriotic enthusiasm of Isaiah, the sorrow and the passion of Jeremiah. The stones of the walls spoke to Him, the gates replied—and when first He saw the mighty mass of the great Temple flashing white in the sunlight upon its uplifted rock, what a thrill!—a thrill of that fine excitement, half of sense and half of soul, which is almost a physical pain, and out of which springs more creative thought than comes afterwards to a man in a year of that 'set gray life' of work which we know so well in London. These are the impressions which kindle latent intellect, which abide with us as living things within the brain, engendering the life of thought; and if *we*, cold northern natures, have felt these things in our childhood, and at a younger age than Christ was now, how must an Oriental child of genius (to assume for a moment a ground which the destructive critics will not deny) have felt their power on His intellect?

Look at another point.

As He drew near to Jerusalem in this journey, various troops of pilgrims must have joined their company. He saw for the first time the great diversity of the human race. Accustomed to one type alone at Nazareth, and that a limited type—for Nazareth was an outlying village; and a somewhat degraded type, for Nazareth had a bad reputation—He was now brought into contact with many types of men.

The same kind of result, we may conjecture, was produced upon His intellect as is produced when a boy

The Intellectual Development of Christ. 129

is first sent out of the narrow circle of home into the varied human life of a public school. The impression which is then made upon the intellect of a boy is one of the most productive which he receives in life. The impression made upon the mind of Christ must have been of equal depth at least, probably far greater; for, first, we know from His after life that His intellect was of the mightiest character, and secondly, the variety which met Him was greater than that with which an English boy is brought into contact. Thus it was not only the realization of the past through the power of association which stirred His intellect; it was also stirred by the contact with the varied national and individual life of the present.

And then there was that wonderful Jerusalem in front where all this variety of life was now concentrated. What wonder if the pure, high-hearted Child, with eager thoughts beginning to move, looked forward with intellectual enthusiasm to His arrival among the throng of men?

More and more, it is plain, the vast idea of Humanity must have unfolded itself within Him during the journey. Then came, to complete and fix this idea, the rush and confusion of the great multitude in Jerusalem during the Feast—men of every nation under heaven in the streets; strange dresses, strange faces. There was the Roman soldier, grave, and bearing in his face the stamp of law and sacrifice; there was the acute Greek countenance, the heavy Egyptian features, the voluptuous lip and subtle glance of the Persian, the wild Arab eyes; every face was a mystery, and the greatest mystery of all was the wonderful world of men.

What kindles thought like this?—the first rush upon the brain of the idea of the diversity of humanity.

It is an idea naturally conceived by a boy. We do not impute to Christ, at this time, the thoughts which arise from it, too numerous to mention. But we find it here in its origin, and in the silent time to come in Nazareth it worked in His intellect, producing its fruit of thought from year to year. Do we trace it in His ministry? 'Other sheep I have which are not of this fold; them also I must bring.' 'Many shall come from the East and West.' 'Go ye into all the world, and preach the gospel to every creature.'

There is another intellect-awakening thought correlative to this of the diversity of humanity, which I cannot but think was first stirred now in the mind of Christ—the thought of the *unity of the race*.

There was one spirit predominant in all the pilgrims to the Feast. They came up to Jerusalem, diverse as they were, inspired by one thought, to perform one common worship, in one place, to one God. It was the form in which the national unity of the Jewish people had been of old embodied. But now, hundreds of other nations had received the Jewish religion as proselytes. Christ, therefore, saw not only the Jews but Gentiles united by the worship of a universal God. We do not say that He clearly conceived the thought of the oneness of humanity at the age of twelve—it was probably too large for His normal development—but we do say that there is nothing unnatural in believing that the germ of it was then first quickened into life. Now there are few thoughts which more than this promote intellectual development. We may imagine it slowly growing into fulness during the maturing years at Nazareth, till at last it altered its form and became personal. This unity of humanity, so broken, so imperfect—this great idea—where is it realized perfectly? And out of the depths of Christ's divine and human consciousness came the answer. It is realized in *me*. All that is human meets in *me*. *I* am the centre where all the diverse and converging lines of humanity meet. *I* am the race.

This is no fancy. He assumed the title of the Son of man. No one has ever dared, but He, to style Himself thus absolutely *man*; no one has ever felt himself thus the realized ideal of humanity, the representative of the whole race to itself, the representative of the whole race to God.

Once more, in tracing the intellectual development of Christ in connection with this one glimpse of His history, we come to the scene in the Temple. Led there by His desire to know, He was brought for the first time into contact with cultivated intellects. He heard for the first time the acute reasoning of the schools; He realized for the first time the vastness of the sea of knowledge. The thought of the diversity of the human intellect was exhibited to Him in the diversity of the opinions which He heard.

When a man first leaves his village for college, and hears opinions, which he has been accustomed to see only in one light, discussed, debated, looked at from fifty different points of view, contradicted, asserted in other and strange forms, a stir is made at once in his intellect, a hundred collateral questions spring to light and ask for a reply; the old bed of his lake of thought is disturbed, and in the disturbance hundreds of new fountains are set free.

This may, generally speaking, represent the crisis which now took place in the intellect of Christ. Feeling deeply that His development was perfect in its several stages, we cannot believe that any of the older thoughts of the Child were negatived by the new thought, or that anything was really disturbed in the sense in which we may predicate that of ourselves. In Him this disturbance was the *orderly* disturbance caused by a multitude of new thoughts being called into conscious being in His mind by the shock given to it by the thoughts of others. But there was more. Here He was made acquainted with the parties among the Jews; with the petrified theology of the scribes, with the conventional morality of the Pharisee, with the conservative infidelity of the Sadducee, with all the false show of religion and the death which lay beneath. There He saw

> Decency and Custom starving Truth,
> And blind Authority beating with his staff
> The Child that might have led him.

Probably these were, at first, only impressions, but we cannot doubt that they produced their fruit at Nazareth. For, starting from these experiences, there grew up within Him that clear comprehension of Jewish life and all its opinions and parties, and of the way in which He was destined to work upon them, which comes out so wonderfully in His ministry. He did not hear in vain the doctors disputing, He did not ask them questions without a great intellectual result.

Such must have been the influence on the intellect of Christ of his days in the Temple. It should be delightful to us to think of Him, whom we reverence as Master and Lord, sharing thus in our curious childhood, listening with engrossed attention, 'both hearing them'—questioning with eager desire—'and asking them questions.' It should be a wonderful thought for us to imagine, with love and awe combined, how idea after idea, existing there potentially, unfolded their germs under this influence in the mind of Christ—germs which, maturing, and, as they matured, generating others, grew up during the years of silence at Nazareth, into that perfect flower of intellect which, shedding its living seeds over eighteen centuries, has given birth to the great ideas which once created, and still create, the greater part of the intellectual life of the world.

One word in conclusion. After this crisis in His history He returned to Nazareth; the same, and yet how changed, how largely widened and deepened must have been His human nature! The thought of humanity had now taken a higher place in His mind than the thought of nature. The thought of God as the Father of man had now succeeded to the thought of God as the Life of nature. His own relation to the race grew into distinctness. The deeper 'knowledge of the world' which He had gained, made, as if by a subtler sense, all the common human life of Nazareth an image of the Life of the great world. He saw—being Himself *the* Man—in every one He met the great common principles of humanity, while He received the impress of their distinctive characteristics. 'Among least things He had the sense of greatest.' There was not a word or action of other men which did not, as He grew in wisdom, touch a thousand other things, and fall into relationship with them under the universal principles which, being the daily companions of His intellect, linked together in His mind the present in which He lived to the past and future of the race. A new interest had arisen within Him, the interest in humanity, or rather I should say, were I not speaking only of His intellect, a new love. It clung to Him, it pervaded His whole thought. That scene in Jerusalem stamped itself on His memory for ever.

With this human centre of thought He lived on in peaceful solitude in the stillness of the upland town. Often He must have wandered to the summit of the hill, when wearied by the petty life of the village, and, as in after life, so now, communed in that prayer which is not petition, but union deeply felt, with God His Father, and seen His life unrolling itself before Him—not devised and planned, but intuitively recognized—as a panorama of which death for truth and for love of men was the sad and glorious close. But He was not deprived of tenderer and more delightful thought. How often must the thoughts of His childhood, of which we spoke last Sunday, the thoughts developed in him by the beauty of His Father's world of Life and Light in nature, have come to satisfy and cheer His inward life of thought! How often, as the turmoil of the world pressed upon His brain, must the stars and mountains and the peace of evening have given to him their silent ministrations! How often as the shadow of His sorrow fell upon His heart, must the quiet joy of His Father's order, felt in nature, have restored and soothed His intellect!

For it were exquisite pleasure to Him to pass (with full knowledge now of the true relation of man and nature) from the contemplation of the weakness and the want of life of the human world into communion with that living spiritual world of God's activity and peace which He saw within the phenomena of nature. This was the one deep solitary pleasure of His life. For though, as we have said, the thought of humanity, and not the thought of nature, was now the pre-eminent thought in His mind —because the redemption of man was His work—yet, the more divine thought must always have been the thought of nature. His labour was inspired by the former; His recreation, joy, and consolation were supplied by the latter.

Brethren, let us part with the solemnizing imagination of this—Christ's silent growth in wisdom in the stillness of the retired Galilæan village. May it calm our noisy lives and our obtrusive interests to realize, if but for one dignified moment, the image of the Saviour of the world, in whom was now concealed from men the regeneration and redemption of the race—living a forgotten life, but ever—'voyaging through strange seas of thought, alone.'

[Feb. 16, 1867.]

THE SPIRITUAL DEVELOPMENT OF CHRIST.

Luke ii. 49.

WE have been engaged for three Sundays on the subject of the development of Christ. We have spoken of His development through the influences of home, of His development through the influences of outward nature, and, last Sunday, of His intellectual development.

This morning our subject is the thoughts which we may derive from the scene in the Temple, with regard to the *spiritual development* of our Lord. These celebrated words, 'Wist ye not that I must be about my Father's business?' afford us a momentary glimpse of the spiritual life of Christ when a child. That spiritual life, essentially in Him from His birth, had been naturally developed in His consciousness by means of external circumstances, and through the growth of His intellect. We have spoken of the way in which the first gleams of the consciousness of His spiritual life may have arisen through the influence of His home and of outward nature. A kindling influence then came upon His intellect in the religious journey to Jerusalem, and the sights He saw at the Feast, and reached its culminating point in the conversation in the Temple. It is well known how the first clashing of our thought

The Spiritual Development of Christ. 137

with other thought makes us conscious of what is in us, how even an inferior man may reveal to our consciousness that which we unconsciously possess. The suggestions of men who only reproduce old thought, of men who are only reflective, arouse the creative energy of one in whom are hid treasures of new thought. The very want of completion in the ideas he listens to makes him sensible of his own power. He begins to know, from contrast, that he possesses finished and universal thoughts.

It is easy to apply this to the spiritual development of Christ. In His spirit lay hid the life of God, limited as to His consciousness of it only by the order of human development. A portion of it had been already developed, but much waited yet to be awakened. The time had now come; the conversation was religious. Remarks, suggestions, explanations of the Law, fell upon His spirit, stirred what was potentially there, till He began to feel, as a child would feel it, His own creative spiritual power, His own union with the Word of God. 'Wist ye not that I must be about MY FATHER'S business?'

Accompanying this dawning consciousness of the spiritual light and life which dwelt within Him, there arose also in His mind the consciousness of His redeeming mission. We seem to trace this in the words 'my Father's business.' It does not appear, however, just to say that this idea was now fully defined and grasped. We should be forced then to attribute more to Him than would agree with perfect childhood; but there is no unnaturalness in holding that it now for the first time became a dim prophecy in His mind. It required for its complete development that the sinfulness of the world should be presented to His growing knowledge as a thing external to Himself. Sin so presented made Him conscious, by the instinctive repulsion which it caused Him, of His own spotless holiness; and, by the infinite pity which He felt for those enslaved by it, of His own infinite love for sinners; and out of these two there rose the consciousness of His mission as the Redeemer of the race from sin. This was the business which His Father had given Him to do. Clearly and more clearly from this day forth, for eighteen years at Nazareth, it grew up into its completed form, till He was ready to carry it out into the action of His ministry.

Let me develope this still more in connection with last Sunday's sermon. We imagined Him, as He journeyed to Jerusalem, realizing in His intellect the past history of His people. He conversed in the imaginative feeling of a child with the great history of the great spirits of the Jewish nation, and in his mind arose a sense of the majesty and power of humanity. He saw the vast tide of men which filled Jerusalem, and He was not free from that impression of awe and dignity which comes to us from the first conception of the multitudinous world of humanity which labours and thinks in London. The first impression is one, and belongs to the universal. As such it is immense, creative, full of awe. It is only when we descend to particularize and divide, that our thought of human nature becomes undignified. We may conjecture, then, that the first

The Spiritual Development of Christ. 139

impressions in Jerusalem awoke in Christ's spirit the elevated view of human nature which we conceive from His after life to have been latent in Him as a child. But when He came to consider classes and individuals, and not the race as a whole—in its idea—He found hypocrisy, selfishness, tyranny, meanness. But the first idea must have remained firm, co-existent with the other sad ideas which followed it.

Man, then, was great, and man was base; man was mighty, and man was weak; man had a divine nature, and man had given himself over to a base nature. But the greatness, strength, and divineness were his true nature; the others were the result of an alien and usurping power. Both existed; but the one existed to be made perfect, the other to be destroyed. Hence, not all the evil Christ came into contact with, not all the blindness, sin, and cruelty which He saw and suffered from, could ever overthrow His divine trust in that which man might become. Here was a real spiritual thought bearing on His mission—*man is capable of being redeemed*.

As His spirit grew more conscious of what it really was, He felt that truth — man's capability of being redeemed—not only without, but within himself. How could He despair of human nature when He knew that He Himself was sinless human nature? His very existence as man was proof that man was destined to be perfect. Conscious thus, from His own sinlessness, of man's possibility of sinlessness, He became conscious, for the same reason, of another truth—that He was the destined Redeemer of the race from the usurping power of sin. Being pure, He knew He could save the impure; being perfect Life, He knew he could conquer the death of man; being perfect Love, He knew He could cast out of the race the devil of self-seeking. Immediately, intuitively, He felt *thus*—was conscious of Himself, first, as sinless humanity; secondly, as the Redeemer of humanity from sin.

We seem, in this way, to see faintly a strange coexistence of apparently contradictory ideas within the spirit of Christ during His life at Nazareth. One would almost think that that impression of the greatness of the human soul would have been worn out by daily contact with the wild dwellers at Nazareth—and yet with what sort of a spirit did He come forth into the world?—With unshaken trust in human nature: recognizing its evil, but believing, as none have ever believed before or since, in its nobility, its capabilities, its infinite power of work. It was not only interest in humanity—that is the way I put it last Sunday, but I was speaking only of Christ's intellect—it was love of humanity, love, the 'business of His Father.'

We come to that by slow degrees—rise into that life by finding out the wretchedness and death of self, but in the Saviour's spirit it rose into being like a flower from a seed already there. It developed itself till it penetrated His whole nature with one great spiritual thought, 'I will give away all my being for the human race.'

This love of man, and desire to impart life to those who needed life, was correlative to another spiritual idea—indignation at evil. It was this which balanced love in Christ, and kept it from the weakness of our affection

The Spiritual Development of Christ.

and the maudlin sentiment of much of our philanthropy. Christ abhorred sin, and saw it in its native darkness. There was in Him, therefore, an agony of desire to redeem us from it, and a pitying indignation for our desolate slavery. He laboured to convince men that they did need a deliverer from sin; and when a man, like Zacchæus, felt his selfishness and desired freedom, it is wonderful how the Saviour's spirit sprang to meet the seeking spirit, clung to it, and poured into it a stream of life and faith and hope. But when men, for the sake of keeping up an ecclesiastical dominion, for the sake of success, for the honour of dead maxims, stopped the way of others, gave men lifeless forms, and persecuted the Light because it condemned their darkness, how the holy anger kindled! As the Child listened to the intolerance of the Pharisee, the dogmatism of the scribe, and the scornful infidelity of the Sadducee, there must have sprung up in His heart an instinctive feeling of opposition; and this spiritual wrath at wrong done to the souls of men, grew and deepened at Nazareth—as the meaning of what He had heard in the Temple was made clear to Him by His after knowledge—till it culminated in the withering denunciations of His ministry.

We have now seen how the consciousness of His having a work to do for men began to dawn in His spirit. He must be about a business in life. But there was something more; it was not *His* work only, it was primarily His *Father's* business. Thus in doing His own work He was doing His Father's work. The thought as yet was dim, childish, not clearly realized, but it was developed afterwards into that clear sense of a united work done as if by one will, by Himself and the Father, which we find expressed in texts like these: 'My Father worketh hitherto, and I work;' 'I have glorified Thee upon the earth; I have finished the work which Thou gavest me to do;' 'If I do not the work of my Father, believe me not. But if I do, though ye believe not me, believe the works, that ye may know and believe that the Father is in me, and I in Him.' There is the full clear consciousness of that spiritual idea of which here we see the germ—that all His work was His Father's work.

Brethren, it is the true thought for us; not only that all true work which we do is God's work, but that work which is not of God is not work, does not properly exist in the universe at all. 'There *is no* work but Thine.'

When we first take up our place and labour, we mistake the meaning of our life. We think we are born to do our own will, and we act upon our thought. Straightway all our work becomes selfish; we toil and struggle for ourselves, we are an end unto ourselves; and the result is that we find our work becoming mean; our view of life contemptuous; ourselves ignoble. But when the root idea of life is changed, when we know that we are here to do God's will, and that His will is love to us and all, the impulse and end of our work are altered. We accept the duties laid upon us, and are not anxious to make them into advantages to self. We think, 'God has placed me here and told me to do this. He is Right, and knowledge and good must flow to all if I am faithful. I am His instrument; through me He

The Spiritual Development of Christ. 143

is making a phase of Himself known to man; through me He is doing a portion of His mighty labour.' The thought transfigures our view of the universe; immediately work becomes unselfish and sanctified, life is ennobled, the commonest drudgery is rendered beautiful, suffering is gladly borne. Men call us aside to the pursuit of pleasure, to the passion of excitement, to the fame and honour we may win, to seek our own will and gain it. 'Hush!' we say, 'we live now in deeper joy than you can know, we have loftier excitements. Fame, honour, they are in His hand and not in ours. My own will! I have my will when I do His will.' O brethren! how magnificent a thing might life become could we but turn away from all temptations to do our own will, and say to the tempters, were they even father or mother— say in the strength of Christ—'I cannot; wist ye not that I must be about my Father's business?'

In tracing the spiritual development of Christ we have thus found in Him the germs of two great thoughts—the first dawning consciousness of His Messiahship, the first dawning consciousness of His peculiar relation to His Father.

We consider, in conclusion, the result of these thoughts upon His life. No doubt, one might say, 'He felt Himself at once separated from common life. He was marked from mankind, and the rest of His existence must be in accordance with this isolation. The marvellous boy would remain at Jerusalem. Why should He go back to remote and vulgar Nazareth, where His rising light would be concealed? There was another career before Him. He would confute the doctors with

His supernatural knowledge and power, and, as He grew up, set up a new religious sect.' This would be, I venture to say, the natural evolution of the history on the hypothesis of the truth of the mythical theory. If Christ's life is the product of the Jewish-Christian imagination, this representation *ought* to be that given us in the Gospels. What do we find? Absolute silence. He went home to common life, to subjection to His parents, and for eighteen years not a word or act betrayed His presence. It is a fact absolutely inexplicable upon the mythical theory, and till it is explained it vitiates that theory. Look at it in another way. Given a tolerable acquaintance with the modes of thinking and feeling of the Jewish Christians of the first two centuries, we ought not, if the mythical theory be true, to be astonished by any of the circumstances attributed to the life of Jesus; all ought to be easily accounted for, easily imagined.

But here is a circumstance quite unaccountable, so strange, that it has awakened the amazement of all ages—this silence of eighteen years. It is exactly the reverse of that which would be accreted by imagination round the person of Jesus. It is devoid of all embellishment, all exaggeration: it is eighteen years passed by without a word, and those years the very ones in a great man's life for which followers and admirers have generally formed the greatest number of mythical stories. It is strange, in reality, to us who believe; it must be of infinite strangeness to the supporters of the mythical theory. It is passed by, and no wonder, by the propounder of that theory.

The Spiritual Development of Christ. 145

This was the case, however; the Child went home with His parents. And was this the end of the aspiration in the Temple; was this to be about His Father's business? We can scarcely understand it, we to whom passiveness, quiet life, seem unproductive. But so it was with the perfect Man. Eighteen years of silent life were the mode now in which He was to do His Father's business. To keep quiet, to live the common life of a labouring man in Nazareth, to wait and develope, this was God's business for His Son.

It is a vast lesson. We complain of the slow dull life we are forced to lead, of our humble sphere of action, of our low position in the scale of society, of our having no room to make ourselves known, of our wasted energies, of our years of patience. So do we say that we have no Father who is directing our life, so do we say that God has forgotten us, so do we boldly judge what life is best for us, and so by our complaining do we lose the use and profit of the quiet years. We cannot be still, cannot be at rest. It is the most natural and yet the most ruinous fault which belongs to men in an age which lives too fast and has almost a morbid passion for incessant labour. O men of little faith! Because you are not sent out yet into your labour, do you think God has ceased to remember you; because you are forced to be outwardly inactive, do you think you also may not be, in your years of quiet, 'about your Father's business'? Receive the lesson of Christ's life—the lesson Milton learnt from God's Spirit in his heart:

> They also serve who only stand and wait.

Lastly, to Christ Himself, His Father's business then

was the development of all His inner self, the maturing for His work. The idea of His mission and the powers for it grew together, and when the time for action came He was ready.

Such times of waiting mark, not uncommonly, our life. Our youth is kept back from the press of labour, or our manhood is forced to pause. It is a period given to us in which to mature ourselves for the work which God will give us to do.

Oh! use it well. Grow in it, do not retrograde. The way we spend it oftentimes in youth is in light indifference or daring bravado, and when the time comes in which the work which God had chosen for us is ready for our energy, we have no instruments to work with, no ideas to expand and express in fruitful labour. The way we spend it oftentimes in manhood is in whining at God's unfairness, as we call it; in complaining regret for past activity, and then, when work is again laid before us, we have lost the time during which we ought to have matured ourselves; enfeebled the will by fruitless wailing; chilled the aspirations which kindle, and the faith and hope which sustain, the toiling spirit of a noble workman for the race; we have missed our opportunity, and now we cannot enter on our ministry. Nothing is sadder than the way in which we wilfully spoil our life.

Brethren, no time of seeming inactivity is laid upon you by God without a just reason. It is God calling upon you to do His business by ripening in quiet all your powers for some higher sphere of activity which is about to be opened to you. The time is coming when

The Spiritual Development of Christ. 147

you shall be called again to the front of the battle. Let that solemn thought of dread yet kindling expectancy fill the cup of your life with the inner work of self-development which will make you ready and prepared when your name is called. The eighteen years at Nazareth, what was their result? A few years of action, but of action concentrated, intense, infinite; not one word, not one deed which did not tell, and which will not tell upon the universe for ever.

Eighteen years of silence, and then—the regeneration of the world accomplished, His Father's business done.

[November 25, 1866.]

JOHN THE BAPTIST, THE INTERPRETER.

Matthew iii. 1.

THERE is something which touches in us that chord of sadness which is always ready to vibrate, when we think that John the Baptist was the last of all the heroes of the old dispensation, that with him closed the goodly fellowship of the prophets. For we cannot look at the last lighting up of the intellect of a man, the last effort for freedom of a dying nation, or the last glory of an ancient institution like that of the Jewish prophets, without a sense of sadness.

> Men are we, and must grieve when even the shade
> Of that which once was great hath passed away.

But if there be some melancholy in the feeling with which we view the Baptist, there is also much of enthusiasm. If he was the last, he was also the greatest of the prophets. That which all the others had dimly imaged, he presented in clear light; that which they had spoken in parables, he declared in the plainest words. Thus, he not only finished the old dispensation, he also ushered in the new. He is, as it were, the bridge between two eras; he represents the transition period between Judaism and Christianity.

Our object, however, is not to dwell on this important

John the Baptist, the Interpreter. 149

view of the Baptist's position, but to connect his work with the collect of this Sunday.

The collect calls upon God to stir up the minds of His faithful people in preparation for the advent of Christ. It is on this account that it is so arranged by the Church as always to be read before the first Sunday in Advent. It marks the condition of mind with which we should anticipate the coming of the Saviour; it was doubtless suggested by the character and the work of the historical forerunner of our Lord. For John the Baptist was called to be the awakener, the exciter of the Jewish world. It is so that he characterizes himself: 'I am the voice of one crying in the wilderness.' And of this we have proof enough. He troubled the whole of Jewish society to its depths. Priests, formalists, infidels, soldiers, publicans, wealth, rank, and poverty streamed day after day into the wilderness to hear and to obey the preacher. It is as the stirrer of Jewish life and thought, as a warning voice to England—awakening our hearts to the advent of Christ—that we shall consider him to-day.

I said that John was the finisher of one, and the introducer of a new dispensation. For centuries the thoughts and passion of the prophets had streamed into and filled the Jewish heart. They kindled there vague desires, wild hopes of a far-off kingdom, passionate discontent with things as they were. At last, about the time of the birth of Christ, these scattered dreams and hopes concentrated themselves into one desire, took form and substance in one prophecy—the advent of the anointed king. It was the blazing up of an excitement which had been smouldering for a thousand years; it was the last and most powerful of a long series of oscillations which had been gradually increasing in swing and force. Now two things are, I think, true; first, wherever there is this passion in a people, it embodies itself in one man, who is to be its interpreter. Secondly, wherever a great problem of the human spirit is growing towards its solution, and the soil of humanity is prepared for new seed from heaven, God sends His chosen creature to proclaim the truth which brings the light.

A great man is then the product of two things—of the passion of his age, and of the choice of God. So far as he is the former, he is but the interpreter of his own time, and only the highest man of his time; so far as he is the latter, he is beyond his age, and points forward to a higher revelation.

Such was the Baptist's position—the interpreter of the spiritual wants of the Jewish people, the prophet of a greater revelation in the future.

'Repent: for the kingdom of heaven is at hand.'

This was John's witness in the wilderness. To this God had brought him after thirty years of education. From his birth he had been a marked child set apart for a peculiar work. For years he had lived with his father, sometimes in the hill country of Judæa, sometimes in Jerusalem. Even in his childhood he had seen almost all the aspects of Jewish society. He could have mingled with the pleasures of the capital, but the strictly ascetic life imposed on him, and the sense that he was elected by God from mankind, kept him as one who

John the Baptist, the Interpreter. 151

stands apart and observes, but does not mingle with, the crowd of men. Such a life has a tendency to make a man judge harshly, too harshly, of the world. But, indeed, as the youth looked round upon Jerusalem, he had some excuse for harsh judgments. The one peculiarity of Jewish religion was its unreality. The Sadducee believed in nothing spiritual, in nothing which he could not test by his senses, or demonstrate by reasoning. The lawyers and scribes spent their time in theological discussions which they mistook for religion, and in investigating the letter of the Scripture while they denied its spirit. The Pharisees were content to seem religious, but to *be* religious was not necessary to support their power.

Jewish religion was a nut without the kernel, a sepulchre, white and fair without, but within full of dead men's bones.

Fancy the shame and pain with which a true man must have viewed all this hypocrisy and unreality! We can no longer wonder at his resolution to leave the corrupted life behind him and to go into the freedom and righteousness of the wilderness. There, at least, he would be alone with God; there, beside the untainted stream of Jordan and beneath the pure eyes of the stars, he could live in the heroic associations of his people, and remember that they were a holy nation once; there he could wait and pray for the time when truth might break again upon Israel from Jehovah. We know at least that many sincere men were of this mind in Judæa, and retiring from the world, like the Christian hermits of a later date, formed a kind of society and called themselves Essenes. It is possible that John may at first have joined himself to these. But if so, it could not have been for a long time, for a new revelation was coming to the Jewish anchorite, and a new revelation, be it of what it may, drives a man into loneliness. Only in quiet, in solitude with God, in unbroken questioning with his own soul, can a prophet of God discover what God is saying to his spirit. The Baptist went apart and brooded over his half-arisen thought. He had heard the wonders of the birth of Christ, he had probably known Christ well as boy and man. Carrying this remembrance always with him, the thought of a great spiritual Deliverer grew in force.

The impulses of his own heart, sorrow for his country's degradation, hatred of his country's guilt and of social and religious lies, his own passionate desire for a Saviour, added fresh fuel to the burning hope within him. Deeper and deeper became his longings, more ardent became his prayers, more intense his solitude with God. At last, one day (for such revelations come suddenly as the crown of long preparation), it flashed on him from God that the Messiah would soon be manifested. He knew within himself that the time was come. Forthwith a fire began to blaze in his heart, and his message rushed to his lips. He left his loneliness, he came forth the preacher, his voice rang far and wide, 'Repent, repent: the kingdom of heaven is at hand.'

And his words found an echo in all hearts, for what had stirred in him had been stirring in the Jews, only they could not give it clear expression. They had had formless ideas, desires for which they had no translation, a void in the heart they could not fill. The desires were translated into words, and the void in the heart was filled, when John, looking on Jesus as He walked, turned and said to his disciples, 'Behold the Lamb of God, which taketh away the sin of the world.'

It is the province of the man of genius in all ages to express the hidden and the speechless in the hearts of other men, to interpret man to himself. The new epoch of thoughts took substance as the Baptist spoke. He threw into words, and in doing so interpreted, the wordless passion of a thousand souls. Brethren, that it is to be a preacher.

The stirring in the heart of Palestine had been but little. It had not strength or consistency enough to become a living impulse in society. It might have died out as a thousand others have perished in national and individual life, for want of an outward push. The *vis inertiæ* of Pharisaism must have been as strong as the sceptical conservatism of the Sadducee. But God did not forsake the searching spirits of Judæa, and just as a young man, who cannot harmonize his life, who cannot discover a dominant motive, who has passionate feelings which he cannot express, and a multitudinous army of thoughts which he cannot arrange or discipline, lights one day upon a noble treatise or an inspiring poem, and is shaken to his depths by finding himself reflected there and there interpreted—becoming then so stirred by this self-interpretation that he finds his true path, and, setting his steps to an ordered melody, sees his goal, and is resolute to reach it — so were the religious-hearted Jews affected by the preaching of the Baptist. They saw the problem of their inner life solved, they were aroused, impelled, stirred to the recesses of the soul.

Of all the blessed works which God gives to man to do in this life, there is none more blessed than that of the awakener—of the interpreter.

It is the work which I would that all who see beyond the present, and whose eyes God has opened, would now undertake in England; for there is a movement abroad in society which ought to be made constant, and needs an interpreter of its meaning. If I desire anything strongly in this life, it is that God may send to us some men of genius, some inspired men, to kindle into a blaze the low fire of excitement which is smouldering here, and to show us what it means; that we may shake off our old life and put on the new. For it is not to be denied that that apparently causeless movement which presages a great change, and which is like the groundswell which rolls on shore before the hurricane, is to be felt in England now. Men are stirred they know not why. Vague hopes of change and reform are drifting before our eyes. A general excitement of thought upon nearly all questions of the intellect and spirit, the characteristics of which are incoherency, irregularity, oddity, prevails far and wide. New theories are born and perish in a month. We know not what to believe, or what to cling to. The old landmarks have been washed away, and we have not settled the new ones. With a general notion of our power and greatness, of our inexhaustible wealth and national courage, and with a pride in our intellect and the omnipotence of reason, there is conjoined a widespread suspicion that our foundations are not sure, a contempt of the times, and a dissatisfaction with society and with the life we lead. Educated, and even uneducated men have lost respect for old things and old ways. Few men can now be found who reverence the old only because it is the old. That false reverence, I rejoice to say, is passing away, and even the most conservative are beginning to be impatient of mouldering abuses. It is curious that the reform agitation arose not so much among the working classes themselves as among the literary and cultivated men of the time. The impulse given has been taken up by others of a different type, but the first impulse arose from the most intellectual class of men in England. Precisely the same thing, though in an immensely greater degree, took place before the French Revolution.

There is, again, a general stir and discontent with the state of the poor. We are awaking at last to the consciousness of our neglect, of the inadequacy of our means of relief; of the shame which lies heavier on us than on any of the leading nations of the West, of the insufficient education of the poor; of their disgraceful housing, of our own indifference to human suffering and neglect of sanitary measures. We feel that our modes of governing in these matters have openly and completely broken down. At no other time do we remember so great an indignation and contempt among just men for official imbecility.

If many of us are stirred into dissatisfaction with things as they are, some of us are more than dissatisfied with much of English life. We used to boast of our business habits, and think ourselves excellent organizers; now we smile somewhat bitterly at our boast.

Public mismanagement has wasted millions of money in works of war. The expenditure has been so reckless as almost to amount to dishonesty. Better organization might have saved at least a fourth of the money for reproductive expenditure. Men do not seem to see that public economy, in order to civilize our degraded classes, is as much a Christian duty for a nation, as private economy, in order to be able to be charitable, is for an individual.

Nor is this all. The standard of social and political morality is far lower than the time at which we live demands. The past seems to have taught us very little. Our elections are so conducted that the future members of Parliament are in many cases wittingly actors of a lie, shutting their eyes, on the pretence that the money is given for expenses which they know is for bribery. The money goes to debase and enslave the voter, and it is plain that those who bribe are morally more guilty than those who are bribed, as much more as the tempter is worse than the tempted. The worst feature in the case is the amusement which this corruption seems to afford to English society.* *There is an old saying that they are fools, men without sense, who make a mock at sin.

Step lower in the social scale, come from Parliament to monetary life. English honesty was once a proverb;

---

* I leave this because it was true in 1866, as the record of the Committees on Yarmouth and Totness prove. It is a proof of the revolution of thought spoken of in this sermon, that in little more than two years the above sentence has become untrue. I wish I could say the same for the sentences which follow.

John the Baptist, the Interpreter. 157

English dishonesty, unless we repent, will soon become the second reading of the proverb. There is no need to dwell upon the dishonesty of speculations—the made-up balance-sheets—the ruin of thousands by selfish greed, which have disgraced our banks, railways, and commercial houses—the false balance and the cruel adulteration, the lying advertisements which dishonour our trade. It is enough to say that no man who loves his country can see this widespread system of theft and falsehood without dismay.

There is much more, but enough of this. The cheerful thing we see in it is, that men's hearts are beginning to be stirred with dissatisfaction and hatred of it all. Increase that dissatisfaction, deepen that hatred, by all the means in your power. Work in society, so far as it is given you, the Baptist's work. Stir, arouse men to see these evils, and cry to them, Repent, for Christ is coming to throughly purge His floor. For come He will to these things, to rebuke and chasten. We know not how His advent may appear; it may be in political or national disgrace, it may be in the bitter punishments of war, it may be in reformation, or in revolution—but one thing we do know, that things so evil cannot last long without their natural penalty. Our widespread dissatisfaction means that Christ is coming to change society, perhaps to shake down the old edifice altogether. Pray that He may come to reform, and not to punish penally, and while you pray act like Christian men against these evils. 'Stir up, O Lord, the wills of Thy faithful people.'

In passing from outward to inward life, we find the

same stir and awaking. For many years there has not been so great an excitement of the human spirit in England, the characteristic peculiarity of which is that no one knows what to make of it or how it will end. We need some one to tell us what it means, to express it for us and to point out the path into which we should direct all its scattered energies — we want a John the Baptist.

The excitement shows itself in many ways. Among many of the laity there is a contempt and neglect of religion as taught from pulpits and books. Thousands never enter a church. They say that what they hear has nothing to do with their daily life, is apart from all their interests. Yet there is a really passionate desire to find truth, to gain some light upon the ever-recurring problems of life, to escape from the unproductive state of scepticism. They are willing to accept Christianity, but they demand, and justly, that it should explain and be applicable to the life of this century. If it is a universal religion, its principles should throw light upon our social, commercial, and political difficulties as well as on our spiritual ones.

Generally speaking, they hear too little of these things. The commandments and doctrines of men are taught rather than the principles of Christ; and even in theology the forms in which the teaching is couched do not belong to modern thought. It is no wonder that our churches do not attract men and women who either think or are disturbed in thought. Until we cease to give them the husks of the theology of thirty years ago as food fit for those to whom the very terms of that theology

John the Baptist, the Interpreter. 159

convey no meaning, we cannot expect our preaching to be listened to. Men are crying out for some teaching which will represent and interpret their own time.

Turn from the laity to the Church, and note the state of excitement in which it lives. There is not a clergyman's house in England in which, after all the labours of the day, the great questions of theology are not discussed with an eagerness almost without former parallel in England. Every new critical book produces a storm of attacks and replies. No well-known teachers of any party can speak on any religious subject without awaking a quite disproportioned excitement. The subjects of prayer, of providences, of the possibility of miracles, of the Eucharist, of the priesthood, are discussed in the daily papers as if they were, and in fact they are, subjects of interest to the British public. It seems as if treasures of passion were laid up which only want an occasion large enough in order to concentrate themselves into an outburst.

In the mean time the clergy themselves run into all sorts of theories without clearly knowing whither they are going. They say they are pursuing truth; but there is no method in the pursuit. They are like men lost in an Australian wood, who run to and fro, and after many hours find themselves at the place they started from. Many, in despair of rest, rush to find it, and only find stagnation, in the Church of Rome.

All kinds of experiments are tried. A bishop sets his face like a flint, and calls in question the authenticity of nearly all the early history of the Old Testament. He destroys, he does not dream of constructing. Some of the younger clergy employ their time in only opposing the old forms of religion, forgetting that they ought to build, and not to overthrow; forgetting that every work of opposition is a negative work, and that a negation has no force. Another body of clergy have fallen in love with the past, and seek by a retrograde movement to find God again in life, forgetting that God is always *in front* of men. They attempt to revive that power of the priesthood which England spent so much blood and so many years in destroying, and they are so blind as to imagine that England will suffer its revival. In a hundred ways the spirit of men is stirred, but how or for what end no one can yet tell.

Once more, observe another curious thing. It is an age of science. The omnipotence of the human reason is declared. The marvellous in religion is discredited; the supernatural is said to be necessarily impossible. And yet, what do we see? The grossest credulity, not among really scientific men, but among those who follow them in their denial of the miracles of the Scriptures, in their denial of the supernatural in Christianity: among the readers and admirers of the negative schools of France and Germany, men and women, led away by charlatans, falling into the oddest and most chimerical supernaturalism, disbelieving in the resurrection, but believing in spirit-rapping; disbelieving in the inspiration of the Epistles of S. Paul, but believing that Bacon writes bad English and worse sense, and that Milton comes from heaven to compose verses of which a school-boy would be ashamed. This class of English society presents the strange spectacle of belief in curious follies in the midst of the decay of religious belief, of men believing in all sorts of supernatural influences except in God.

In all we find the same sort of general and undefined excitement which prevailed in the world before Christianity, and which has prevailed before any great revolution in thought.

There is no possibility of affixing a particular cause to each of these developments of excitement. There is but one cause for them all. It is simply this, that old things, old thoughts, old institutions are ready to perish; that the old forms do not fit the new thought, the new wants, the new aspirations of men; that new wine has been poured into old bottles, and that the old bottles are bursting on every side. At present the new thought is too strong for the old moulds, and men, sick of their condition, and finding it insupportable, are everywhere hungering and thirsting for a change. There is a stirring of all the surface waters of English life and thought, but no one can tell why they are stirred; there is something at work beneath which no man sees, which causes all these conflicting and commingling currents, all this trouble on the upper waters.

There is, however, in it all that which is inexpressibly cheering. It tells us plainly that Christ is coming, not in final judgment, but in some great revolution of life and thought. 'England,' to quote of it a French writer's words on Europe before the outburst of the French Revolution, 'resembles a camp which is roused by the first rays of the dawn, in which the men, moving to and fro among one another and agitated, are waiting till the sun, rising in full radiance, points out to them the path they have to follow, and lights it up for their march.' We are waiting for the Sun of righteousness to rise, and to illumine the new way on which we are entering.

Lastly. It is the cry of some, Repress all this stir, all this inquiry; it is dangerous. Hold fast to the old forms; they are the only safe ones.

No, brethren; it is this very thing which we *will* not do if we be wise. Stop inquiry? Stop the Ganges in full flow to the sea! Try it, and the result is only the roar of the river, the overflow which devastates the country, the sweeping away of your feeble barrier and the rush as before of the great river to the ocean. Hold fast to the old forms! What, when they are dead, when the Spirit inspires them no more? No; we wish to live—and we die spiritually if we cling to what is spiritually dead, as we perish politically if we cling to what is politically dead. We do not want to be without forms; but a new spirit is coming on us, and it will create new forms for itself. For, to make use of S. Paul's words in a different meaning, but in an analogous one, we do not want to be 'unclothed, but clothed upon, that mortality may be swallowed up of life.'

Therefore we are bound to keep up this stir of life, this excitement of thought. Let us be ready for our John the Baptist when he comes; let us pray for the interpreter and the awaker who will come and say to us, 'The kingdom of heaven is at hand.' 'Behold, the Bridegroom cometh! go ye forth to meet Him.' Let us live in prayer, and progress, and patient watching for his presence. Before long he will arrive in a great, though perhaps a slow revolution in English religious thought, and when once we have been moved by that, there will be a great revolution in English life, and once more we may be proud of a regenerated country.

'Stir up, then, O Lord, the wills of Thy faithful people, that they, plenteously bringing forth the fruit of good works, may of Thee be plenteously rewarded, through Jesus Christ our Lord.'

[June 14, 1868.]

DEVOTION TO THE CONVENTIONAL.

Acts vii. 51—53.

THE rejection of Christ by the Jewish people was a national sin; it was the act of the whole nation. His death was the result of the full development of the then Jewish mode of looking at the world—the spirit of the age, among the Jews, killed Him.

I put it in that way because the term, a national sin, wants a clear definition. It is used at present in a way which is quite reckless of any settled meaning. Every party, even every sect in the country, declares its opponents guilty of a national sin. But a national sin is not an evil done by any one party to the nation, but an evil done by the nation itself, a direct evil consciously chosen and adhered to; or an evil neglect or blindness which take their rise from the whole tone and spirit of the mass of the people. I might mention courses of political action in which England has persisted for years, through all changes of party, which are of the character of national sins, but I will content myself with an illustration, which will not stir up anger. Apart from political acts or political opinions, on which the generality of the people act, the national sin of the England of to-day is extravagance, waste of money.

Devotion to the Conventional. 165

From the administration of the army and navy down to the administration of the household of the poorest dock labourer, there is, generally speaking, no conscientious, educated, cultured expenditure or care of money. The poor are even more extravagant, more reckless, than the rich. And the dreadful punishment which follows on the sin of waste of money is this, that the nation becomes blind to the true uses of money. It spends nearly 15,000,000 a year on its army, and a little more than 1,000,000 on education—so intense an absurdity that it only seems necessary to mention it to expose it. It spends 10,000,000 a year upon its navy, and is so stingy towards the science which developes the intellect of the whole people, and towards the art which exalts and refines the soul, as only to vote about 100,000 a year for these objects; so that things the value of which cannot be represented in money, and on which great sums have been spent, are perishing for want of a little wise expenditure. We are extravagant where we ought to be economical, and economical where we ought to expend freely. This is our punishment, and future Englishmen will look back with amazement upon this time, when we spent millions on war-ships the guns of which cannot be served in a fresh breeze, and left, to take one example, for want of a few thousands, the noblest specimens of Assyrian art to rot rapidly away in a damp cellar in the British Museum. Not many months have passed since the great representation of a lion hunt, carved thousands of years ago by an artist who puts our animal sculpture to shame, and who worked from personal observation of the lion in his vigorous contest and in his agony, has been placed in that deadly vault. Now, so rapid has been the destruction, that in certain parts there is scarcely a vestige left of the labour of the noble hand, and a white fluff of damp, gathering upon the stone, has eaten away all the delicate lines and subtle carving over a great part of the work. In a few years or so, in spite of the glazing, the whole may be corrupt dust. I have mentioned this partly in the hope that it will be taken up by some one who has some interest left in these subjects, and some influence to use upon them, and partly to show how a national sin, like extravagance, avenges itself by stinginess in matters where stinginess is destruction and disgrace.

But one of the worst of national sins is the rejection or the neglect by the mass of the people of the great men whom God has sent to save the nation, to teach the nation, or to give ideas to the nation. It is a proof of the perfect culture of a people, of its being truly civilized, in intellect and spirit as well as in prosperity, when it recognizes, as it were intuitively, its great men, puts them forward at once as rulers, and obeys their guidance. It is a proof of its failing power, of its retrogression, of its diseased condition, when it neglects, despises, or kills its great men. Of this proposition, for the two are one, history supplies a thousand instances. For the man of noble genius, the prophet, or whatever else you call him, is the test of the nation. He exists not only to do his own active work, but to passively prove what is true gold or false; and as many as he saves he dooms. Those are lost who reject him—the whole nation is lost if the whole nation rejects him—for it is not he so much whom it rejects as the saving ideas of which he is the vehicle.

Hence, when such a man appears, the question on which hangs the fate of the people is this : Will the nation recognize him or not; will it envy and destroy him, or believe in him and follow him ?

That question which has again and again been placed before the nations of the world, was placed in the most complete manner before the Jews at the appearance of Christ, the perfect Man—is placed in Him before each of us as individual men—since He was not only the representation of that which was noblest in the Jewish nation, but of that which is noblest in humanity. Christ was the test of the Jewish nation, and His rejection by them proved that they were lost as a nation. Christ is the test of each of us, and our acceptance or rejection of Him proves that we are worthy or unworthy of our humanity. This passive unconscious work of Christ was recognized by the wisdom of the old man Simeon when he said, 'This child is set for the fall and the rising again of many in Israel.' It was recognized by Christ Himself in many of His parables, notably when He said, ' For judgment,' i. e. for division, for sifting of the chaff from the wheat, ' am I come into the world.'

And so it was, wherever He went He was the touchstone. of men. Those who were pure, single-eyed, and true-hearted saw Him, clung to Him, and loved Him; those who were conscious of their need and sin, weary of long searching after rest and not finding, weary of conventionalities and hypocrisies, believed in Him, drank deep of His Spirit, and found redemption and repose.

They flew to Him as naturally as steel to the magnet. Those who were base of heart or false of heart, proud of their sin, or hardened in their prosperous hypocrisy, men who worshipped the mummy of a past religion, naturally hated Him, recoiled from Him, and, to get rid of Him, hanged Him on a tree.

In doing so—and this was the deed of the mass of the people—they destroyed their nationality which was hidden in their reception of Christ. It is at least a curious coincidence with this view, that when the priesthood before Pilate openly rejected Christ as king, they did it in these words—words which repudiated their distinct existence as a nation—'We have no king but Cæsar.'

He did nothing overt to produce this. He simply lived His life, and it acted on the Jewish world as an electric current upon water; it separated its elements.

It will not be without interest to dwell upon some of the reasons which caused this rejection of Christ among the Jews, and to show how the reasons of the rejection or acceptance of Christ are not primarily to be found in certain spiritual states or feelings which belong to a transcendental region into which men of the world cannot or do not care to enter, but in elements of action and thought which any man may recognize at work in the world around him, and in his own heart; in reasons which are identical with those which cause a nation to reverence or neglect its really great men, to lead a noble or an ignoble life.

The first of these is *devotion to the conventional.*

It is practically identical with want of individuality, one of the most painful deficiencies in our present society.

Now the rectification of that evil lies at the root of Christianity. Christ came to proclaim and to ensure the distinct life, the originality, of each man. All the principles He laid down, all the teaching of His followers as recorded in the Epistles, tend to produce individuality, rescue men from being mingled up, indistinguishable atoms, with the mass of men; teach them that they possess a distinct character, which it is God's will to educate; distinct gifts, which God the Spirit will inspire and develope; a peculiar work for which each man is elected, and in performing which his personality will become more and more defined.

Now the spirit of the world, when it is conventional—and when is it not?—is in exact opposition to this. Its tendency is to reduce all men and women to one pattern, to level the landscape of humanity to a dead plain, to clip all the trees which are growing freely, 'of their own divine vitality,' into pollards, to wear all individuality down into uniformity. There must be nothing original—in the world's language, eccentric, erratic; men must desire nothing strongly, think nothing which the generality do not think, have no strongly outlined character. The influence of society must be collective, it must reject as a portion of it the influence of any marked individuality. Custom is to be lord and king; nay, despot. We must all dress in the same way, read the same books, talk of the same things; and when we change, change altogether, like Wordsworth's cloud, 'which moveth altogether if it move at all.' We do not object to progress, but we do object to eccentricity. Society must not be affronted by originality. It is a rudeness. It suggests that society might be better, that there may be an imperfection here or there. Level everybody, and then let us all collectively advance, but no one must leave the ranks or step to the front.

This is the spirit which either cannot see, or, seeing, hates men of genius. They are in conflict with the known and accredited modes of action. They do not paint pictures in the manner of the ancients, nor judge political events in accordance with public opinion, nor write poems which the customary intellect can understand, nor lead a political party according to precedent. They are said to shock the world; as if that was not the very best thing which could happen to the world. So it comes to pass that they are depreciated and neglected; or, if they are too great and persist, persecuted and killed. And, indeed, it is not difficult to get rid of them, for you have only to increase the weight of the spirit of custom and bring it to bear upon them, and that will settle the question, for men of genius cannot breathe in this atmosphere, it kills them; the air must be natural in which they live, and the society must be free. The pitiable thing in English society now is, not only the difficulty of an original man existing in it, but that society is in danger of becoming of so dreadful a uniformity that no original man can be developed in it at all. This, if anything, will become the ruin of England's greatness.

There is, it is true, a kind of re-action going on at pre-

Devotion to the Conventional. 171

sent against this tyranny of society. Young men and women, weary of monotonous pleasures, are in rebellion, but the whole social condition has been so degraded that they rush into still more artificial and unnatural pleasures and excitements; in endeavouring to become free, they enslave themselves the more.

Those who might do much, do little. It is one of the advantages of wealth and high position that those who possess them may initiate the uncustomary without a cry being raised against them. But even with every opportunity, how little imagination do they ever display, how little invention, how little they do to relieve the melancholy uniformity of our pleasures, or the intense joylessness of our work!

Now this was precisely the spirit of the Jewish religious world at the time of Christ. Men were bound down to a multitude of fixed rules and maxims; they were hedged in on all sides. It was all arranged how they were to live and die, to repent and make atonement, to fast and pray, to believe and to worship, to dress and move. It was the most finished conventionalism of religion, in spite of the different sects, which the world has ever seen.

Then came Christ, entirely original, proclaiming new ideas, or, at least, old truths in a new form, making thoughts universal which had been particular, overthrowing worn-out ceremonies, satirizing and denouncing things gray with the dust of ages, letting in the light of truth into the chambers where the priests and lawyers spun their webs of theology to ensnare the free souls of men, trampling down relentlessly the darling customs of the old conservatism, shocking and bewildering the religious society. And they were dismayed and horrified.

He did not keep, they said, the Sabbath day. He ate and drank—abominable iniquity!—with publicans and sinners. He allowed a fallen woman to touch Him. Worse still, He did not wash His hands before He ate bread. He did not teach as the scribes did. He did not live the time-honoured and ascetic life of a prophet. He dared to speak against the priesthood and the aristocracy; He associated with fishermen. He came from Nazareth: that was enough; no good could come from Nazareth. He was a carpenter's son, and illiterate, and no prophet was made, or could be made, out of such materials. And this man! He dares to disturb us, to contest our maxims, to set at nought our customs, to array Himself against our despotism. 'Come, let us kill Him;' and so they crucified Him. The conventional spirit of society in Jerusalem, that was one of the murderers of Christ: they did not see, the wretched men, that in murdering Him they murdered their nation also.

So far for this conventional spirit as that which hinders the development or obstructs the work of genius, and as that which, in strict analogy with its work to-day, killed the Prince of Life long ago in Jerusalem; let me take the question now out of the realm of thought and history, and apply it practically.

Ask yourselves two questions: first, what would be the fate of Christ if He were suddenly to appear as a teacher in the middle of London, as He did of old in the middle of Jerusalem? How would our orthodox religious society and our conventional social world receive Him? Desiring to speak with all reverence, He would horrify the one by His heterodox opinions, as they would be called; the other by His absolute carelessness and scorn of many of the very palladia of society. Supposing He were to denounce—as He would in no measured terms— our system of caste; attack, as He did of old in Judæa, our most cherished maxims about property and rights; live in opposition to certain social rules, receiving sinners, and dining with outcasts; tear away the flimsy veil of words whereby we excuse our extravagance, our vanity, our pushing for position; contemn with scorn our accredited hypocrisies, which we think allowable because they make the surface of society smooth; live among us His free, bold, unconventional, outspoken life; how should we receive Him? It is a question which it is worth while that society should ask itself.

I trust more would hail His advent than we think. I believe the time is come when men are sick of falsehood, sick of the tyranny of custom, sick of living in unreality; that they are longing for escape, longing for a new life and a new order of things, longing for some fresh ideas to come and stir, like the angel, the stagnant pool. What is the meaning of the vague hopes everywhere expressed about the new Parliament? It really means that England is anxious for a more ideal, a more true and serious life, a reformed society.

Again, to connect this first question with the religious

world: suppose Christ were to come now and proclaim in Scotland that the Sabbath was made for man, or to preach the Sermon on the Mount as the full revelation of God to men accustomed to hear the Gospel scheme discussed each Sunday; in the first case He would be persecuted as an infidel, and in the second as a heretic. Supposing He were now to speak against sacerdotal pretension, or the worship of the letter of the Bible; against a religion which sought to gain life from minute observances, or against a Sadducean denial of all that is spiritual (a tendency of the religious liberals of to-day), as strongly and as sharply as He spoke at Jerusalem, how would He escape? The religious world could not crucify Him, but they would open on Him the tongue of persecution.

I believe there are thousands who would join themselves to Him, thousands more than recognized Him in Judæa—for the world has advanced indeed since then—thousands of true men from among all religious bodies, and thousands from among those who are now plentifully sprinkled with the epithets of rationalists, infidels, heretics, and atheists; but there are thousands who call themselves by His name who would turn from Him in dismay or in dislike, who would neglect or persecute Him, for He would come among our old conservatisms of religion, among our doctrinal systems and close creeds, superstitions, false liberalisms, priesthoods, and ritualisms, as He came of old among them all in Jerusalem, like lightning, to consume and wither everything false, retrograde, conventional, restricted, uncharitable, and superstitious; to kindle into life all that is living, loving, akin to light and full of truth within our religious world. If we *could* accept the revolution He would make, our national religion would be saved, if not it would be enervated by the blow and die:

Brethren, we ought, realizing these things as members of society, or members of any religious body—realizing, I say, Christ speaking to us as He would speak now—to feel our falseness, and, in the horror of it, to act like men who have discovered a traitor in their camp, whom they must destroy or themselves perish. We may save our nation if we resolve, each one here for himself, to free ourselves from cant, and formalism, and superstition, to step into the clear air of freedom, individuality, and truth, to live in crystal uprightness of life and holiness of heart.

And lastly, ask yourselves this second question, how far the spirit of the world, as devotion to conventionality, to accredited opinion, is preventing you personally from receiving Christ?

Is your sole aim the endeavour to please your party, running after it into that which you feel as evil, as well as that which you feel as good; forfeiting your Christian individuality as a son of God, that you may follow in the wake of the public opinion of your party? Is that your view of manly duty? Then you cannot receive Christ, for He demands that you should be true to your own soul.

Are you permitting yourself to chime in with the low morality of the day, to accept the common standard held by the generality, repudiating, as if it were a kind of Christian charity to do so, the desire to be better than your neighbours, and so coming at last to join in the light laugh with which the world treats social immoralities, reckless extravagance, the dishonesty of trade or the dishonesty of the exchange, or the more flagrant shame, dishonesty, and folly which adorn the turf—letting evils take their course because society does not protest as yet, till gradually the evils appear to you at first endurable, and then even beautiful, being protected by the deities of Custom and Fashion, which we enthrone instead of God? Are you drifting into such a state of heart? If so, you cannot expect to be able to receive Christ, for He demands that life should be ideal; not only moral but Godlike; not the prudence of silence about evil, but the imprudence of bold separation from evil.

And, leaving much behind, to come home to the inner spiritual life, is your religion only the creature of custom, not of conviction; only conventional, not individual? Have you received and adopted current opinions because they are current, without inquiry, without interest, without any effort of the soul—orthodox because it is the fashion to be orthodox, or heterodox because it is the fashion to be heterodox? How can you receive Christ?—for where He comes He claims reality, the living energy of interest, the passion of the soul for light and progress. Ye must be born again; born out of a dead, Pharisaic, conventional form of religion into a living individual union with the life of God. Some may tell you not to inquire, lest you should doubt; not to think, but to accept blindly the doctrines of the Church, lest you should end in scepticism. Counsels of cowardice and faithlessness, productive of that false sleep of the soul which is ten times worse than scepticism—which takes from man the activity of thinking, of doubting, of concluding; which destroys the boundless joy of religious personality, the pleasure of consciously willing, of full conviction, to be a follower of Christ, a man at one with God. Our faith, when it is accepted only on the word of others, is untried and weak. It has the strength of a castle which has never been attacked, of a chain which never has been proved. It may resist the trial, but we are not sure about it. We are afraid of search, afraid of new opinions, afraid of thought, lest possibly we lose our form of faith. Every infidel objection makes us tremble, every new discovery in science is a terror. Take away the old form, and we are lost, we cry out that God is dead and Christ is overthrown.

In reality we have no faith, no religion, no God. We have only a superstition, a set of opinions, and instead of a living God, a fetish.

The true religious life comes of a clear realization of our distinct personal relation to God. The views of society, the accredited opinions of the Church on religion, the true man does not despise; he seeks to understand them, for perhaps they may assist him in his endeavours; but he does not follow them blindly, he puts them even aside altogether, that he may go straight to God, and find God for himself, and as a *person* know that God is his, and that he is God's. His faith is secure, because he has won it by conquest of objections, because he has reached it through the overthrow of doubt, because he has proved it in trial and found it strong. He has come at truth by personal thought, reflection, by personal struggle against falsehood, through the passion and effort of his soul. His love of Christ is not a mere religious phrase, it is a reality. He has applied the principles of the Redeemer's life and words to his own life; to the movements of the world; as tests and direction in the hours of trial, when duties clash, or when decision is demanded; and he has found them answer to the call. He has studied the Saviour's character and meditated on His life, and of conviction he has chosen Him as the highest object of his worship, as the ideal to which he aspires.

Prayer is no form of words to him; he has known and proved its power to bring his soul into blest communion with the Highest. He does not hesitate to speak the truth, for he feels that he is inspired of God.

Such a man's religion is not conventional, has no fear, is not superstitious; it is individual, it is *his*, inwoven with his life, part of his being; nay, it is his being. He is consciously at one with God. He has freely, with all the faculties of his humanity, received Christ Jesus.

Two things, then, are laid before you this day—conventional religion, a whited sepulchre; personal religion, a fair temple whose sure foundations are bound together by the twisted strength of the innermost fibres of the soul; —a religion of words accepted from others, which begins in self-deception and ends in blindness, superstition, and the terror of the soul—or a religion at one with life, begun in resolution, continued in personal action towards Christ the Ideal of the soul, and ending in the conscious rest of union with God.

Choose; and may God grant us all grace to choose that which makes us men, not the puppets of opinion— that life which frees us from the slavery of following the multitude, and makes us sons of God through Jesus Christ our Lord.

[June 21, 1868.]

DEVOTION TO THE OUTWARD.

S. John xviii. 36.

This sentence contains in a condensed form the reasons of the rejection of Christ by the Jews, the reasons of His rejection by us. It was the spirit of the Jewish world which delivered Him to death; it is the spirit of the world which meets Him now, sometimes with the contempt of indifference, more rarely with the activity of hatred. There can be no peace between His spirit and the worldly spirit; they are naturally antagonistic. 'My kingdom,' said He, 'is not of this world.' 'I am not come to send peace on earth, but a sword.'

Now this is one of those declarations which is seized upon as challengeable. 'If His kingdom,' says the objector, 'be not of this world, then what has He to do with us? For we want a religion which will serve us in the world, which will enter into our daily life; we do not want a mysterious, transcendental, sequestered religion.'

The answer to that is that the spirit of the world is not identical, as the objection seems to say, with the spirit of humanity. The former is devoted to that which is conventional, visible, transitory; the latter in its highest form is represented in the life of Christ Himself.

Devotion to the Outward.

Now the essential difference of that life is its natural humanity, not mysterious or transcendental, except so far as our human nature is itself so ; not sequestered but eminently social, eminently interested not only in the great movements of humanity but also in its trivial trials, even in its meanest wants, and that to such a degree that we may almost assume *à priori* that whatever Christ supported and encouraged is a useful and vital element in the race, and that the spirit which He opposed is as much opposed to the true interests, as it is deadly to the perfect development, of humanity.

This we endeavoured to prove, in one particular, last Sunday. We showed that devotion to the conventional was an element of the spirit of the world, and that not only did it destroy the life of Christ in Judæa, but that wherever it exists at present it retards the development if it does not altogether destroy the life of genius, and in so doing delays the advance and injures the health of the race.

Now the second element of the spirit of the world which is at once opposed to the advance of humanity and to the spirit of Christ is *devotion to the outward* to the exclusion of the spiritual.

The chief form which this takes in England now is the love of material prosperity, the passion for wealth.

Nearly the whole of the energy of the vast middle class in our country is absorbed in money-getting, and the consequence is that no nation except America has such a preponderant mass of monotonous prosperity as England.

To belong to this class most people give their whole soul ;

to be excluded from it by poverty is to be excluded from society. A man, however rich in thought, has but little chance of large social influence unless he possess a certain amount of money.

The evil results of this in checking the development of the nobler powers in the mass of men, and in injuring individual genius, are plain. Physical prosperity being the ideal of the nation, and the generality of society giving more honour to the man of 10,000*l.* a year than to a great thinker, a great artist, or a great poet, there is not stirred in those who have fine powers that great enthusiasm which comes when the interest of a whole people, as it was of old in Athens, watches over and cheers on his way the rising genius. He feels that the battle against the general dulness and apathy is almost too hard for him to fight, carelessness begins to injure his work, despair creeps towards him, his wings are stained with dust, his soul is tainted, he works for a public he despises, and he despises himself because he condescends to flatter their taste; his art, his literary labour, suffer from his self-contempt, till at last he becomes hardened, and often ends, worst result of all, by prostituting his genius to the public cry—by painting pictures, for example, to be bought, not to teach and elevate—by placing his powers under the feet of public opinion instead of assuming his lordship, and educating public opinion. He too must become wealthy; we force him to follow us, but in doing so we corrupt his nature and we ruin his genius. He is our slave, he too must work for the material. And what is genius without freedom, without aspiration towards the ideal? It is an eagle caged in a splendid garden. The kingly bird is praised and fed by admiring visitors who glance and go by; but the lustre of the eye is dimmed, disease is at its heart, and the worst disease is its contentment: it has ceased to think of the mountain liberty, ceased to aspire to the sun.

That is the picture of our work upon the men whom God has sent among us.

Again, it is not only devotion to money-getting, but devotion to material ease, which prevents the development of original character, and opposes it if it should exist. The men who are immensely wealthy have all they want. They do not care to work; they have nothing to work for. Their energies are left undeveloped except in the exercise of a strenuous idleness. They live habitually in that comfortable ease which grows less and less inclined to those great struggles by which a man, with pain and passion, steps forward to the front as a king and guide of men.

And with the comfortable mass of the people, it is the same in a different way. Their circumstances are so easy that, except in the self-imposed agony to be rich, they have nothing to contend against. They have but little pain, except that of disease, none of the personal contest of neighbour with neighbour which made life in the middle ages so dangerous, so suffering, and so interesting. Everything which shocks our sensibilities is done for us; mechanical, scientific discoveries have made life so easy to be lived that it runs smoothly down its polished grooves. We become effeminate; a change in the weather prostrates our energies, a severe trial makes us wish to die, or to escape from duty; we are indignant with God and life if our roses are crumpled. This is not the soil in which the heroic virtues grow. There is but little heroism now exhibited in England, however much there may be latent. There is but little of that passion for the doing of noble things which makes a man not only willing but joyful to do and suffer much, to face pain and danger with that spirit which makes pain the spur of energy, and danger the drop of spice in the cup of life.

There broods over the generality an atmosphere of torpidity and slothful comfort in which it is becoming more and more impossible for a man of genius or of heroic character to develope himself. The spirit which lives in this atmosphere sets itself at once in opposition to any man who is rash enough to overcome the general effeminacy and step forth to challenge the general monotony. The world finds that this man cannot be borne. His ideas are novel, and novel ideas are vaguely felt to be dangerous to the general ease. We do not understand him, and everything which is incomprehensible is, as such, not only insolent to half-developed intellects, but also afflicts them with the same sort of blind fear with which a savage nation looks upon any great exertion of the forces of nature, the cause of which it cannot comprehend. The general mediocrity becomes angry with a particular exhibition of excellence. The man himself increases this anger; for he will not bow down to the great golden image, he will not subscribe to the articles of commerce, nor swear allegiance to my Lord Prosperity. We either treat him as a heretic, and, if we cannot persecute him, neglect him, ridicule him, or, worse still, we let loose upon him the overwhelming river of misplaced and ignorant praise. We blame him for what is greatest in him, we praise him for that which is common or conventional, and so it comes to pass that he either succumbs, if weak, under our praise, and does only what is common, or he struggles on, panting for breath in the atmosphere of dull panegyric, till at last he dies of the infliction. He cannot fawn and flatter those whom he knows to be inferior to himself, except in the matter of wealth, and if he wants success he must on the whole crawl for it. If he refuses to follow the line marked out for him, no one buys his work till he has, after many years of exhaustive struggle, conquered. When the victory comes the man is outworn. He feels himself called upon to oppose the views of common men, to traverse their cut and dried opinions, to *teach* them what is beautiful and just and heroic in art, in politics, in thought, in action, and they resent the impertinence instead of reverencing the master. To teach *them!* in whom lies hid all the greatness of England, that wealth, that comfort, that commercial force, which every other nation envies and adores. It is incredible audacity. 'What is his one voice to the grand tone of our collective wisdom? The man must be put down.'

So it is (for I need not dwell on it longer) that men of genius, of individuality, are becoming rarer and rarer; their influence, when they happen to exist, of less and less power upon the money-getting masses.

Devotion to the outward kills the unseen things which

belong to genius as much as the unseen things which belong to the Christian life. It is as deadly to imagination as it is to spirituality. It is as destructive of the true interests of humanity as it was in old time of the life of Christ.

This latter part of the subject is now our theme.

It was, I repeat, this element in the spirit of the world—devotion to the outward alone—which helped to crucify Christ Jesus.

The form it took among the Jews was in appearance noble. It was not a passion for wealth, but it was a passion for the restoration of their freedom. It was a splendid outward empire for which they longed, a fierce Jewish pride which they indulged. They cried out for the Messiah to come as a triumphant Jew, to make Jerusalem the capital of the world, to tread the hated Gentile under foot. They were not, as we are, sunk in comfort; they were not sluggish, the fierce Jewish spirit blazed in them; they were not unheroic, no greater heroism has ever been recorded than that of the last struggle with Rome; but the outwardness, if I may coin a word, the worldliness of their conception vitiated its nobility. Even within their own circle the same spirit prevailed. Each party struggled for political precedence till their patriotism was stained and its success destroyed by their greed of power. Worldliness gnawed at the root of the Jewish heart, and when Christ appeared among them, proclaiming Himself the Messiah, they could not believe their ears. This poor Galilean their glorious king! this carpenter's son, the companion of fishermen, the friend of publicans and

Devotion to the Outward.

sinners, low born, opposed to the ruling sects, preaching no crusade against the Romans, refusing the proffered crown, proclaiming in the eloquence of every act that God's true kingdom came not by violence nor by fraud, was not established by conquest over the bodies of men, nor by dazzling the sensuous in men, but by obedience and suffering and self-sacrifice; was to be established only by the spiritual power of pure truth over the souls of men, to be splendid only by nobility of spirit, by purity of life, by death for love of men—this their Messiah! this the end of all their hopes! It was not to be borne.

The moment it was clear that He was resolved to preach that His kingdom was not of this world, there rose against Him the insulted spirit of the world, the injured worshippers of outward glory. They tried at first to induce Him to take up their ideas; they offered Him the crown, they even went so far as to flatter Him. 'Good Master,' they said falsely, 'we know that Thou art true and teachest the way of God in truth.' Even His disciples hoped that He would restore the kingdom to Israel. But He was proof against all; He rested on the Invisible; He looked far forward to a kingdom in the hearts of men; He proclaimed the lordship of Truth and Goodness and Love. He did not care for lordship over either Pharisee or Sadducee, or for the world-wide empire of Jerusalem; all this He ignored as if it existed not, and this tacit scorn they could not bear. They hated Him, they called Him infidel, they said He had a devil and was mad. Thus inspired by the spirit of devotion to the outward, they crucified Him, as the spirit of devotion to money-getting and ease ignores or resents now in England the man whose life and speech condemn it.

For if Christ were now to come among us, it is that which He would denounce and contend against with a force which would soon raise up the cry of revolutionist, insane enthusiast, against Him. For He would not modify His expressions, nor smooth His sentences, in order not to shock the temper of the world. Ask yourselves how you would as a nation receive a man who should say to you—as, indeed, with less cause He said in Palestine—saying it too with a living earnestness which should force you to believe at least that he meant what he said, that those of you who gave your whole life to accumulation of many goods were *fools;* that it was *impossible* for you to serve God and to serve mammon; who, looking on your devotion to luxuries, should call on you to leave all and follow Him; who, seeing your careful watch over your comfort, should say to you in all seriousness, 'Be not anxious for your life, what ye shall eat or what ye shall drink, nor yet for your body what ye shall put on. Seek as the first thing the kingdom of God and His righteousness;' who, looking at the pomp of your charity, should say that the penny given to God out of her penury by the poor widow in the lane was infinitely more than the 500 guineas given out of your abundance; who, surveying the restless weariness, the unrelenting joyless fervour with which men, day after day, allowing themselves no relaxation, no wise moments of passiveness, sometimes scarcely any natural joy, make haste to be rich, and when rich, make haste to be more rich, should suddenly touch them and make them hear, like a solemn knell of warning, this—' What advantageth it you, if you gain the whole world, and lose yourself?' How would the nation bear such teaching now—not spoken in faded accents, in worn-out sentences from the pulpit, but driven home to each man's heart, so that the whole people could not get rid of the teaching except by getting rid of the man? It is a solemn question, for on it hangs the continuance of England's greatness. For when wealth is preferred to honour, when honesty is sacrificed to speculation, when duty is put aside if it stands in the way of fortune, when love is choked by selfishness, when the spiritual powers are left uncultivated in the absorbing haste for gain, or in the slumber of physical comfort, then—unless there be growing up a counteracting influence, the nation must die, and it is better that it should die. I do not say we are yet in that condition, but we are tending to it, and it behoves every man who loves his country to recall to his heart the teaching of Christ, and to live it out in opposition to the spirit of the world.

Lastly. Ask yourselves personally how far this money-getting spirit, this devotion to physical comfort, is preventing you from receiving Christ. Has that feverish ardour in pursuit of wealth seized upon you, so that your inward life is deprived of all moments of calm; so that even in this church you are thinking of buying and selling and getting gain; so that even at night you dream of your daily chase after wealth? Oh! what hope can you have of being a follower of Christ? How can you receive Him? for he demands the first worship of the soul; he demands the growth of the spirit, the sacrifice of time and wealth, for love of man. And you have no time to give Him, and no wealth to spare. You have no sequestered moments during which His gracious influences may flow upon you, there is no stillness in your soul during which aspiration may rise to drink the air of heaven, and prayer seclude an hour for communion with the infinite peace of God's unworldliness. Devoted to the visible, spending all your life on the material, how can you live for the invisible, how can you develope within you the spiritual? 'My kingdom is not of this world.' Has that no echo in your heart—you, whose kingdom *is* of this world—does it awake no longing for a higher life; no note of sadness, not even of self-pity, in your soul; no desire to escape from the noise and meanness of your life, the slow extinction of your immortality? Then indeed it is ineffably, infinitely pitiful. You are deaf to Christ; you have gained the world, but lost yourself.

And you who, being wealthy, do not run this race of wealth, but repose upon the silken cushions of your life, whose every wish is fulfilled, whose every caprice is satisfied, to whom every moment unamused is misery, passing through life half slumberously lulled by unvarying comfort, the lotus-eaters of society, how can you come to Christ? For He demands an active interest in humanity which will give you trouble and disturb your ease. He dreads for you the sleep of the soul, the paralysis of resolution, the absorption of aspiration in the ease of life. He bids you wake out of your dreamy being to face the stern realities of the world, arise and sacrifice yourself, stand up and make your life alive.

Devotion to the Outward.

And you who, being also wealthy and at ease, are yet more impetuous at heart, who do not eat the lotus, but seek in ceaseless excitement relief from the maddening monotony of comfort—if you really wish to know Christ, take up the nearest duties of life which you now neglect because they do not excite; assume the cross which you now push impatiently from your shoulder because it interferes with your pleasure. There are certain uninteresting or unpleasant duties which you know you ought to do; your nature grown craven and hating pain, your will powerless from dissipation of effort, recoil from the struggle. Re-invigorate your nature and your will with the spirit of Him whose kingdom was not of this world, and believe me that, though there must be suffering in your endeavour, there will be no lack of that higher and grand excitement which, born of difficulty met by a will set in resolute tension towards victory, makes life worth living, and leaves behind it no bad taste in the mouth, no sore place in the heart.

To all I say, in the name of Christ, your true kingdom, the true kingdom of your humanity, is not of this world, not of the conventional, the visible, and the transitory. Come away from its mean pursuits, its indolent ease; cease to breathe its atmosphere, to live in its spirit. Unite yourself to the things eternal in Christ Jesus. Then you will not only be saved yourself, but—and this is the higher motive—add an element of salvation to your nation. You, at least, will not be partaker of that spirit which slew Christ of old, and now threatens to corrupt and to destroy all men of genius in this country.

[June 28, 1868.]

THE RELIGION OF SIGNS.

Luke xi. 29.

From the ancient days of the people of Israel, when Moses, knowing the character of his nation, asked of God that He would vouchsafe to him a sensible sign to show as proof of His mission, until the time of Christ, we find among the Jews the craving for signs and wonders.

They desired material proofs for spiritual things, they demanded that every revelation should be accredited by miracles. It was through the gate of the senses and under the guidance of wonder, not through the gate of the spirit and under the guidance of faith, that they entered the temple of Religion.

Now this was absolutely a childish position. The child is the scholar of the senses, but it is a disgrace to a man to be their slave. The child may believe that the moon is self-luminous—it is through believing the error that he finds out its erroneousness—but it is ridiculous in the grown-up man who has examined the question not to say, 'My senses are wrong.'

It is spiritual childishness which believes that a doctrine or a man's life are true because of a miracle. The miracle speaks for the most part to the senses, and the senses can tell us nothing of the spiritual world.

The Religion of Signs.

It is spiritual manhood which out of a heart educated by the experience arising from the slow rejection of error, can say of any spiritual truth 'It *is* so, it *must* be so. I have the witness of it within, and though a thousand miracles were to suggest the denial of it, I should cling to it unswervingly.'

Now, the position of mind exactly opposite to this was that held by a large number of the common Jews and apparently by the greater part of the chief men. The latter demanded signs of Christ as proof of the truth of His teaching; the former displayed an absolutely sensual craving for miracles. And yet, on neither of these classes did the miracles, *per se*, produce any lasting effect. The Pharisees confessed, we are told, the reality of the miracle of the raising of Lazarus, and then immediately met to take measures to put Christ to death. The common people were so little impressed with one miracle that they immediately demanded another, as if the first had had no meaning.

This is the plain spirit of Fetishism, or the worship of sensible wonders without any knowledge why the worship is given, without any attempt to discover why the wonder has occurred.

It was the temptation to yield to this passion of His time and to employ His miraculous power for the sake of winning the favour of the multitude; or for ostentation; or for the sake of establishing His kingdom rapidly; which Christ conquered in the trial called that of the pinnacle of the temple. In that temptation was gathered up the whole meaning of this part of the spirit of the age, and in conquering it at the outset of

His career, He conquered it for His whole life. Again and again it met Him, but it met Him in vain. Even at the last, the voice of this phase of the spirit of the world mocked Him upon the cross. 'If He be the King of Israel, let Him now come down from the cross, and we will believe Him.' They fancied, even then, that an outward sign could secure their faith, as if those men *could* believe, who were blind to the wonder of love, obedience, and martyrdom for truth, which, greater than any miracle, was exhibited before their eyes on Calvary.

His greatest utterances, where all was great, were spoken in the spirit contrary to this religion of the senses. He threw men back upon the witness of their own heart, 'They that are of the truth hear my voice.' He declared that His true followers know Him by intuition, 'My sheep know my voice, and they follow me.' He made eternal life consist, not in the blind faith which came and went with the increase and cessation of miracle, but in the faith which recognized Him as the Son of God; in the spiritual union which He expressed in the words, 'He that eateth my flesh and drinketh my blood, dwelleth in Me, and I in him.' God, in His view, was not the wonder-worker of the Old Testament, but a Spirit who demanded a spiritual worship arising out of a deep conviction of His necessity to the soul. 'God is a spirit, and they that worship Him must worship Him in spirit and in truth.' He swept away with fiery and pregnant words all the jugglery of superstitious ceremonial with which men had overloaded the simple idea of God, and He called them back to natural life and feeling; to child-like trust in a Father

The Religion of Signs.

ever near to them; to a simple and pure morality. But at the same time He presented to their effort a grand ideal which, though it seemed too high for human nature, has yet stirred and exalted men as no other ideal has ever done—'Be ye therefore perfect, even as your Father in heaven is perfect.'

It was all too high, too simple, too spiritual to please the Jewish taste. It is true he condescended in a certain degree to their weakness of faith, and He did many mighty works, partly because He felt that some men must be first attracted through the senses, and partly, as in the case of Nathanael, in order to confirm a wavering faith. But on the other hand, He always refused to do any miracle without an adequate motive. Where the miracle could establish no principle, where it was not preceded by faith, or where it did not teach a universal lesson, Christ would not pander to the Jewish craving for a sign. This was His stern answer, 'An evil and adulterous generation seeketh after a sign. There shall *no* sign be given it,' &c.

Stung with His righteous scorn of their passion for the visible, they slew Him, and signed in His death the warrant of their nation's ruin.

Now I have been endeavouring to show that the spirit of the world in its several developments, which killed Christ, is identical with the spirit which in every nation has neglected, enfeebled, and persecuted all individuality, originality, or genius, not only in religion but in philosophy, poetry, art and science. We have seen this in the case of the worship of the conventional and of the worship of gain, ostentation, and comfort. We have seen how these phases of the spirit of the world have corrupted, ruined, and killed the life of men who rose above the common standard. I do not say that this result is due altogether to the spirit of the world; much is due to the weakness of the men themselves; but we who are not gifted men have no idea of the subtlety and awful force of the temptations of the world to men of genius; we, who have not the strength nor the weakness of genius, can scarcely conceive how cruel and how debasing the influence of the world may be when it masters that strength, or flatters that weakness into folly.

The phase of the spirit of the world of which we speak to-day is that of devotion to signs and wonders.

Men of genius are themselves signs and wonders in the world. How does the world treat them? It does not help them, it does not bring out what is best in them; it makes a show of them, and then dismisses them with a sigh of weariness. They are taken up and flattered till all their strength is drained away. They are polished down till all the angles which made them of use, which jarred upon the splendid dulness, or irritated into some life the lazy indifference, of common society are smoothed away, and the man offends no more by originality. It fills one with pity and anger to think how many who might have been Samsons, and have smitten our modern Philistinism to its death, have been ensnared by the Delilah of fashionable society, and set, 'shorn of their puissant locks,' to work in the prison and to make sport for the Philistines. We mourn, and with just cause,

The Religion of Signs. 197

the loss of many who, born to be kings, have sunk into willing slaves.

Look at the way in which this devotion to signs and wonders in the world acts now upon the literature of the country. In that sphere it is represented by a craving for 'sensationalism' which results in intellectual sloth. Men ask for books which excite but give no trouble. They have not time, they say, to read slowly, much less to read a book twice over. A book genuinely thought out but not brilliant, in which the experience of a life of intellectual work is concentrated, has scarcely a chance of success. The public are too indolent to read even a thoughtful review of such a book, unless it be written in a sparkling style and flavoured with a spice of sensation. Except they read signs and wonders, they will not read at all. What are the consequences? Men of thought, who are strong of will and believe in themselves, refuse to submit to this tyrannical cry for signs. They persist in writing books of worth and weight, but they do it in a kind of despair, and their work suffers from the dogged dulness which despair creates. Unlistened to and hopeless, they cannot write with the joy which enlivens expression, with the uplifting sense of a public sympathy.

Men of thought, who are weak of will, and whose self-confidence depends upon the public voice, write one book of power and then surrender their high mission. They enter on the career which demoralizes the finer powers of genius—the career of the reviewer and the magazine contributor—and too often end by drifting into the mere sensationalist, writing a book which, like an annual, grows, blooms, and dies in a season. They strain after brilliancy; not brilliancy for its own sake, but brilliancy for the sake of show or favour. They fall into the very temptation which Christ resisted in the case of miracles.

I might illustrate the subject in other spheres than the sphere of literature, but enough has been said to show the operation upon men of genius of this element of the spirit of the world which as a craving for signs and wonders among the Jews hurried the Saviour to the Cross.

Now, a society tainted with the diseased passion for this class of writing is drifting away from that temper of mind which can frankly accept Christ Jesus, for His is not the life which can satisfy the sensationalist.

Separate it from the moral glory, the spiritual beauty, which rose from it like a sea of light out of inner fountains, and it is a common life enough. Uneventful for thirty years, the story of it, even in the midst of its miracles, is marked by nothing especially exciting. It was in itself eminently natural, unartificial, deep, cool, and quiet as a garden-well, passed by preference among rustic, uneducated men, amid the holy serenity of the mountain and the desert, among the gracious simplicities of natural beauty, beside the ripple of the lake, upon the grass-grown hill—seeking even at Jerusalem refuge from the noise and passion of the city in the peaceful village of Bethany or among the shadows of the silent garden of Gethsemane.

We cannot understand it, we cannot understand Him, we cannot enter into the profound simplicity and truth of

The Religion of Signs.

His teaching, if we have habituated our mind to morbid excitement, our moral sense to a continual violation of it in both French and English novels, and our emotions to a mental hysteria which destroys the will. This may seem a slight evil, but it is more than we imagine. We should look with fear upon the growth of this temper in English society; it is denaturalizing it. It renders both mind and heart corrupt. It will end by making the life corrupt and society impure. Sensationalism in literature is closely connected with sensuality in society.

Again, take in the present time as another form of the Jewish passion for signs and wonders, the existence among us of men and women with a passion for the false supernatural. The true supernatural is not the miraculous but the purely spiritual, not the manifestation of things which astonish the senses but the revelation of things which ennoble the spirit. In neither of these ways are the things with which we have been lately favoured truly supernatural. They are abundantly material, and they do not ennoble. The last appearance of the chief prophet has not been characterized by a surplus of spirituality

Every day, however, fewer persons are likely to be swept away by this spiritual quackery, for as the ozone of scientific knowledge is added to our social atmosphere, these corrupt growths dwindle and die. But it is worth while perhaps to say that they enfeeble the intellect and do harm to Christianity. No man can long float in the misty region of pale speculation in which these exhibitions involve him—speculation which starts from no fixed point and aims at nothing—nor be tossed about by the inconsequence of the so-called phenomena without feeling his intellect ebbing away and its manliness departing. They render the reason a useless part of our being.

So doing, they do evil to Christianity; for to conceive Christianity grandly, to expound it nobly, to develope it within our own souls as fully as possible, and to work for its perfect kingdom, we need to unite to its spiritual power within us 'the power of a free, vigorous, manly, and well-cultured intellect.' We need for the work of Christ, not only spiritual life as the first thing, but intellectual light as the second.

Again. One of the greatest evils which arise from the encouragement of charlatanry of this kind in connection with religion — and it is *so* connected—is that it protracts the period when the work of science and religion, by consent of their several professors, will advance together. It causes scientific men to think that everything connected with religion is inimical to the methods of science; it intensifies their opposition to the thought of the supernatural by setting before them a false supernaturalism. It throws contempt upon and degrades the notion of a spiritual world. It increases a credulity on the one hand which leads to gross superstition; it increases an unbelief on the other which leads to gross materialism. The extremes of the two sides are set into stronger opposition, and in the noise which the extreme parties make, the voices of wiser men remain unheard.

One element of good hope, however, attends its appearance among us. The spirit in society which it feeds has almost always, in conjunction with a spirit of unbelief with which it is connected, preceded a revolution of thought. It was so before the teaching of Christianity. It was so before the rise of the Reformation. It was so before the outburst of new ideas which gave force to the early days of the French Revolution.

I have hope that this blind confusion, this tossing together of the elements of credulity and unbelief, will create, in a reaction from them, a rational and liberal faith.

Analogous to this is the endeavour to awake and excite religious sensibility either by the overwrought fervour of the revivalist, producing an hysterical excitement which is mistaken for a spiritual manifestation— or by the sensual impressions made by the lights, incense, music, colour, and all the paraphernalia of the ritualists. I do not deny the real enthusiasm, however cruelly mistaken in its mode of action, nor the good which many of the revivalists have done ; nor the good and the enthusiasm which follow the efforts of the ritualist, but in a certain degree they both agree in this —they try to produce spirituality from without. They make use of stimulants which are unnatural in relation to the spirit, though natural in their relation to the body.

Precisely the same thing is done by those who hunt after exciting sermons, who imagine they repair the ravages of the devotion of six days to the world by an emotional impression on Sunday as transient as the morning dew; who mistake a thrill of intellectual excitement for a spiritual conviction, a glow of aspiration for a religious act, and pleasure in a sermon for the will to conquer evil.

Now all these things are, under one form or another, the products of the same spirit which in the days of Christ sought for signs and wonders.

The melancholy superstition which is called so ironically spiritualism unfits its devoted votaries for their daily work. Some play with it, and it does them little harm; but others, embarking in it with energy, get into an excited, inoperative, unhealthy condition, in which a quiet Christian life becomes all but impossible, in which duty becomes a burden if it separate them from their experiments, in which it seems better to sit at a table slothfully waiting for a spiritual communication than to go with Christ into the middle of the arena of life, and do our duty there against the evil. It is there, in faithful following of Him, that we shall have spiritual communications; it is there, in self-sacrificing action, that we shall feel inspired by God to act and speak; it is there that we shall realize our communion with the host of all great spirits, in enduring like them all things for the truth; it is there, by faithful prayer and resistance to temptation, by the warfare against sin within and wrong without, that our hearts will begin to beat with the excitement which ennobles and the enthusiasm which does not decay; it is there, loving our Saviour's spirit above all things and aspiring to reach His Divine perfection, that we shall enter into the true spiritual world, and feel, not the miserable presences of beings which, on the impossible supposition of their existence, it is a disgrace to associate with, but the very presence of the Spirit of God within us;

hear, not a futile and laborious noise, but the voice of God Himself, saying to us, after the conquest of sin or the performance of duty in His strength, 'Well done, good and faithful servant.'

And as to the attempts of revivalists or ritualists to influence the spirit through the flesh, there is this plain evil, that all stimulants of this character produce each their own peculiar reaction, and are followed in the reaction by exhaustion. Then the passionate emotion must be worked up again by another and a fiercer address, or the æsthetic impression which produced the thrill must be again received, but this time by means of a more exciting service. It follows, then, that the exhaustion of reaction is greater since the stimulant has been more violent. So it proceeds, till at last the limit of stimulation has been reached and the excitement can be aroused no more. Only the exhaustion remains, the craving is still there, and the worn-out votaries of the religion of the nerves and the senses turn back—unable to do without their thrilling sensations—to the old excitements, and go back in the case of revivalism to sin, in the case of ritualism to the world.

Of course we only speak of tendencies, not of persons. It would be absurd to deny that many faithful men have been made by revivalism. It would be far more absurd to deny that there are thousands of devoted men who attach a living meaning to ritualistic observances, and to whom these things are not a form without a spirit, but the natural expression, and therefore to them the right expression, of spiritual feelings—who use them not to create from without, but to embody from within, their inner life with God.

But, making this allowance, it seems clear that this form of religious life is not the highest nor the truest form of the Christian life. It encourages that temper of mind which demands signs and wonders as proofs and supports of faith. It is in bondage to ceremonies; it is against our full freedom in Christ Jesus. It says to men, in principle, 'Except ye be circumcised, Christ shall profit you nothing.' It denies the equal holiness of all times, of all places, to the Christian heart, by asserting the especial holiness of certain times and certain places. It places the priest between us and God as a necessary means whereby alone we may hold communication with God. It asserts the absolute necessity of certain symbolic observances for the reception of any higher spiritual grace from God.

This is not the purity and simplicity of Christianity. It is a rehabilitation of those elements in Judaism which Christ attacked and overthrew. It is opposed to the whole spirit of His teaching. He removed the barriers of ceremonies, of sacrifices, of authority, of localized and exclusive sanctities, and He brought the heart of each man into direct communion with the Heavenly Father. As to a priesthood, and its pretensions to interfere between us and God, Christ swept it away with every word and action of His life, and by uniting the individual soul to God, made every man his own priest, and the daily spiritual offering of each man's love in feeling and in action the acceptable sacrifice. 'If any man love me, he will keep my words; and my Father will

The Religion of Signs. 205

love him, and we will come to him, and make our abode with him.'

There is the charter of our freedom, and there is not a word in it of the necessity of God's grace coming to us filtered through the medium of a priest, or a ceremony, or a sacrament, or a symbol.

To some men these things may be necessary; for some men signs and wonders of one kind or another, ceremonies, symbols, or outward excitements may be required. Let us not deny their needfulness at times, for even Christ made use of miracles. Because some of us can do without them, we must not impose our liberty on others. But we must not allow that they can *give* life, though they may support it; we must not make them of the *first* necessity, we must not imagine that a Christianity not adorned but encumbered with them is anything but a low type of Christianity. We must avow that the insistance on, or the craving for, any form of the religion of signs or the religion of superstitious wonder, is an element of disease in the Church analogous to the spirit which helped to bring Christ Jesus to his death.

Sometimes He gave way to it when He saw the heart was true, as when He touched Nathanael's wavering faith through wonder, or when He condescended to the doubt of Thomas. But He led Nathanael to a more spiritual region, 'Thou shalt see greater things than these,' a divine union between heaven and earth through the medium of the Son of man. And He marked out Thomas's faith as weak, 'Blessed are they who have not seen, and yet have believed.'

Yes, brethren, blessed is he, in these times of devotion

to the sensible, who can behold the obedience and the deep self-sacrifice of the Saviour's life and death; who can watch, unfolding in Him, perfect love, undaunted courage, stainless purity, the simple nobleness of truth, the union of mercy and justice, and recognizing that as God in humanity, throw himself upon it in a pure passion of love, and with a solemn force of faith, and clasp the perfect Man to his heart as his unique possession, as his living impulse, as his Redeemer, in whose love his sin is drowned, his lower self annihilated.

Signs, wonders, excitements, observances, I need them not to make me trust in Thee. I feel Thy power in my heart, Thy presence moving in my life. I hear Thy voice; it is enough, my spirit knows its sound, claims it as the voice of the rightful Master of my being. I have not *seen*, but, O my Saviour! I have *felt*— and I believe.

Individuality.

[Dec. 6, 1868.]

INDIVIDUALITY.

Luke ix. 24.

THIS is one of those sayings of Christ which have aroused in men opinions of the most opposite character. It has been received on one side with scorn, on the other by reverence. It has been considered as a piece of unpractical sentiment, it has been hailed as the very inmost law of all life.

We may ask why it was that Christ expressed Himself in so mystical a manner. It was partly because He spoke not only for the period in which He lived, but for all periods of the history of the world. He gave to men seeds of thought which were to be developed in proportion as the world developed. Much has been wrought out of them, much remains to be discovered. Some say that Christianity is effete: it seems to me that we have but begun to understand it. But the plain reason for the mystery of Christ's sayings is this, that all the highest truths are by their nature mystical, above and beyond the power of the intellect *acting by itself.* The super-intellectual lies beneath our science, our theology, our philosophy, even our art.

Many of the conclusions of science as well as those of theology and philosophy are deduced from intuitions, which we cannot demonstrate. In chemistry, e.g., though the law of definite combining proportions has been demonstrated, yet the atomic theory which answers the question —as well as many others—why combination takes place according to that law, remains undemonstrated, beyond the region of the reason. It is 'a backward guess from fact to principle.'

So also with astronomy; the laws of Kepler express demonstrated facts, but the theory of gravitation, which explains why those facts are so, lies outside of demonstration. We know nothing of that quality of matter—if there be such a quality—which enables matter to attract matter.

These theories, like spiritual truths, are intuitions, and the mode of proving the one and the other, so far as they are capable of proof, is the same.

The man who lives much with Christ, that is, with divine humanity, feels the principles which rule the spiritual life of man. These principles were felt and stated by Christ. Do they explain the facts of the spiritual life; are there none of those facts which contradict the principles? Then we infer that the principles are true. It is not necessary that they should explain *all* the facts, for in theology, as in science, many facts are waiting for further knowledge before they can be ranged under the principles; it is only necessary that they should not be contradicted by the facts.

The man who lives much with Nature, that is, with the form of God's thoughts, feels what is true of her, has intuitions of her secrets. He calls his intuition a theory, and then reasons back to it by experiment; and if the facts occur as if the principle were true, he keeps his theory though he may not be able to bring *all* the facts into harmony with it. It is sufficient if the greater part are explained and no contradiction occurs. He waits, like the theologian, for further light. And as he always holds his theory so as to be ready to take up another which embraces a larger number of facts, so we should hold our spiritual principles, ready, nay, hoping for the revelation of higher ones which may more fully explain the facts of the life of the soul. Indeed, many of Christ's sayings and the whole tendency of the doctrine of the second advent declare that more all-embracing principles than those we have at present are destined to become ours hereafter.

But the main point of the analogy on which I insist, laying aside the rest, is this, that both science and Christianity proceed from intuitions which are not brought to the test of the pure intellect. Both Faraday and S. Paul worked from principles which they could not demonstrate.

It is no argument, then, against Christianity, that the principles laid down by its Founder cannot be brought to the test of the pure intellect, any more than it is against science that its theories cannot bear the same test.

Assume the truth of the principles of Christ, and though we cannot as yet explain all the facts of spiritual life by them, yet they explain a vast number, and are not contradicted by any of the facts in their own sphere.

Assume the truth of certain scientific theories, and they explain the operations of nature up to a certain point, and are not contradicted by the facts which belong to their sphere. But you have to assume, you cannot demonstrate at present in either case. The theories of science and the principles of the spiritual life are both proved backwards, not forwards, and as the proof is never complete, they always remain to a certain degree without the limits of the pure intellect. Both pass into a belt of shadow.

We work then upon intuitions in the realms of science and of spirit by the same method, the intellectual method of experiment. But the facts on which we work are of a different kind. We must not confuse our scientific work by introducing into it spiritual feelings; nor our spiritual work by introducing conclusions drawn by the intellect from the sphere of criticism or science. Else we fall into spiritual absurdities, and either lose the use of, or travesty, our intuition. Take, for example, the unproveable spiritual truth of my text. Whenever an attempt has been made to subject it to the dry action of the mere intellect, to limit it by rules, to reduce it to maxims, or to act on the motive of the *utility* of sacrifice, it has been made ridiculous in practice, or lost its power, or ceased to be itself, or been travestied into Pharisaism. Unless its action comes fresh and free from the heart, it becomes selfishness in the end.

Among all men before Christ, it was dimly felt as true, but it was not recognized as the only law of life. Its recognition as such was due to Christ. He saw it as the one universal idea of the universe; He knew that it was the expression of the very life of God; He seized on it, and embodied it in His life, in His

Individuality.

words, above all in His death. It was *the* one truth to which He bore witness; it was the one truth in which all the other truths which He taught were contained. This is the full, inexhaustible meaning of His career. He could truly say of Himself that He was the life, because He was the sacrifice.

But I am now asked what is meant by self-sacrifice.

Self-sacrifice means that the motive power of true life is not our own interests, passions, wealth, or reputation, but the interest and advance of others. It means the clear recognition that God has no self-life, never, in our sense of the terms, acts, thinks, or *is* for Himself, for His own glory, never considers Himself at all; has therefore no jealousy, no anger, no caprice, no petty motives, none of those accursed selfish passions which have been imputed to Him by mistaken men—but realizes His life in the life of all, and in giving of Himself away becomes the life of all—it means the clear recognition of this by the heart, and such an action following on the recognition as unites us in similar sacrifice to the life of God, till we too find our only being along with Him, in the being of all which lives by Him.

But you will say 'This destroys my individuality, and to that I cling. I do not care to live if I am to be mingled up with the universe. It is one of my deepest instincts to desire to be, and to recognize myself. I am a distinct person, and I wish to continue distinct for ever. I have no interest in immortal life, and I can conceive no interest in a future life with others, unless

I and all preserve each our separate and different being.'

We reply, that any spiritual theory of life which tends to destroy and not to assert the individuality of man is an inhuman theory, and as such false; that Christ and His Apostles proclaimed the separate individuality of each man in proclaiming the personal and distinct relation of each man to God. Any explanation of this text must therefore account for the fact of this desire of individuality.

We must keep up our individuality, but we ought to take care that it is true and not false individuality. The key to distinguish them from each other is given to us in the text. It speaks of a double nature in man; one which asserts self, the other which denies it. The first has a seeming life which is actual death; the second has a seeming death which is actual life; and therefore, as life is inseparably connected with individuality, the development of the selfish nature is false individuality; the development of the unselfish nature is true individuality.

Take for example the case of the selfish man. He grasps all he can, he accumulates, but only for himself. He has little connection with the race, except so far as he can use men for his own purposes; he lives among men, but it is with the suspicion and hard heart which divide him, not with the trust and love which unite him to his fellows. He lives alone, he dies alone, and the wind and rain which wear out the letters on his tomb are the only haunters of his pretentious grave.

There are many who, seeing this self-sufficing, separate

man, will say that he possessed a strongly marked individuality. But it is not *individuality*, it is *isolation*. The sense of life is inseparable from the sense of individuality, and this man has only felt a fiery craving which he mistakes for life. Love for self, sympathy for self, activity for self, do not produce life or the sense of life; they produce self-disease, the satiety which consumes, the dreadful loneliness which corrupts the soul, that passionate lust for more which is itself the unsatisfied worm which eats away the heart. No vivid or exalted sense of individual being can ever fill the heart of this man until he escape from the curse of self-involvement, and spread his being over all the world. But if the habit should become too strong, then, finally, even the last sign of possibility of life passes away, for the craving is dulled, the pain of satiety is lost, and the heart ossifies. Isolation has produced the death of individuality. 'He that loveth his life shall lose it.'

Now turn and look at that Divine Figure who came at this advent time to lose the life which the selfish man has cherished. His worst opponents have never dared to say that He lived for Himself, that He sought His own interest or His own glory. Those who have not believed in Him as the Christ have honoured Him as one who gave His whole life up to the service of men. His enemies who slew Him gave in scorn their unconscious testimony to His self-sacrifice: 'He saved others, Himself He cannot save.' There is no need to dwell upon the exquisite service of His years of work; their self-surrender is known. I mention only, as less dwelt on, the manifold sympathy with different characters which could only arise out of His having lost His own being for the time in that of the person to whom He spoke; the intense patience with littleness, and interruption, and misunderstanding; the absolute want of that anger at being continually mistaken and at want of insight on the part of followers, to which philosophers and teachers are subject.

When the minor incidents say so much, with what a fulness do the greater events declare that Christ never even acknowledged the existence of a self in His nature! He lost His life; but in losing the life of self He bruised the head of the deathfulness in human nature, and claimed and won for us the eternal life.

And what was the result—one result of this, at least? That no personality is so unique as His; no one figure in history stands out so accentuated, so distinct; no individuality is so individual. And yet—is it not strange?—no universality is so universal, no figure is so blended up with others, no personality is so unlimited. The double thought is true of Him, that none lived so much in others, and yet none was so truly himself. For true individuality, like true life, is gained by the loss of that which seems individuality. It is gained by the loss of consciousness of self, or, to express it otherwise, it is secured when we become naturally incapable of self-isolation. It is not difficult to illustrate these statements from the sayings of Christ. He never distinguishes His own personality from that of God. He knows nothing of Himself except as in union with God. 'I proceeded forth and came from God'—observe the clear

Individuality.

recognition of individuality — 'neither came I of myself, but He sent me.' Observe how the former is balanced: Christ was conscious of individuality, but only so because He had no separate consciousness of self. Again. 'He that believeth in me, believeth not on me, but on Him that sent me.' 'He that seeth me, seeth Him that sent me.' 'I have not spoken from myself. Even as the Father said to me, so I speak.' 'I and my Father are one.'

From these and many other passages you see that Christ the Man rejected altogether the notion of an independent being in Himself—was only conscious of Himself as in God and united to Him—could not even for a moment isolate Himself so as to desire anything for Himself alone, or to contemplate and admire Himself, or think of His own thoughts as His alone, or feel the feeling of His feelings as we do till we are sick of the false individuality which we create. He was freed from the slavery which forces the selfish man to revolve for ever round himself, free to live in God, free to unite Himself to the universe, free to pour His spirit forth on the world. Now in this freedom of life in the life of all, in this self-abandonment, He found the intense consciousness of life which is the best expression of the meaning of individuality. For the life He felt was not His own particular life, but the life of God in Him; the being He was conscious of was the being, and therefore the activity, in Him of the whole universe of spirits who received their life of God. His individuality was perfected in the loss of self.

This is the main statement; but in order to make it

clearer we will look at it through the light of a few illustrations.

Take S. Paul, the man of active work. He is remarkable among religious teachers for a want of that isolated self-consciousness of which I have spoken. No jealousy of others, no posing before the world, no morbid self-examination spoiled his nature. Self was lost in 'spending and being spent' for others. Willing even to lose his own soul for his kinsmen, how does he describe his being?—'It is not I, but Christ who liveth in me.'

And yet what an individuality! How he stands out in the history of the Church, how marked in character, how vividly distinct in feeling! It is astonishing what an impression of fulness of life we gain, if we only glance over one of his Epistles, how convinced we are that he must have felt the opulence of Being in every hour of his life. He lost his lower life to find a higher individuality in union with the life of Christ, with the life of all whom he had taught and loved. The life of Christ in God, the life of all the race in Christ, the life of every Corinthian, Roman, Ephesian, whom he had met—all these varied existences became part of him by love, their life the life he lived, the guarantee and source of his individuality.

And *you*, when has life been dearest to you? when have you felt the fine thrill of intense Being? when have you realized your personality most vividly? Has it not been when God has enabled you to lay aside some guilty pleasure, or to put by the crown of prosperity that you may, in being true to duty, lose your sinful self in union

Individuality.

with His righteousness? In the very moment in which you have trodden down your lower nature and refused to isolate yourself from God—then it is, I venture to say, that, though life seems ruined with pain, yet a sense of other life begins to rush through your being; not life as it is known here, but a touch of something ecstatic, keen, intense. It is that you have entered into the outskirts of God's life; and in denying self, and in asserting the will of your Father as your own, have become conscious of a personality in Him, such as you have never realized before.

Or again, has it not been when in intense love you have merged your being in that of another, when another is the life of your life, when self is drowned in the sea of feeling? Was it not then that the meaning of Being became known to you, that you felt yourself a person, but felt it somehow in another? Was it not then that life even in its meanest details became not only worthy but exquisite, that you were somehow admitted into the secret of that correlation of things in which everything is great, that nature spoke to you as to an intimate friend, that God drew nearer, that the soul of the universe seemed to pulsate in harmony with yours, that the dread and weight of eternity were lifted off, because you were yourself dwelling in eternity? Isolation had perished, and out of its ruins arose individuality. You lost and found yourself.

Let that be multiplied; let the loss of self in one be multiplied into the loss of self in love of all men; let the same intensity belong to the universal love which belonged to the particular love, and we then possess some conception of the individuality of Christ, of how it is possible to say of Him that He was not a man, but humanity. He lived, and is living, not in Himself, but in all men. Love has made Him, as it were, transformed into the being of all. Into His individuality He has therefore taken the individuality of all, and He feels His own being in the being of the whole race. Do you not see how infinitely rich, how intensely living, how inexpressibly various, must be His individuality?

Do you not see how the more lives you yourself manage to live in intensely, how the more you lose your isolated self and the thoughts and feelings which cluster round it, and take instead into you the thoughts and feelings of others, the richer and the more varied, the more complex and the more interesting, and therefore the more vividly individual, becomes your being?

It is difficult to make this clear; I cannot express it as I wish. Perhaps a personal illustration may repeat the experience of some among you, and bring home the thought. It was my fortune last year, in going from Torcello to Venice, to be overtaken by one of the whirlwinds which sometimes visit the south. It was a dead calm, but the whole sky, high overhead, was covered with a pall of purple, sombre and smooth, but full of scarlet threads. Across this, from side to side, as if darted by two invisible armies, flew at every instant flashes of forked lightning; but so lofty was the storm —and this gave a hushed terror to the scene—that no thunder was heard. Beneath this sky the lagoon water was dead purple, and the weedy shoals left naked by

Individuality. 219

the tide dead scarlet. The only motion in the sky was far away to the south, where a palm-tree of pale mist seemed to rise from the water, and to join itself above to a self-enfolding mass of seething cloud. We reached a small island and landed. An instant after, as I stood on the parapet of the fortification, amid the breathless silence, this pillar of cloud, ghostly white, and relieved against the violet darkness of the sky, its edge as clear as if cut with a knife, came rushing forward over the lagoon, driven by the spirit of wind, which, hidden within it, whirled and coiled its column into an endless spiral. The wind was only there, at its very edge there was not a ripple; but as it drew near our island it seemed to be pressed down upon the sea, and unable to resist the pressure opened out like a fan in a foam of vapour. Then, with a shriek which made every nerve thrill with excitement, the imprisoned wind leapt forth; the water of the lagoon, beaten flat, was torn away to the depth of half an inch; and as the cloud of spray and wind smote the island, it trembled all over like a ship struck by a great wave. We seemed to be in the very heart of the universe at a moment when the thought of the universe was most sublime.

The long preparation, and then the close, so unexpected and so magnificent, swept every one completely out of self-consciousness; the Italian soldiers at my side danced upon the parapet and shouted with excitement. For an instant we were living in Nature's being, not in our own isolation.

It taught me a lesson; it made me feel the meaning of this text, 'Whosoever loseth his life shall find it;' for it is in such scanty minutes that a man becomes possessor of that rare intensity of life which is, when it is pure, so wonderful a thing that it is like a new birth into a new world, in which, though self is lost, the highest individuality is found. I am conscious now, in looking back, though the very self-consciousness involved in analyzing the impression seems to spoil it, that it is in such a moment, when, as it were, you find your individuality outside of you in the being of the universe, that you are most individual, and most able to *feel* your being, though not to *think* it.

Take that into the spiritual world. Put the heavenly Father and the Spirit of Christ, and the race of men as seen in Him, into the place of the grandeur of Nature—lose your lower self, all thought, all feeling of it in union with them by love, and—that is the Christian life; for it is the life of Christ Himself—nay, it is the very life of God. No life can be so infinite, so creative, so entire as God's, because none is so given, so utterly lived in all—and all the ecstacy of joy and self-forgetfulness which comes on us in such moments as I have described, of sacrifice to duty—of love to another—and of absorption in natural sublimity—are but the faintest shadow of that unspeakable joy of life and intensity of individuality which God possesses in never knowing what self is, in possessing, of choice, His being in the being of the spiritual universe. It is to *that* that we look forward; not to a heaven of selfish rewards, not to a world of self-enjoyment; but to the loss of all consciousness of our lower being in union with the being of God; to the loss of all thoughts and feelings which for an instant tend to isolate us from the whole universe of spirits akin to us; and to the gain of our true individuality in the feeling that we are at one with the individuality of all.

'For whosoever will save his life shall lose it: but whosoever will lose his life for my sake, the same shall save it.'

[Trinity Sunday, 1868.]

THE CREATION.

Genesis i. 1.

It is not very long ago since an eminent high priest of science undertook, before an assembly of clergymen, and at their invitation, to expose the relations of the clergy to science, and he began with this proposition, or words to the same effect: 'that he supposed he might assume, without fear of contradiction, that nine-tenths of the clergy believed that the world was created in six days.' It would be hard to say whether extreme astonishment or extreme amusement was the predominant feeling with which his declaration was received: astonishment that any man (however so immersed in his peculiar business as to prevent his knowledge of the business of other men) should be so ignorant of the position and feelings of the persons whom he came to enlighten; amusement, that he should, being thus ignorant, expose his ignorance with such innocent simplicity. It was plain that he looked on the mass of the clergy as sharing in the spirit of the priests who persecuted Copernicus and Galileo, or at least as sharing in the wilful blindness of their persecutors; and the result was, that the lecturer was placed in the undignified position of having created a man of straw, against which he tilted for an hour, while the real opponent, with the real points of opposition, was left absolutely untouched.

Now all this comes of some scientific men having fallen into the errors and evils of that priestcraft of which they have accused, and with some good reason, the clergy for many years. Priestcraft, brought into contact with opinions which oppose its own, or which it fancies oppose its own, becomes unreasonably excited, loses its head on the point in question, and rushes to trample down its opponent as blindly as a bull in the arena excited by a red flag. It refuses to see the position of its adversaries; it calls their arguments evasions of the question; it will admit no possible premises but its own; it will not take the slightest trouble to find out what its opponents really hold, and the natural consequence is that being ignorant, it makes mistakes; that being sure of its own right, and seeing no right but its own, it becomes intolerant, contemptuous, and would be persecuting if it had its way. It is an extremely melancholy thing to see how some of the masters of science are exhibiting, under another form, so many of these characteristics of priestcraft, and how by doing so they are retarding the progress of the world.

If we, both clergy and scientific people, were to try not to live solely in our own atmosphere, but also a little in the atmosphere of one another, there would be some hope of that reconciliation of science and religion for which the progress of the race is waiting.

The first chapter of Genesis has been one of the battle-grounds on which science and the received theory of inspiration have met in contest. Because its statements conflict with the discoveries of geology, the whole inspiration of the Bible has been denied; and many declare that when we maintain that the Bible is inspired, we are evading the question and false to our creed. They take up the ultra theory of inspiration, and ignorantly declare that we all hold that theory—that if we do not hold it, we ought to hold it, and other intolerances of that kind.

It shall be my work to-day to endeavour to show that it is possible to believe this chapter inspired, and yet to leave a free field to science; nay, more, to show that the principles which underlie this chapter are identical with the principles recognized by the geologist.

There is no need to weary you with recapitulating the well-known objections to the truth of the details given in this chapter. They are known to all. It will suffice my purpose to say that I am one among many in the Church who believe those objections to be fatal not only to the theory of verbal, but also to that of plenary inspiration. Many theories of reconciliation have been published; but, first, they continually evade the real points, or they do not see them, and secondly, the theories answer themselves by contradicting one another.

Are we, then, to say that this chapter is uninspired because the account given in it of the Creation cannot be reconciled with the discoveries of science? No; for we deny that the writers of the Bible were infallible upon scientific and historical questions; and it does not follow

The Creation.

that error on these points proves that they were in error on spiritual questions, any more than the errors of the man of science in matters of theology prove that he is in error upon matters of science. On the contrary, that the writers of the Bible are proved to have no higher knowledge about scientific and historical questions than that which they could gain at the time in which they lived, is a mark, not of the want, but of the wisdom of inspiration. For if the writers had brought forward scientific truths in the childhood of the world's knowledge, their spiritual revelation would have been disbelieved. If Moses, for example, had told the Israelites that the earth went round the sun, when they daily seemed to see the sun going round the earth, they would have rejected his declaration of the unity of God. The one assertion would have reflected, in their eyes, falsehood on the other.

We must judge the Book by the times. It was necessary that a spiritual revelation should be given in harmony with the physical beliefs of the period; and when we demand that the revealed writings should be true to our physical knowledge in order that we should believe in inspiration, we are asking that which would have made all those for whom the Bible was originally written disbelieve at once in *all* it revealed to man. We ask too much: that book was written on wiser principles. It left these questions aside; it spoke in the language, and through the knowledge, of its time. It was content to reveal spiritual truth; it left men to find out scientific truth for themselves. It is inspired with regard to the first; it is not inspired with regard to the latter. It is inspired with regard to universal principles; it is not inspired with regard to details of fact. The proof that it is inspired with regard to principles is that those principles which it lays down or implies are not isolated but universal principles. They are true of national, social, political, intellectual, as well as of spiritual life, and above all, and this is the point which I especially wish to urge, they are identical with scientific principles. Let us test this in the case of this chapter.

The first principle to be inferred is that of the *unity of God*. One Divine Being is represented as the sole Cause of the universe. Now this is the only foundation of a true religion for humanity. Starting from the Semitic peoples, it has gradually made its way over the whole of the Aryan family with the exception of the Hindoos; and even among them, and wherever else the worship of many gods exists, it is gradually driving out polytheism and establishing itself as the *necessary* religion for humanity.

It is also the only true and ultimate foundation of international, national, social, and family union. The deepest possible ground of unity which nations and bodies of men can possess is that they should all, however different otherwise, be one in the worship of the heart. Community of worship consolidates nations, societies, and families.

And now observe, that it is at this point that geology and revelation meet in principle. Out of all the investigations into the past life and growth of our globe, there emerges the conviction of One Divine Reason at

The Creation. 227

the root of all organization, and of all processes of change in the crust of the earth. We find the same primary ideas appearing in the oldest and in the latest plants and animals. We can reduce all the infinite forms of animal life to a few primitive types of construction; nay, the very last hypothesis put forward confirms this, by declaring that all the varieties of life have been developed, without a break, in accordance with one law. Again, with regard to the growth of the earth itself, we have discarded the notion of agencies different from those which now exist; we explain the various changes which have taken place during infinite myriads of years on precisely the same principles, and by the same agencies, on and by which the present changes, elevations, depressions, and depositions are taking place. The plan and mode have not altered; there is unity of purpose throughout.

The next principle in this chapter is that *all noble work is gradual*. God is not represented as creating everything in a moment. He spent six days at His work, and then said it was very good. Now there is no principle more universal than this—that in proportion to the nobility of anything, is it long in reaching its perfection. The summer fly is born and dies in a few days; the more highly organized animal has a long youth and a mature age. The inferior plant rises, blooms, and dies in a year; the oak transforms the storms and sunshine of a century into the knotted fibres of its stem. The less noble powers of the human mind mature first; the more noble, such as imagination, comparison, abstract reasoning, demand the work of years. The greatest ancient nation took the longest time to develope its iron power; the securest political freedom in a nation did not advance by bounds, or by violent revolutions, but in England 'broadened slowly down from precedent to precedent.' The greatest modern society —the Church of Christ—grew as Christ prophesied, from a beginning as small as a grain of mustard-seed into a noble tree, and grows now more slowly than any other society has ever grown—so slowly, that persons who are not far-seeing say that it has failed. The same law is true of every individual Christian life. Faith, to be strong, must be of gradual growth. Love, to be unconquerable, must be the produce not of quick-leaping excitement, but of patience having her perfect work. Spiritual character must be moulded into the likeness of Christ by long years of battle and of trial, and we are assured that eternity is not too long to perfect it.

Connected with this universal principle is another—that this gradual growth of noble things, considered in its general application to the universe, is from the lower to the higher—is, in fact, a progress, not a retrogression. We are told in this chapter that first arose the inorganic elements, and then life—first the life of the plant, then of the animal, and then of man, 'the top and crown of things.'

It is so also in national life—first family life, then pastoral, then agricultural, then the ordered life of a polity, the highest. It is the same with religion. First, natural religion, then the dispensation of the Law, then the more spiritual dispensation of the Prophets,

The Creation.

then the culmination of the external revelation through man in Christ, afterwards the higher inward dispensation of the universal Spirit, to be succeeded by a higher still—the immediate presence of God in all.

So also with our own spiritual life. First, conviction of need, then the rapture of felt forgiveness, then God's testing of the soul, through which moral strength and faith grow firm; and as these grow deeper, love, the higher grace, increasing; and as love increases, noble work and nobler patience making life great and pure, till holiness emerges, and we are at one with God; and then, finally, the Christian Calm—serene old age, with its clear heaven and sunset light, to prophesy a new and swift-approaching dawn for the emancipated spirit.

And from both these universal principles, the mighty principle is born of God as the Divine Order. We see Him in this chapter bringing the forming light out of the formless void, separating sea from land, dividing the waters above from the waters below and light from darkness, calling out the sun and moon to determine days and years, allotting to His creatures their habitations, and setting over them the ruling mind of man as lord and king.

It is a picture of that which He has always done in the history of humanity: bringing redemption out of sin, settled government out of revolution, peace out of war, law out of anarchy; till, finally, we shall see the perfect universe born out of the travail of the imperfect universe.

Now all these principles are identical with those which

support geology. The growth of the world on which we live was slow. Geologists have now given up the idea of rapid transitions, of great catastrophes initiating a new age. Each geological period melted slowly into the next; and the more complex in appearance the earth grew, and the more noble in varied life and varied landscape, the slower was the progress of its movements. All geology, all the story of ancient life, is witness to the truth of the principle of this chapter, that great work is slow in proportion to its greatness.

The ancient history of life bears witness also to the next principle, that progress is from the lower to the higher. We cannot force it into particulars, for some of the ancient fishes and reptiles seem to have been more complex and more highly organized than the latter ones, but broadly and largely it is true. For first appears the zoophyte, then the shellfish, then the fish, then the reptile, then the bird, then the higher animals, and last of all Man, the highest. This is the testimony of science to these two principles of which we have spoken, and from them arises, as in other things so in physical, the principle of a Divine order in creation.

The next truth to be inferred from this chapter is that the universe was prepared for the good and enjoyment of man. I cannot say that this is universal, for the stars exist for themselves, and the sun for other planets than ours; and it is a poor thing to say that the life of animals and plants is not for their own enjoyment as well as ours! but so far as they regard us, it is an universal truth, and the Bible was written for *our* learning. Therefore, in this chapter, the sun and stars

The Creation.   231

are spoken of only in their relation to us, and man is set as master over all creation.

It is on the basis of this truth that man has always unconsciously acted, and made progress in civilization. Out of our humble yet kingly investigation of this world and its laws, out of our lordship over the animal creation, out of our scientific study of the sun and moon and stars as set in the sky for our direction, has grown the mighty fabric of our civilization.

Out of our reverence and love for the beauty of nature and the beauty of form and life, have been developed the poetry, the sculpture, the painting, and the architecture of the world, the humanizing and the softening arts of life.

On the varieties of climate and their influence has depended much of the variety of national character, and on this in turn the progress of the race; for it is by mutual antagonism and reciprocated submission of diverse nations to one another that the race advances.

Out of quiet and tender watching of the life of animals and plants, of the deep quiet of the night and the sunny radiance of the day, of the harmony, beauty, and sublimity of nature, have flowed in all ages to the human spirit deep lessons for life, soothing influences, kindly impulse, the enthusiasm which is wisdom, and the life which is unworldly.

I need scarcely urge the force with which this truth is taught by geology. Every one knows that the whole of its revelations allow us to assume, that if the earth was not designedly prepared for us, it could not be better arranged if it had been designed. The various rocks have been so upheaved as to present themselves easily to our working. The different strata have been so exposed as to create different soils for all the varieties of vegetation. The great material of our prosperity has been taken especial care of, and preserved in great basins of rock from excessive denudation.

The next principle is the *interdependence of rest and work*. The Sabbath is the outward expression of God's recognition of this as a truth for man. It was commanded because it was necessary. 'The Sabbath was made for man,' said Christ. And the same principle ought to be extended over our whole existence. The life of Christ, the type of the highest human life, was not all work. 'Come ye into the wilderness, and rest awhile.' Toil and refreshment were woven together. But as in this chapter there were six days of work to one of rest, so in His life, as it ought to be in ours, 'labour was the rule, relaxation the exception.' Labour always preceded rest; rest was only purchased by toil.

This also is universally true. Nations and men take their rest after periods of great national, intellectual, or spiritual excitement, during which creative ideas have been struggling with corrupting ones, and the work of a century has been done in a few years. A pause ensues; a Sabbath comes, and the nation or the man sink back nerveless to recover their strength, and to realize their new position, in repose.

Geology teaches us that the same principle has ruled the history of the earth. Great activity has always been followed by repose. When one agent has been at work for a long time at a certain place or period, it

The Creation.

reposes, and gives place to another. When one family of plants or animals has prevailed for a lengthened period, it pauses, and another becomes dominant. For myriads of centuries the earth has rested in the sabbath of night from the destructive force of the sun, and its inhabitants from their own fierce activity of life in the sabbath of sleep.

Thus everywhere the principles laid down in this chapter are identical with the main principles of geology.

This, then, is the ground on which we meet the impugners of the inspiration of this chapter—on the ground of universal principles. We say, that if the Bible and Nature came from the same God, there must be a point where the principles revealed in the one coincide with the principles observed in the other. We have found those principles to be identical. In its deepest depths the Book of Revelation is in harmony with Science. We stand at one point of the circumference of a great circle, the scientific man at another. There seems an immense space between us, and if we go on producing our lines of thought without reference to each other, we get farther and farther away. But let us, for once, turn back, and go towards the Centre. We shall draw closer and closer together, and finally meet in the mind of God.

Lastly, there is one specially spiritual principle which glorifies this chapter, and the import of which is universal, 'God made man in His own image.' It is the divinest revelation in the Old Testament. In it is contained the reason of all that has ever been great in human nature or in human history. In it are contained all the sorrows of the race as it looks back to its innocence, and all the hope of the race as it aspires from the depths of its fall to the height of the imperial palace whence it came. In it is contained all the joy of the race as it sees in Christ this great first principle revealed again. In it are contained all the history of the human heart, all the history of the human mind, all the history of the human conscience, all the history of the human spirit. It is the foundation-stone of all written and unwritten poetry, of all metaphysics, of all ethics, of all religion. It is a universal truth whose dependent truths are too long to enter upon here, but which I have endeavoured in many ways and at many times to teach from this pulpit. It is the glory of this chapter that it proclaimed in the earliest times a truth which it was the object of Christianity to reproclaim. But it is a truth so great that its growth in man is of infinite slowness. If in five thousand years more our race should realize on earth the full meaning of this divine principle, it will be well for it indeed.

These are the universal principles which are to be found in this chapter.

And this, we are told, is not inspiration; this is not the work of a higher spirit than the spirit of defective and one-sided man. This illuminating constellation of all-embracing truths; stars which burn, eternal and unwavering, the guides and consolers of men in the heaven which arches over our spiritual life; their light for ever quiet with the conscious repose of truth, 'their seat the bosom of God, their voice the harmony of the world'—to which, obedience being given, nations are great, souls are free, and the race marches with triumphant music to its perfect destiny—this is not inspiration! Brethren, it *is* inspiration.

[February 24, 1867.]

THE BAPTISM OF CHRIST.

Matt. iii. 13.

The baptism of Christ was the point of transition between the silent life of thirty years and the active life of His short career. It was not, justly speaking, the beginning of His work, for His life had been work throughout. The labour of His ministry was the exact result of thirty years of inner labour. But it was the beginning of His public work. It was the first outward expression of the inward development of which we have been speaking for four Sundays.

Before we endeavour to find a resting-place for thought in the baptism of Christ, there is one point in His development at which we only glanced last Sunday, which had some consequences worth our consideration.

We said that it was owing to the external presentation of sin to His holy heart, that there was stirred in Him, first, the consciousness, by contrast, of His own perfect righteousness, and secondly, the consciousness of His power, as the sinless One, to redeem the race from sin. What do these involve? They involved suffering; and suffering as He suffered involved obedience, and

The Baptism of Christ. 237

obedience produced in Him two of the most remarkable characteristics of His ministry—His freedom and His force.

Let me trace in outline the meaning of these points. Consider what the character of the village was, out of which no good thing could come. How He must have suffered there!—suffered from the immoral life of the outlawed Nazarenes, suffered from the bigotry of those who afterwards would have cast Him down from the hill precipice, suffered from their blindness to His character, too true a type of the blindness of His countrymen. In this way He bore the pain of the contact of a holy nature with sin. At times, the keenness of this pain must have aroused an overwhelming desire to go forth and do His work; but no! He must be still, He must obey; not one step forward till His Father gave the sign. In this way (and it is to this period of His life I refer the text), in this way 'learned He obedience by the things which He suffered.'

Obedience to whom? To His Father's will. And here we dimly see how the consciousness of His intimate relation, as Son of man, to God increased. Day by day His spirit urged Him forth, day by day He found within Himself no sign that as yet He was to issue from retirement. Thus it was not only from the contact of a holy nature with sin that He suffered, He suffered also from the self-restraint which repressed the natural feeling which, sinless in itself and spontaneous, would yet have been wrong, under the circumstances, to indulge. Every act of *that* obedience had in it natural pain, every act had in it exquisite pleasure, for it made Him more and more conscious that His will was at one with His Father's will.

This was the spiritual result of His obedience. It developed day by day within Him an increasing consciousness of what He always was—one with God. In these years grew up the deep conviction—not as the result of reasoning, but of impassioned intuition—of that which afterwards He expressed, 'I and my Father are one.'

Self-restraint, therefore, repression of natural and righteous impulses, because their expression *then* would not have been in accordance with His Father's will, in other words, obedience, marked His life at Nazareth.

Now there were two especial characteristics of the life of Christ which flowed from this—His force and His freedom.

It was the source of His force. The habit of self-restraint increases concentration of will, and concentration of will gives force to all action and all speech. Look at His words. What a quintessence of thought, what infinite meaning, what weight, what awful force within them! How they kindled, penetrated, and glowed in some men! How they smote the hard hearts of others! 'Never man spake like this man.'

'I will give you rest.' Think of that as a type of His words. The quiet sense of power in it is almost supernatural. The secret which ages had only hidden deeper, the pursuit of all alike, of the fool and the philosopher, of the merchant and the poet, the shepherd and the king, the savage and the civilized, of this secret a despised Jew boldly declared He was the possessor and

The Baptism of Christ.   239

the revealer. And such was the splendid force in His words, that men believed them. It was too audacious not to be true. He who dared to say that, must have been more than a mere man.

Look at His acts. He put Himself in opposition to the whole power of the Jewish priesthood, and though apparently subdued, finally conquered it. He sent forth twelve unlearned men to overcome the world, to overthrow all the old philosophies and old religions, and they did it in His spirit. He lived out perfectly everything which He taught. He gave humanity a universal religion. He saved the world. It was the power won by years of quiet self-restraint.

What a lesson for our hurried, self-assertive life! We rush into the strife of existence before our mental powers are braced and trained for battle, and we either fail, or do but half we might have done, or in a year or so we are jaded and outworn. There is then no force in our words, they are not the results of any slowly acquired principles. There is then no living power in our acts, they are wavering, irresolute, hasty.

Brethren, if we are to do anything in life, we want for it concentration of will, and concentration of will is the heroic offspring of the patient waiting of self-restraint in obedience unto God.

The second result was *freedom*. I have described the force, the vast reserve of power laid up through obedience in Christ's nature. Well, that in itself must minister to freedom. Power, when power is of an evil will, produces wild license; power, when power is governed by a righteous will, is one of the highest elements of noble liberty. But with a passing glance at that, let me trace for a moment how freedom came to Christ out of His obedience. That which the wise German said, Christ knew. Only within the circle of law is freedom learnt or freedom won. The physical philosopher learns what are the laws of nature and their work. He finds out where he is limited, and he knows that in *that* direction he cannot move. But knowing his limitations, he freely acquiesces in them, for he has boundless room to act within the circle of laws he knows, and on the side of which he has ranged himself. The impotent struggler against law is a slave to his own anger and folly; and he remains a slave. As long as he fights against law, he cannot know it and become its freedman by his knowledge.

Apply this to the life of Christ. Through obedience to His Father's will He was at one with His Father's will. He stood on the side of the Lord of the universe, and then the whole sphere of God's action lay before Him, in which to freely act. His spirit could expand with liberty in all directions. It is true if He had wished to do that which God did not wish, He would have found Himself limited. But He could not wish anything but His Father's will, and therefore there was no barrier anywhere to His thought and action. He was entirely free—free with a joy in His freedom, for so perfect was the union of His will to God's that His feeling was not I must, nor even I ought, but I delight to do Thy will, 'my meat and drink are to do my Father's will;' for there is no restraining law to him who loves the lawgiver. But you may say, If He was limited on any side He was not free. I answer, He was at least as free as God Himself, whose will is self-limited by right. So were the three great qualities which make any action great developed in Christ Jesus: union through obedience with the highest will; force of character; freedom of character. In silence was wrought this wonderful maturity. For eighteen years in still retirement the mighty heart, the universal spirit of Christ, elaborated within them the conditions necessary for His action on the world. For eighteen years the all-embracing love, the all-embracing intellect, the spirit whose depths centuries have not exhausted, and whose Life will be our life for ever, was content to remain at rest; was satisfied to be tied down to quiet obedience to His parents, to the common duties of household life, to the restricted life of an apathetic Jewish village.

And yet towards the end of this period at least, the divine love and pity were yearning to go forth and act. The holy indignation was struggling towards its utterance; the inspiration of something greater than human genius, but akin to it, was glowing in His heart and intellect. But He would not move. He believed and therefore did not make haste. There was no hurry, no confusion, but perfect order in that divine existence. It was the noble self-restraint of noble temperance. In silent obedience He waited for the summons to go forth, and live out in action that which was within Him. At last, when He was about thirty years old, the call of God was heard.

Our first question is, How did the summons come?

It came through the natural course of events. The whole course of history had been a preparation for the ministry of Christ. We are told that there was a stir over all the world about this time, a pause of expectation. Systems of government and systems of philosophy had been exhausted. The world lay dying of that worst starvation which results from want of new ideas, and an unconscious prophecy arose, traces of which we find in heathen literature, that a new king of thought was coming to renew the spirit of the world. This prophecy, vague and unconscious among Gentile nations, was clear and conscious in the Jewish people. For centuries their prophets had given it form and substance; their sufferings had brought it more vividly before them, and, as the futile efforts of Theudas and Judas before Christ's coming seem to prove, it was now a general expectation among the Jews that the Messiah was on the point of appearing.

Now it frequently occurs that the longing of a nation concentrates itself in one man who becomes its voice. This was the work of John the Baptist. He came forth from the desert and proclaimed that the kingdom of God was at hand. But every one felt that the kingdom must have a king, and the question was put to John by the passion of the Jewish people, Are you the King? Are you the Christ? And John answered, 'I am but a voice; there cometh One mightier than I.' The answer quickened expectation, and far and wide over Palestine there spread the cry, 'Where is the King of the Jews? We desire our Messiah.'

The fulness of time had then come; Jesus heard the

The Baptism of Christ. 243

summons. He heard in it His Father's voice. His heart beat responsive to the cry of humanity, and the Son of God and Son of man came forth 'to do His Father's will and to finish His work.' We will say nothing of what may have passed in His secret soul. These are things before which the truest attitude to take is that of reverent silence.

We pass on to His baptism. I need not here repeat the story. We have to consider what is more important, the meaning of the act.

It was, *first*, the proclamation of His human relationship to man, and of His human relationship to God.

His development had reached its height. He was clearly conscious of His divine nature; He was clearly conscious of His complete union with our nature. But His divine nature, so far as its omnipotence, omnipresence, and omniscience, so far as all that could separate Him from sharing perfectly in our humanity, was concerned, was to remain uncommunicated as yet to His natural, growing humanity; while the perfect holiness, the perfect spiritual character of God, were to be exhibited unmarred, through the medium of His humanity. Hence His baptism was the formalized proclamation of His sinless human nature. First, He declared by that act that as man He submitted Himself to the will of His Father, as shown in the mission of the Baptist. He put Himself, that is, into communication with God's existing plan for the spiritual education of the race. He connected Himself with the whole of the Old Testament history by connecting Himself with John, the last of the Old Testament prophets, and after this momentary contact with the old, He passed on to found the new. By this act He bound together in submission to His Father's will the old and the new dispensations, and recognized Himself as the central point of history; the Man to whom all the past history of the race had tended, the Man from whom all the future history of the race was to flow. He declared Himself not only to be a Man, but the archetypal Man.

But there was more in it than this. How could He most plainly declare to men, at the very entrance on His work, that He was at one with their nature; a sharer in all its sorrows and joys, its infirmities and its duties; not removed by any unhuman powers from its sphere? How could He best throw into form this cardinal idea of His manifestation? By undergoing the ceremony to which all men who were devoting themselves to a new life in Judæa were now submitting. In the same way He is represented as undergoing circumcision in obedience to the Law.

We find this idea in His own words. John objecting to baptize Him, Christ replied, 'Suffer it to be so now; for it is fitting to fulfil all that the law demands.' Observe the word used: not it is necessary, that would imply that He needed a rite of purification, which would infer that He was sinful; it is it is fitting— 'there is a propriety in what I do. I do it to declare my submission to the laws of my human nature; I do it to show that while I am on earth my manifestation will be strictly Jewish, worked out in accordance with the Jewish law.' He was entering on a new sphere of action; and submitted for the sake of fitness, and not

The Baptism of Christ.

to disturb the harmony of life, to the initiation which then was reckoned as the best; and such a submission no more implies, as some have said, a consciousness of sin in Christ, than the taking of the oath of allegiance on entering upon an official post implies in an Englishman's heart disloyalty to his sovereign.

This leads me to the last meaning of His baptism. John's baptism prepared those who underwent it for admission into the kingdom which was at hand, it consecrated them to the new work of the new kingdom. In their case two conditions had to be fulfilled—repentance and a sense of sin.

But these conditions were impossible to Christ. He had no sense of sin. He needed no repentance. The import of the rite was then different in His case. It consecrated Him King of the theocratic kingdom, and proclaimed to all men that His organization of that kingdom had begun.

Thus, while the historical meaning of the rite varied with the subjects to whom it was administered, there was an element of preparation in it which was common to both. It consecrated the people to be members of the theocratic kingdom, it consecrated Christ to be the theocratic King; but it marked for both the commencement of a new course of life, in which the subjects of the kingdom were to receive pardon and life; in which the King was to accomplish the work of salvation, and to bestow life upon His followers.*

So began the new life of our Saviour. Instead of silence, golden speech; instead of quiet village life,

* See for this explanation Neander's *Leben Jesu*.

action in the great world; instead of inward development, outward expression of the results of development; instead of domestic peace, stormy opposition; instead of dangerless existence, the path of the witness for truth, of the self-sacrificing Love to the goal of death.

In conclusion, how does Christ's baptism speak to us? for in the light of His life can we alone understand our own.

We have rites of consecration. In baptism we are claimed by the Church for God, and dedicated to His service. In confirmation we publicly assume the duties which have long been ours, and the Church consecrates us afresh to the work of God. But these are not the parallels in our lives to this moment in the life of Jesus. Our truest baptism and our truest confirmation are often unrepresented by any outward ceremony. There are hours of consecration in our lives of which none know but God and ourselves, hours in which our whole inward being is moved and trembles like a flower born at night, in expectation of the morning it has never seen as yet. Such an hour sometimes comes in youth, when youth has in it most of the poetic temperament. It is generally some solemn and beautiful aspect of nature through which God does the work of reminding us of our immortality. We are living thoughtlessly; our youth, a medley of all tempers, is sometimes grave and sometimes gay, sometimes idle, sometimes active. Our life, the sport of every passing gale, without an object or an aim, is content to drift upon the breeze, and to enjoy its careless freshness.

Then it is that some night, as we go home by the

The Baptism of Christ.

starlight, or some morning as we watch—in that dewy coolness which is so exquisitely pure that the sense of it is as a feeling in the heart—the awakening of life beneath the uprising sun, that God touches us through the solemnity and sweetness of His world. We feel our own nothingness and vanity before this mighty calm and beauty. It is so purposeful, so attuned to harmonious work, so full of latent force and ease; seems so alert and watchful to do its master's will, that we are startled out of our vain existence, and, vague and undefined as the feeling is, realize for an instant the infinite of labour, and feel that God has for us a future. That is one of the consecrated moments of life, a baptism. 'I made no vows,' said one who had known what such an hour was,

> But vows
> Were then made for me; bond unknown to me
> Was given, that I should be, else sinning greatly,
> A dedicated spirit.

It is a more solemn moment when youth is over, and, with stores of thought and feeling unexpended, our work in life is presented to us by God. The path of duty lies before us now, untrodden, and as yet unsullied. If we be anything of men, we cannot look forward then unmoved. An enthusiasm comes upon us. There is with us the sense of a Presence higher than that of any man, who, we dimly feel, has chosen us for our work, and is sending us forth to do it. We are lifted above ourselves into a higher region where thought is not, but only inspiration. We grasp with our greatest strength the new world of our aspiration. We do not wish, we *will* to be pure, and true, and faithful. We consecrate ourselves to duty. It is a partial exhibition in us of the meaning of Christ's baptism.

O brethren! keep the passion of these hours of consecration in youth, in opening manhood, fresh within your heart. They are the times when the soul has escaped from its death and has become alive. In them we have entered into the realm of the infinite, and breathed its invigorating atmosphere. They are given to show us what man truly is, and what we may become. Woe and misery to the man who, having once possessed them, falls utterly short of their ideal. Yes, when life loses its colour, and the days of existence are dull and apathetic, when 'use and custom have bowed down the soul under a growing weight of vulgar sense;' when we are tempted to be false to God or man, to be impure and base, and so to die eternally; when sloth creeps on us and counsels neglect of life's earnest labour; or when still subtler trials warp the soul, when 'the light which leads astray is light from heaven;' when art lures us to make life nothing but a scene of beauty; or when science makes us in love with a universe of death, and blots out the old world 'which moved with light and life informed' in which we walked with God; oh! then look back, recall these consecrated hours, say to yourself, Then I was alive, then I was truly myself; I will not be unworthy of the vows then made for me; I will not fall below the promise of my hour of consecration to a true and holy life for God and man.

And having thus conquered temptation, you may then become aware, in that moment of high resolve, of

The Baptism of Christ. 249

a still more solemn consecration. Awakened out of the danger of losing your true self, startled by your own weakness, your soul is open to the deeper influences of the Spirit of God. You become conscious of God in a nearer relation than before. You feel that He has been with you, giving you, and educating you by, your work. You realize that you are His son, and that He is your Father in Christ Jesus. Moreover, you have been convinced by failure of your weakness and sin, and you cannot rest till you have found a Saviour. That is *the* great baptism of the soul—the great hour of consecration. Life takes then a new aspect. The old duties remain, but they are held in a higher service. You have not only a work to do for man, you have a work to do for God, and the two spheres of labour mingle into one. You understand then something of the deep import of the baptism of Jesus, something of the thoughts and feelings which filled His spirit when in the stream of Jordan He began in self-devotion, sad and resolute and calm, His ministry of love. There, in that ministry, if you want an impulse, you will find it, an impulse which, though you falter in the battle, will never leave you nor forsake you.

Child of God, consecrated to do the work of God, look, when the heart is weary and the spirit jaded, at the life which followed this consecration of Christ. The work He then undertook was completely done. There was no sorrow like His sorrow, yet duty was never refused. There was fiercer opposition than you can know, yet there was not one failure. There were more obstacles than you can ever meet, yet ever nobler and more firm, ever wiser, tenderer, and stronger rose the spirit of Christ Jesus to accomplish His Father's business, till in the hour of triumphant death He could say with majestic truth, 'It is finished. Father, into Thy hands I commend my spirit.'

There is our motive power, there our aspiration. Bring the force of all the consecrating hours of life to bear upon that ideal. Look not back then to recall old feelings and to win a power from their memory. The time for that is gone by. You are now on a higher stage of life, for the follower of Christ who is baptized into the work of Christ does not find force and freedom for the duty of life within himself. He escapes from his own weakness and slavery to lose his lower nature in the strength and liberty of Christ. He finds his truer being in union with the work of Christ. The child of God does not look backward to gain fresh energy. His energy is the energy of hope, and not of retrospection. He presses forward; his glance is ever onward. He anticipates revelations of God more and more glorious, consecrated hours of deeper and deeper joy, till, at last, the hour of death baptize him into perfect life, and consecrate him to be a partaker of that ampler and mightier work which God accomplishes for ever, in love and righteousness, upon His spiritual universe.

THE FORTY DAYS IN THE WILDERNESS.

Matthew iv. 1.

THE baptism of Christ was the culminating point of that spiritual development of His inner life of which we have spoken, and it is symbolically described as reaching its completeness by the descent of the Spirit upon Him.

It was a moment then of ecstatic joy, of the highest consciousness of inspiration. Two dominant thoughts, as we have already suggested, were with Him: the first, that He was the very Son of God, perfectly at one with the Father; the second, that He was the destined Redeemer of the race. These were realized by His human soul at the hour of the baptism with an overwhelming sense of inspired joy.

We may have felt this ourselves in a less degree. Conscious of some great idea which has lived with us a hidden life for months, there has come a time when it seems suddenly to complete itself and to issue forth upon us clothed in light, warming and irradiating the whole of life, recreating our whole conception of God and of humanity. It is an hour of ecstasy and inspiration. Everything seems possible. We are lifted above the ordinary level of humanity, above the customary powers of our nature.

What is our first impulse? It is to go forth and make known to men our thought, to quicken them with our life and inspire them with our message. But at first we find that impossible. The enthusiasm is too great for wise action; the joy is too fine for contact with the rugged world. Our passion must subside, we must realize our inspiration in thought, we must grasp our new conception as an instrument of action rather than as a subject of contemplation, before we can bring it to bear upon the world. Therefore it is not action which follows at once on such a revelation as I have described; it is a period of silence, a period of loneliness filled at first with deep restfulness of being, with repressed enthusiasm of joy. But we cannot expect these feelings to last. The very strength of our delight causes a reaction, and in the reaction we become aware of the other side of our enthusiasm. We realize the image of our original conception in contact with the old and outworn conceptions accredited by lapse of time and habit in the world. We are forced to look in the face the gigantic difficulties of introducing an original idea among those which are by the very nature of the case its enemies.

Such is the general representation of that crisis which all men who have reinvigorated the world with a new conception must have more or less experienced. When it came in the life of Christ, it came as it would come to a perfect man. It was clearly defined. It was consciously accepted. It was concentrated. It was apart

The Forty Days in the Wilderness. 253

from the errors, the fluctuations, the mistakes, which belong to it in the case of ordinary men. It shared in all that belonged to pure human nature. It was freed from the disturbing influences of sinful human nature.

Now, if our representation be true, we make a mistake when we think that those forty days in the wilderness were all days of temptation and sorrow. They must have been, on the contrary, days, at first, of peaceful rest, of intense joy.

Alone with God, driven by the Spirit into the wilderness, the Saviour dwelt in the peaceful thought of His union with His Father. The words spoken at the baptism, the fulness of the Spirit's power within Him, had filled His human heart with serene ecstasy. He went into the wilderness to realize it all more fully, to expand within Himself through meditation the ideas of which He had become so deeply conscious, to devote Himself in depth of solemn forethought to work out in active life the message of His Father.

It was then in this spiritual rest and joy that we may reverently conceive the beginning of the wilderness life was passed. As such, it was the first pure poetry of the perfect union which was to arise between the heart of man and the Spirit of God; the spring-time of the new life; the first clear music which ever flowed from the harmony of a human spirit with the life of the universe. Both sang the same song—the song of self-sacrifice.

But now we meet the question, How did this become test, temptation? To understand this we must recall the two great ideas in His mind: the first, that He was at one with the Father—that gave Him His perfect joy; the second, that He was the destined Redeemer of the race, the Messiah long desired by men.

Now observe, that in Him the second thought followed naturally upon the first. He could not remain in mere self-enjoyment of this fulness of life with God. Life must of its very nature pass beyond itself to give life, and the infinite joy of the Saviour's life in God became coincident with infinite longing to communicate that joy to men. The two great ideas of His spirit mingled into one—His fulness of life was fulness of love.

To the first peaceful days had now succeeded days when desire to begin His redemptive work filled His soul. And the voice in His own soul was echoed by the cry of the Jewish people for their Messiah. He was urged, then, by two calls, one within and one without.

But — and here is the point at which suffering and test entered—these two voices directly contradicted one another. As soon as Christ turned to the world with the greeting of His love, He heard coming from the world an answering greeting of welcome, but the ideas which lay beneath it were in radical opposition to His own. The vision of an omnipotent king and an external kingdom was presented to His spirit as the ideal of the Jewish people. It came rudely into contact with the vision in His own heart of a king made perfect by suffering, of a kingdom hidden at first in the hearts of men. It is not difficult to see the depth and manifoldness of the tests which arose from the clashing of these two opposed conceptions.

The Forty Days in the Wilderness. 255

But it was not only test, but temptation—which He rejected without having cherished it for a moment—which came to meet Him in these two opposed conceptions.

How was this? We have spoken of His joy. Now observe the sorrow which followed it.

For years of silence at Nazareth he had observed and felt this false ideal of the Messiah and His kingdom among the Jews. His sympathy with the universal heart of His people made Him comprehend it clearly. It accompanied Him from Nazareth to Jordan, and in the cries for a Messiah which He heard from the crowds round John the Baptist, it was brought more prominently before Him. In the moment of His self-dedication to His work at baptism, it necessarily took even a stronger form and presented a sharper contrast to His own conception of His Messiahship. But the more He realized it, the more powerfully rose the Holy Spirit within Him against it in strong repulsion. This repellent force of the Spirit against the Jewish thought drove Him away from men into the desert.

And now began the contest. His love of men urged Him to go forth. His shrinking from their evil thought of Him drove Him back into the waste. As often as He turned to men, so often was He met with the false image they had made of Him, so often was presented to Him the temptation of throwing Himself into their ideas, of founding His kingdom at once in splendour over a people delivered by miraculous power from the Roman tyranny. He never received the thought of yielding for a moment into His spirit, but presented to His intellect and heart it tortured Him. He saw Himself in necessary conflict with those He loved. He saw Himself hated and despised by those He meant to save. He saw that the conflict of His ideas with those of the world must end in death. For many days the suffering of this temptation lasted. He could not go forth till all the possible phases which this temptation—*the* temptation of His ministry—could assume, had been realized in thought and conquered.

This is the second thought we must connect with the wilderness life of Christ—His humanity plunged into the deepest sorrow, engaged in the pain of a tremendous struggle against the evil conception formed by men of His mission and His work.

Combine those two thoughts, the joy and the sorrow in the desert, and we find Christ's mingled being, Son of God and Son of man. One and the same impulse, the impulse to be the Redeemer of men, afforded Him at once the deepest joy and the deepest pain: deepest joy, because in that impulse He recognized most fully His union with His Father; deepest sorrow, because in that same impulse He was made conscious of His woful separation from the humanity He loved.

We discover, then, in Christ that strange union of two human passions of which we ourselves are sometimes conscious: joy so keen as to be pain, sorrow so deep as to be cherished as a pleasure. For there is a blessedness which arises out of sorrow, and there is a spiritual peace in which 'all the joys of heaven meet and interchange greetings with all the sorrows of humanity.'—It was in this state of heart that Christ may have been during the forty days in the wilderness. In the overwhelming rush of these feelings, meeting, mingling, clashing, He lost all perception of the usual wants of the body. The spiritual life in its intensity kept the physical in abeyance, and out of this majestic but unforced predominance of the spirit over the body was partially born His victory.

Such is the general, large idea of the solitary contest of Christ in the wilderness, before the three particular temptations were presented to Him.

What does it represent to us? It represents the great law of the history of man's nature—that every one of us must, in order to realize our true work and moral position in this world, meet and contend with the powers of evil.

At one time or another our Father makes us aware that we have a work in this world to do against evil. We become conscious of ourselves as the soldiers of God. And the moment that occurs we find ourselves driven by the Spirit into the wilderness; we find ourselves in opposition to the false ideas of the world. The whole aspect of life is changed. We feel the weight of a new responsibility. We begin to acknowledge that we are fellow-workers with God, that we too, like the Saviour, are called upon to do a redeeming work. To realize that fully is to be partaker of a great joy and of a great sorrow; of the joy of getting near to God; of the sorrow which is born as we look forward to the weary warfare we must wage against the world with Christ.

It is a solitary time, a time in the desert, and we must meet it in resolute silence; gathering up strength through prayer and quiet communion with our Father's Spirit for the strife of the Christian warrior's life.

It is an hour of temptation, for to us as to Christ the spirit of the world presents itself alluringly. The siren song of pleasure lures us from our labour at the oar. The self and the flesh within us raise with joy their heads in answer. 'Duty is hard,' they say, 'life is short, too short for enjoyment. You have fine senses, high gifts and powers, why employ them in labour which will only bring you pain? Employ them rather in turning the stones of life into bread. Throw yourself into the ideas of the world; why should you wear out your life in opposition? Float down the stream, take your ease, eat, drink, and be merry.'

And the voice of Christ whispers in reply, 'My brother, take up your cross and follow me. Duty is severe, but it is the greatness of the soul. Obedience is difficult, but it is the path to freedom. Suffering and the battle against the world are hard for flesh and blood to bear, but out of them is wrought high honour, true manhood, likeness unto Me. My strength is made perfect in your weakness. My life is found in the destruction of your baser self; and your perfection like mine own is won through suffering for righteousness.'

That is the crisis. How many of you have passed through it? Whose voice have you listened to?

It is conversion to come out of it having chosen the side of Christ. You are changed from one of the victims of self into one of the noble army of martyrs.

It is by changes such as this—by men selecting the good, rejecting the evil—that God's regiment of warriors is formed; and through their battle taken up by a succession of spiritual heroes, and carried on from age to age, righteousness and the great realities of God are slowly being set up as conquerors of the evil and death and nothingness of this visible world. This is the deep undercurrent of power which underlies history. The temptation and victory of any man is an example for the moment of the law which gives this current of progress force. The temptation of Christ was the embodiment, in a representative example, of this law. It is the central point to which all previous examples converge, from which all future examples diverge, and in which the meaning and the force of all were concentrated.

He is then the King, by victory, of all the warrior host of God. He met the very first principle of evil, and He drove it back into its native nothingness. And He did this in the might of holy and suffering humanity. Our nature has therefore triumphed over evil, and though it was with agony, 'with strong crying and tears,' yet even that is matter to us of adoring joy, 'for in that He suffered being tempted, He is able to succour them that are tempted.'

I suppose no truths can be dearer to a human heart than these two—the sympathy of the Son of man in temptation; the victory of humanity in the Son of man over evil.

For we are so tried and tossed, so compassed round with pain, so much apparently the sport of fanciful passion, so curiously framed as it were for temptation, with high aspirations living in us along with base desires; so hovering ever on the verge of good and ill, and so weak to choose the good; so troubled by the necessity of battle when our heart is weary with the passionate longing for rest; so sick of ourselves and of the vile cravings which at times possess us, that God knows we do want some sympathy higher than any one on earth can give us, some sympathy which will not weaken but strengthen, some certainty that the Eternal Love and Righteousness can feel with us and assist us. Therefore it is the deepest blessedness to know that one who shared in our nature—the proper Divine Man—was in the days of His flesh a partaker of 'our strong crying and tears,' and 'learned obedience by the things which He suffered,' for then we know that He can, in His triumphant nature, be still 'touched with the feeling of our infirmities.' Brethren, who are struggling with evil within you and without, you have with you the exalting, power-bestowing sympathy of the Son of God and Son of man.

Lastly, the other consoling truth is that humanity has conquered evil. Take that great fact as the foundation of all action. There has been human temptation without human fall. There has been one Man at least who has met sin on its own ground, and has baffled the tempter. He is your brother and your God. Sin is at His feet, and death and Hell. Brethren, if we love Him, they shall be at ours. We look forward, then, not to defeat, but to victory — to individual victory, to universal victory. The conquest in the wilderness is the earnest of a greater conquest yet to be. The time shall come when evil shall have no place in the universe of God, and holiness be all in all. Ah! why should we faint, and falter, and despair, when that is so divinely true? We are fellow-workers with the Almighty Goodness to that majestic end. Therefore, conquer evil in yourselves in the strength of Christ. Personally, that is the only thing worth living for. And once you have begun to conquer evil in your own heart, you will be able to contend to the death against evil without you in the world. Publicly, that is the great work of man. Let us pray this day with added fervour, that He who fought and won the battle in the wilderness may give us power to do our duty against all wrong and all sin, with our whole heart and soul and mind and strength.

[February 2, 1868.]

THE TRANSFIGURATION.

Luke ix. 28—33.

This remarkable story divides into two parts the ministerial life of Christ. It is the central point of His public career. It is connected, in thought, with His baptism by the voice from heaven. It is connected with His death by the conversation with Moses and Elias, 'who appeared in glory, and spake of His decease which He should accomplish at Jerusalem.'

It was in the evening that Christ ascended the mountain slopes with three of His disciples, and sought a solitary place in which to pray. The mountain chosen by tradition for the scene is Mount Tabor, but there are reasons for denying this random choice, and for identifying Mount Hermon instead as the scene of the transfiguration. The summit of Tabor was inhabited, and Christ sought for solitude. Six days before the transfiguration the Saviour was close to Cæsarea Philippi, and though in a week He had plenty of time to reach Mount Tabor, there is no mention of such a journey to Galilee till a week after the transfiguration. He was then about this time in the very shadows of the chain of the Anti-Libanus, and the marked expressions in the story, 'upon *the* mountain,' on 'a very high moun-

The Transfiguration. 263

tain,' agree with the conjecture that it was the lofty side of Hermon which He ascended in the evening; not to its exposed summit, but to some secluded nook among its grassy uplands. We must not forget the appropriateness on this supposition of the comparison of the whiteness of Christ's garments to snow, for above the Apostles' heads was the dazzling snow which illuminates the peak of Hermon.

Such, then, we may conjecture, was the place and such the time; a lonely mountain recess on the side of Hermon quietly touched by the evening light.

Observe, first, Christ's love for mountain solitudes. This is only one instance out of many, and it brings before us the sensitive humanity of Christ. We watch Him as, wearied and overwrought in the warm oppressive air of the lowlands, He ascended oftentimes at evening to a higher range of atmosphere, where the breeze came freshly over the mountain side, bringing with it strength, refreshment, and enthusiasm. It is pleasant to feel, even in this, how we sympathize with Him, for none of us have passed from the stifling air of a London summer into the winds of the Alpine uplands without feeling not only the physical, but also the moral influence of the change.

We have felt, moreover, the deep quiet of the hills, when even the sounds which are heard, the whirr of a bird's wing, the drip of water from a rock, are not conceived as interruptions, but as expressions of the silence; we have felt the strange impressiveness of this living silence which brings to pure hearts—and how much more to Christ, the purest—a mysterious but real sense of exalted power, a sense of solemn joy in communion with the stillness of nature which is work, and the beauty of nature which is order.

And if something akin to this, but infinitely deeper, did not influence the soul of Christ, how are we to account for this marked preference of mountain solitudes when He desired with all His soul, to commune in prayer with His Father?

It does not seem to be without meaning to us. Christ loved nature. There are those who take up the words of Cecil, the great Evangelical, and say with him, 'I want to see no more sea, hills, fields, abbeys, or castles; I feel vanity pervading everything but eternity and its concerns, and perceive these things to be suited to children.' I think we may feel that this was not the way in which the Saviour's human nature felt. He could not have been a one-sided man. All that is best and purest in our life He must have entered into in a better and purer manner. And when have many of us felt that we were most divided from the mean and sinful elements of life: when have we most realized our deliverance from the burden of the body, and, through humility, our dignity as sons of men? It was in mountain solitudes alone with the sky and God; or deep in the heart of the woods; or by the side of the lake when the ripple washing in the reeds made its wild metallic music, the loneliest, coolest sound in all the world, in which Nature seems to utter her most secret passion.

These were the very haunts, the very places where Christ loved by preference to wander when He would

The Transfiguration. 265

most realize His union with His Father—on the hills of Palestine when evening fell; among the olive shades of Gethsemane; by the shores of the Galilean lake. There everything spoke to Him of His Father's character. There all the world to Him was sacramental.

It should be so with us. Celestial messages and grace should flow to us through every sight and sound which touches and exalts the heart. Alone with Nature in her sublimity or tenderness, as many of you will be in the coming autumn, standing on the highland moor, the wind your sole companion as it races over the heather; reaching at last the Alpine ridge with the silent world of peaks below; looking up into the purple depths of night upon the solitary sea; let the stillness creep into your heart and make you conscious of your God; let prayer rush to the lips, not the prayer which is petition, but that which is communion. Realize your God through His eternal Word in nature, and it is not too wild a hope that on you too, in that moment of felt communion, there may come an hour of transfiguration to form an epoch in your life, an impulse for the future, a foundation for higher and more serious work.

The next thing we consider is the transfiguring glory. As the Saviour prayed, His whole appearance changed. His countenance shone like the sun, His garments even seemed to shimmer with light, and appeared dazzling white like snow.

Possibly the explanation of the rationalist may be partly true, and the radiance of an eastern sunset may have gleamed around Him as He prayed, and given an additional element to the glory which transfigured Him, but that was not the source of this appearance, nor did it add much, if it occurred, to the wondrous sight. The light which irradiated Him came from within.

We know how joy and love will, at their height, transfigure and change a man; how noble feeling kindled by high enthusiasm will make the ugliest look beautiful; how strangely on the features of the dying inward blessedness will seem to create a heavenly light of joy. That which occurs at these times to us, happened now to Christ, and in the greatest possible degree of which sinless humanity is capable. He had been rapt into intense communion with God. He felt the deepest, nearest union with His Father, unintruded upon by the noise of men, undistracted by the troubles which surrounded His ordinary life. And this fulness of the spirit, this ecstasy of communion, this celestial joy, streamed forth over His whole being and made His appearance glorious. He seemed to the Apostles another man. His very garments seemed to shine with the light of His countenance. Awestruck, they bowed before the revelation of His inner nature freed for the moment from the limitations of His humanity. Let us but grant the divine nature of Christ, or even grant only perfect spiritual purity, perfect life in union with God, and there is nothing præternatural in the radiant glory in which Christ appeared to the Apostles.

At least, it supplies us with a principle. The outward form takes its glory or its baseness from the inner spirit. Look upon a child's face! Is that nameless innocent brightness ever seen in after-life? Can you not read in a base man's face his baseness? In the most carefully masked countenance there are casual expressions which betray 'the passion and the life whose fountains are within.' Nature refuses to lie, in spite of all our efforts. And if this is the case when the spirit is mean or selfish and there is the careful suppression of expressions which betray, how much more is it the case when the spirit is pure and true, and there is no need of concealment!

In this way we arrive at a real conception of that which S. Paul meant when he spoke of a glorified body; of the meaning of those passages which speak of the saints shining like the sun and arrayed in white robes. The form which we shall have in the world to come will be beautiful and radiant, because the spirit will irradiate it with the light of God. Inner purity, glowing love, the clear light of truth, the ecstasy of undivided life with God, will glorify our form into that supreme beauty which is not physical but spiritual, in which the thought of merely physical beauty will be altogether lost. That which transfigured Christ on earth will transfigure us in heaven.

Thirdly, we have to consider the vision. 'And behold there appeared to them Moses and Elias, talking with Him.' Now, however we may interpret the circumstances, either as objective or subjective, the meaning seems tolerably clear; Moses and Elias represent the Law and the Prophets, and Christ is the end of them both. All the revelation given in the past culminated in the revelation which He gave. The glory of the Law and of the Prophets was fulfilled and expanded in

His perfect glory. The whole of the Old Testament was, so far as it was spiritual, taken up into the New. The unity of the Old Testament with the New was declared, and the superiority of the New Testament over the Old.

With regard to the Law, Christ destroyed it so far as it was temporary and preparatory, while He fulfilled its real spirit. The Law, as a set of literal maxims, of negative precepts, culminated in Pharisaism. The Law as holding in it spiritual principles which were contained in the maxims, culminated in Christianity. Christ destroyed the former and fulfilled the latter. The Pharisees deified the husk, the shell; Christ rejected the shell and discovered the kernel. Take one example. The Law said, 'Thou shalt not kill'—a negative precept, leaving the heart untouched. Christ touched and expanded the inner meaning; made it into a principle, and applied it to the source of murder in the heart. 'He that hateth his brother is a murderer.' 'Love your enemies.' Love, and you *cannot* murder either in intention or in act.

And if Moses stood with Christ as recognizing in Him the fulfiller of his law, Elias stood there and saw in Christ Him of whom all the race of prophets had spoken. Again and again, in various ways, sometimes obscurely, sometimes clearly—but ever more clearly as the prophetic spirit developed—did the Jewish prophets tell of a deliverer, and a king, and a revealer of God who was to come. Of all the nations of antiquity they alone looked, not backward but forward, to a brighter age. And that brighter age was concentrated for them in the appearance of one Man. And here in the vision of the Transfiguration Elias seems to stand by Christ and say, 'This is He whom we the prophets have for centuries past proclaimed as King and Saviour.'

Again, all the teaching of the prophets culminated in the teaching of Christ. They proclaimed the spiritual character of God. He *was* that character. They depreciated ceremonial righteousness in comparison with rightness of heart. It was the one great battle of His life. They (and in this Elijah was pre-eminent) drove home by personal appeal, and with astonishing daring, the arrow of conviction to the heart of the sinner, revealing him to himself till he trembled and repented. Through Him the thoughts of many hearts were revealed. Every chapter of the Gospels exhibits to us Christ as the denouncer and the convincer of sin, and the awakener of men to self-knowledge and to penitence. They were patriots of Israel; Christ was the patriot of the world. They stood alone against their age; Christ stood alone against the spirit of the world. They bid men look forward and watch for a higher revelation; they denounced despair of life, despair of nobler times, despair of God. They saw into the heart of things by their union with God through holiness, and they prophesied of all things working together for good to a glorious end. And He, far more at one with God than they were, has for ever lifted off the heart of humanity the doubt which obscured the future, and the despair with which men regarded it. By the one act of the resurrection He has made immortal life a magnificent reality. All hope for the race, all impulse to work, all belief in progress, has directly arisen from His teaching. In Him we look ever forward, never backward. Resting on His life and its teaching, on His death and its redeeming love, we can believe that He will never cease to labour and redeem, till in the large eternity of charity God shall gather together all things in Christ.

This is what we see in the figure of Elias standing by the Saviour in the vision of the transfiguration—the concentration in Christ, in all its fulness, of the whole spirit and power of the prophetical order.

Lastly, the Apostles not only saw a vision, but they heard a conversation. Moses and Elias spoke together with Christ of His death which He should accomplish at Jerusalem.

Thus strangely in the midst of radiant glory, of ecstatic joy, intervened the thought of death and sorrow. We found the same intermingling of passions in the hour of the temptation. We find it here again, and we find it haunting us with its mystery in every human life. It is only when joy is most passionate that we are dimly conscious how awful sorrow may be in its supremest depths. Is it only when pain of heart is most passionate that we catch a faint glimpse of that exquisite ecstasy of delight of which we are capable, but which eludes us always. But in both these cases the dim consciousness of which I speak is only ours when the pain and joy, though passionate, are not base but pure.

What is the meaning of this? Why did Christ at the

The Transfiguration.

most ecstatic moment of His earthly life speak of the hour of His greatest pain? Is it possible that they are both one, that joy when it is noble and pain when it is noble are identical? Is Christ's sacrifice the very essential expression of God's joy? Is our sacrifice, in which we feel acutest pain, that which should be delight? It is not an improbable solution of the mystery.

For what is the ecstasy of joy in which God lives but this, that He is for ever giving Himself away? Now, in His perfect life that sacrificing is without pain. But suppose that God were to limit Himself by our weakness, to take upon Him our nature, what would be the result? That very thing which we find in Christ. He *could* not cease to sacrifice Himself, and to find in that His joy and life, but—and here is the point—the sacrifice being made through the channel of an infirm nature would be made with pain. It would be joy *and* pain; both would intermingle and run into one another, so that at times the pain would seem joy, and the joy seem pain. Now suppose, further, that a moment should come in such a life in which the feeble human nature should be all but overwhelmed in the pre-eminence of the divine nature, in which the spiritual should entirely predominate over the physical and the sensitive elements. At such a moment this Being would live only in the pure idea of sacrifice, feel none of the pain and all the joy.

We may so perhaps conceive of Christ at this moment of His life. For once He had passed beyond the limitations of His humanity and entered into the life of perfect joy in sacrifice, which He had for ever

with His Father. At such a moment what wonder if
His face did shine like the sun, and His raiment became white as the light while He talked of His *death*,
the crown of His long self-giving to the world? He
was transfigured with the exquisite joy of sacrifice. It
was not sorrow but the intensity of joy which He realized
in speaking of His death. Conceive that, and then
we can understand the voice which followed, 'This is
my beloved Son: hear Him.' This is my life, my joy
in giving which transfigures Him. In this perfect
sacrifice of love for others He is my beloved Son. 'Hear
Him.' Follow Him in His life. Learn that eternal life
is giving, that eternal joy is sacrifice of self; that the
human is only then transfigured into the divine life when
the pain of sacrifice is felt as the most passionate
ecstasy.

Brethren, that is the transfiguration power. That
thought transfigures the world of humanity. We see it
groaning and travailing in pain. What if all that pain
were only the necessary form under which the race offers
to God the continual sacrifice through which it is being
redeemed by Christ, through which it is being trained to
feel sacrifice not as agony, which it must be to an imperfect nature, but as joy, which it will be to a perfect nature?
The world is transfigured to our view in the glory of that
thought.

It transfigures man. Look at the mother who gives
her health, her hopes, her very life to her sick child.
She suffers, but the suffering is a joy which she would
not surrender for worlds, a joy almost exquisite in its passion. She 'moves with inward glory crowned,' she has

entered into the eternal life, the eternal joy of God's existence, the joy of losing her own life to find it in that of another.

See Moses descending from the mountain with his face gleaming with the light of God. What had transfigured him? It was that in sublime self-sacrifice he had offered up in deepest earnestness his whole being for his people, and had in the offering become at one with the life of God.

Look at Stephen, his face like the face of an angel. How was he transfigured? He had seen his Saviour, and becoming at one with Christ's spirit at the moment of the consummation of the most perfect sacrifice, had learned to cry, in sublime forgetfulness of self and all its passion, 'Lord, lay not this sin to their charge.'

Lastly, brethren, to give all, to live in others, to do this no longer with pain as we do here, but with exquisite joy, is the life of heaven with God. It is that which will transfigure every redeemed soul, and make true life a passionate delight. We shall be freed from the deathful nature which makes us give up ourselves with pain. We enter into God's life of love, that life of love which is in itself the glory by which He irradiates the universe. It is eternal life to be united to that; and to possess even a sparkle of it here is to possess something of that glory which,' streaming forth from the inner life of Christ, transfigured Him in the days of His flesh upon the mount of Hermon.*

* The idea which I have applied here, in explanation of the Transfiguration, will be found fully drawn out in a thoughtful little book, entitled *The Mystery of Pain*. Smith, Elder & Co.

[May 17, 1868.]

THE ASCENSION.

S. John vi. 62.

THE ascension of Christ, to celebrate which the Church dedicates the Thursday of this week, is the crown of the life of our Lord. Our belief in it is bound up with our belief in the other supernatural events of the history. If we disbelieve the resurrection, we must disbelieve the ascension. If we believe the resurrection, we must believe the ascension, for it completes the resurrection.

Now, our belief depends upon the previous conception we have formed of Christ. If He had been only a man— only a particular phase of humanity, and not the universal humanity, concentrated in essence in one Being (a concentration which the Unitarian conceives as possible without divinity, but which in itself seems to us necessarily to imply divinity)—then indeed resurrection and ascension are incredible. But if He was something more, if, as we hold, He was the incarnation of God; or if, as some Unitarians hold, in Him the everlasting Word, the effluence, but not the equal of God, came on earth to realize for man the ideal of humanity—then, starting from that point, the resurrection and the ascension are to us both, the Trinitarian and the Unitarian alike, not only credible but *à priori* to be expected. Or, to put

The Ascension.

it perhaps more truly, the resurrection and the ascension, when we are told of them, commend themselves to our reason, prepossessed with this high conception of Christ.

Ah! some one says, you allow, then, that you come to the question with a prepossession? Certainly; a prepossession with regard to these acts, but a prepossession which has its own particular and just grounds; a prepossession founded on the study of the whole character and life of the Man who has done these acts — a sort of prepossession on which we act continually in our own life when we refuse, for example, to believe in a crime, however supported by evidence, which is imputed to one whose character we have known. 'It is impossible,' we say; 'he could not have done that.' A prepossession which is, in the case of Christ, like a scientific hypothesis which is considered as a law because it explains all the phenomena which come under it; and lastly, a prepossession which we have as good a right to as our opponents have to theirs. Those who start on their investigation of the life of Christ with the theory that the supernatural is impossible, have no right to complain of us who start with the theory that the supernatural is possible. The test of the probable truth of both our theories is whether they explain the facts. Is the life of Christ, and all that has resulted from it, more explicable on the natural or the supernatural hypothesis? I confess that the hypothesis of the destructive critics seems to explain nothing, not even the residuum of facts which it accepts; certainly not the stupendous historical results which followed, and still follow, on His revelation; certainly not the distinct existence of a peculiar spiritual life in individuals, which has made them conquerors of the worldly spirit in all its forms, and capable of radiating this peculiar life to others.

Holding, then, the possibility of the supernatural, though not of the præternatural, I should expect, à priori, the resurrection and the ascension. It is not my intention to attempt an explanation of the how and the whither of the ascension. It is evident from the account, that Christ's form was not the natural body which He possessed before death. Ascension would then have been præternatural. It was a 'spiritual body,' not subject, then, to what are called natural laws; it was, in other words, a supernatural body, and as such, the ascension was appropriate to it. But leaving this aside, we will pass to more profitable, as more practical, thoughts. The ascension was, if we consider its spiritual meaning, the return of Christ's essential being to that life which He had before He came on earth. During His life here, the connection between it and the perfect life of God had never been broken, but it had been modified by His union with the defects and infirmities of our human nature. He took upon Him the defectiveness and death of our nature, and made them, through obedience and sacrifice, into perfectness and life. And His union with our defectiveness* appears especially in two things—first, in this, that the only actual world, the spiritual world,

---

* I use the words *defective*, *defectiveness*, without, of course, implying any moral or spiritual defect in Christ.

was partly seen by Him as we see it, as the phenomenal world; and, secondly, that the essence of God's life, the ceaseless giving of His life for all, in which God finds the joy of His being, was, in Christ, accompanied with pain. The same sacrifices which God makes, Christ made; but Christ, making them through a defective, though not a sinful nature, made them sometimes in the agony of His soul. But there was this difference between His humanity and ours, that He knew, and could realize, that which we never fully know, and only realize at moments—that the phenomenal world is only the form of the spiritual; and that sacrifice is not, rightly, pain, but impassioned joy. In knowledge, then, though not in daily experience, He was never divided from the higher life; and ascension meant the re-entrance into that life, the re-coincidence of knowledge and experience, the passage from the defectiveness which feels sacrifice as pain to the perfectness which feels it as joy—the passage from a life lived partly in the phenomenal to a life lived entirely in the spiritual world.

But the higher life was reassumed with this addition —that the experience of the phenomenal state and of the defective nature was interwoven with the experience of the perfect state and the perfect nature; so that, we might almost say, God's own consciousness was enriched by that of the infirm humanity. The words in which this is stated are open to theological objections, but the thought is not; it naturally arises out of the apostolic statements of the continued sympathy of Christ with men, of the union of God through Christ with men. The fact may not have been caused by the ascension, but it is, at least, made known to us by the ascension.

This, then, is one of those truths which, flowing directly out of belief in the ascension, make, when felt in the heart, the consolation of this strange and bitter life of ours. God knows and can feel with our life. His perfection is conscious of, and therefore can sympathize with, our imperfection. He knows with what an awful weight the mysteries of being press upon our weakness, and how deep is the gloom which at times comes shadowing across our path. And we feel, through our knowledge of His transient union with defective humanity in Christ, that he can identify Himself with our joy, pain, and effort, and live in our most secret heart; till, in the darkest and loneliest hour, we are aware of a Presence of sympathy, love, and power, sitting with us, hand in hand, in the silence which is more comforting than speech.

This is the exquisite spiritual comfort which comes of faith in the truth of the ascension of Christ into perfect reunion with God.

But to change from the consideration of the ascension of Christ to the consideration of our ascension—that is, of our passage from the imperfect to the perfect life—of that, what shall we say? It is no abrupt change of subject, for it is the doctrine of the Apostles that when our particular humanity is united by faith to perfect humanity in Christ, all that He did is repeated in us. We die with Him, we rise with Him, we shall ascend with Him. What hope and what belief is there in us that we shall pass into the heavenly life with Him?

The question brings before us two other questions which have relentlessly forbidden us to rest, relentlessly forced on us the riddle of their solution—Whence we are, and whither we are going? It is easy to say we come from God and we go to God; but men have never been satisfied with this general answer. Speculation has wearied itself for ages in pursuit of the flying problem.

Whence do we come? what was our previous state? in what world, and how did we live, if we lived at all? What relation does our present life bear to our past?

It has been the poetic thought of many that we come here out of a past existence, in which we were nearer to the source of Light and the source of Love; that Life here is but a wearisome recalling of knowledge once possessed, a wearisome effort to re-attain a holiness once enjoyed; that the child being but lately departed from that imperial palace, has with him still at times swift visions and fair gleams of its hidden splendour, but that with the man these fade away, too proud and too delicate to bear the light of common day. These are poetical answers to the question, 'Whence we are?' but they will not do when the soul is passionate with God and with life.

For it does seem the worst of cruelties, if having been at home with light and goodness, we are sent down to the twilight and selfishness of this world, only to get back again with difficulty to the point from which we started. To have lived in the imperial palace, to have seen from its portals the landscape of the universe, and then to be exiled to a cabin, into the dull windows of which glance only now and then gleams of the excellent sunshine we once enjoyed—that is a thought unworthy of a poet's inspiration. It is unworthy, first, because it supposes a useless waste of material and a mere capricious test, and God never wastes one or applies the other; and secondly, because no soul having once attained such a measure of light and love, retrogrades. The law of the universe is progress; or, to express it better with regard to us—God's work in us is education, and education pushes on, not backward, its pupils. If we have existed previously, we existed, it seems to me, in a state inferior to our present one, and we are here for further development.

This brings before us the next enigma—What relation has the present to the future?

The view which at least appears to maintain that our whole education is finished here in thirty, forty, or seventy years, grows more and more impossible of belief as thought deepens, and as the sense of the infinity in which we live increases. The character of a man fully developed in seventy years! Think of the very best and noblest we have known—how unfinished, how one-sided, how unequally grown, even to our eyes, they were when death summoned them to change. Think again, not of the best but of inferior men, and we cannot help feeling that half or two-thirds of their being is only in a rudimentary condition. We see mental and spiritual organs which as yet have no function; we see what *may be* centuries hence, but it is as we see in the fore-fin of the whale the perfect organization of the human hand.

The Ascension. 281

There are other men, nothing of whose nature seems to be developed. They are the zoophytes of humanity, with a spiritual and intellectual being entirely incomplex, whose education, if they are to continue at all, will necessarily take thousands of years. Seventy! Seventy thousand years are not too much to bring some men to perfection.

And as to this life—this short sentence in the volume of our being—we may be sent here just to get the better of only one failing in our nature, one wry twist which needs sixty years or so to set it right. Or we may be sent here, not to better ourselves, but that we may be sacrificed for the sake of some few backward souls; for our personal education by God is in subordinate harmony to the education of all. There is the case of those who seem to come to earth only that they may suffer, who die all their lives long that others may live; who endure for Christ's sake, without a murmur, that others may learn what spiritual peace and courage mean. I can fancy the unspeakable joy of one of these who have been offered up for the race, when, in the next stage of his life, it is revealed to him that his past thirty or forty years of pain have been impulse and redemption to many of his fellow-men.

There is the still stranger case of those poor souls who are so wicked and wretched here that all men shrink from them in dismay and hopelessness; who do not seem to be born for anything but to be examples of evil; who have not a chance given them from birth to death—why, perhaps these too are sacrificed for others, perhaps they *must* be so bad in order to touch the moral sense of society and to wake it to consider its injuries to men, its neglect of righteous dealing to the poor.

That would be miserable, insufferable doctrine, if the education of these outcasts began and ended here; but if it goes on from state to state, the doctrine has a wild gleam of comfort in it. For I can fancy the marvellous change, the rush of softening tears, the penitence-bringing tenderness, which might come to some poor, wicked, ruined criminal when it was given to him to know, in the world to come, that his evil life had stirred a philanthropist to better his whole class, or that his punishment had been overruled to bless and save even one of his brother-men.

But however these things may be, it seems plain that, if we have lived before, we are not worse here than we have been, that we are advancing, even the worst of us; always, however, in subordination to the welfare of the whole. For if any of us do retrograde here, it is for the good of the great Humanity, and if the entire mass of humanity is moving onwards, we shall hereafter, in some form or other, get or give the good of our voluntary or involuntary sacrifice.

It would scarcely be unjust to accuse these speculations of being disjointed, crude, and wild, perhaps even of unfitness for this solemn place. But they are subjects on which all men think; and how else than with a certain crudeness and wildness can we speak, when we get below the surface of conventional thought, and come face to face with the mystery of life, only to chafe beneath the mocking smile with which it greets our effort to solve its riddle?

The Ascension.

Everything seems to our weak eyes so entirely wrong, so inexplicably mournful, so oddly awry, that even vague suggestions, provided they have some ground in the nature of things, may not be valueless.

I do not know what we should do, we who feel the 'burden of the unintelligible world,' if we had not the hope of our ignorance becoming knowledge, our failure victory, our selfishness self-sacrifice in a new and better life. I do not know, I cannot realize, how the atheist can endure to live in face of the things which we see every day. Unless there be a secret solution of it all, there is indeed no God whom man can worship. But the atheist looks into the dreadful eyes of the mystery, and says that it has no solution.

It is clear, however, if His life be true, that our Saviour Christ had hold of some explanation which we cannot find, at least, in the fulness with which He possessed it; and believing in Him, we can wait for light.

S. Paul, S. John, and many of the true and saintly hearts of earth saw something of it, and passed on through sorrow and trial, with a smile of triumph, to do their work, believing in the evolution of perfection from imperfection; and we—oh! now and then, even to us, weak and sinful men, there comes a sudden flash, a mystic hint; the clouds open for an instant, and we seem, far up in a depth of transcendent blue, to read in a moment of revelation, in the strength of which we go many years of our pilgrimage, the meaning, vaguely, of it all. It is the soul asserting its claim to the ascension life, and God allowing the justice of the claim.

Again, it is not only the sorrow and guilt, and, above

all, the hopelessness of a great part of humanity which torture us with trouble of spirit, but also the cold insensibility, the epicurean carelessness of tranquillity with which Nature seems to look upon our pain. We feel that we ought to be at one with her; we are conscious that we are apart. She looks on it all, and weeps and rages in rain and tempest, but it is not for us. We may be torn with grief or passion, but her skies are as blue as ever, and her sun as unpityingly bright. We may chance to be in harmony with her moods, but it is but a chance after all. We do not know the secret which should make us at one with her; it belongs to the ascension life.

I do not know whether our philosophic poet is right or not, that in childhood we see nearer into the life of things. It is true there was then, to some of us at least, a joy in the pure glitter of the stars, an exultation of heart as we watched the crystalline flash of the breaker on the beach, which now has passed away; but I doubt whether the touch of infinite sorrow and the awful sense of homelessness which come upon us now when we lift weary eyes to those calm watchers of the night, have not more of God as more of humility, have not more of real insight into being as more of depth of feeling in them, than the fresh delight of the child. So passionate, so piercing a pang, how could it be felt save by those who are destined for a more perfect life? The 'thoughts that lie too deep for tears' bear witness to a fuller life to come. Depth of feeling is proportioned to glory of destiny.

It is in hours like these, after the exhaustion of the pain of speculation, that we throw ourselves with a cry of faith, voiceless from the depth of the passion from which it springs—a depth of passionate human feeling which only once or twice in life we fathom, driven down into it by the greatness of the pain, like the huge whale, which, struck, plunges into depths of the Atlantic profounder than ever it had sounded before,—that we throw ourselves upon the resurrection and ascension of Christ, and claim them as our own. Our proper humanity has escaped in Him from imperfection into perfection. We do not then ask the questions how and where. We do not think of the supernatural. The consolation, the relief of believing it is too great to permit us to doubt. One of us, a Man like ourselves, has solved the riddle of the world, and destroyed its power to dismay and to devour our souls.

We rest on the fact, and have peace.

But then we are traversed with the other question— Whither are we going? Ascended up to heaven! What is it? Death is infinitely strange, but beyond the strangeness of death is the strangeness of the other life. When we look on the corpse of one whom we have seen, heard, loved day by day, and realize that the whole wonderful machine has run down and will go no more; but crumble into dust of corruption, and nothing be left of all that energy and movement but a few gases, a little dust and water, we ask ourselves in a wonder which for the moment kills our grief, Where is *it*? Is this thing, so chill, so irresponsive to my passion of grief and love, the man I knew, or is he far away living a new life? If so, what *is* that life; can I in any way make it mine?

And the answer is, No! But it is accompanied with

a passionate curiosity to discover the secret, to grasp in thought, even in the slightest way, the outline of the other life. We paint heaven out of the colours of our existence here on earth, only adding to them brilliancy; we realize, or fancy we realize, in imagination the perfect life, but each man makes his own heaven to suit his own temperament, and we know, deep down, by a consciousness which we repress, that we know nothing at all, that we are all wrong, that we cannot, as defective, conceive an indefective life.

And yet, day by day, we still go on painting that which we know we cannot paint, weaving, in the clash of contradiction between our effort and the conviction of our ignorance, a subtle torture for our souls.

What is it? Is it turning a corner and going on where we left off on earth?—is it another seventy years in another world, another weary spell of slow education; or is it sudden development, like a flower which, transplanted to a kindlier clime, blossoms in a night?

Behold, we know not anything. 'It doth not yet appear,' said the Apostle, 'what we shall be;' but he did not leave the question there—we do *not* know; we *do* 'know that when He shall appear, we shall be like Him, for we shall see Him as He is.' Yes, that is the true answer. 'We shall be like Him, for we shall see Him as He is.' We can afford to let all other questions go, 'all subtle thought, all curious fears,' and rest only on the bosom of this truth, clear at least if nothing else be clear, that if we have been growing into Christ here we shall be made like Him there, for we shall see Him—Truth, Purity, and Love—as He is.

The Ascension. 287

Most true and glorious for the saintly warriors of goodness ; but for some of us, who are conscious that we want so much to make us capable of seeing Him, it is a thought dashed with despondency, especially in hours when intellect is strongest and faith is weakest.

The slow, slow work of God, there is something in it terrible to flesh and blood. We ask, bitterly enough, 'Must there yet come years and years of education, and we so weary already?'

Weakness of heart, and the desire which outflies the labour necessary for the right reception of the perfect good, incline us to believe that swift development follows upon death. Yet the belief is contrary to all that we know here of the manner of God's working. If we leave this world unfinished, untrained, there seems nothing for it but much patient toil for us on the part of God, and slow development on ours. And it is an overwhelming thought to have to go on so long—to live, and live, and live, and have no rest from toil and struggle, no sleep in the grave to refresh us. Infinity! It is a dreadful thought for weakness of will to bear; and it comes upon us sometimes with a weight heavy as frost upon the polar sea. Perhaps the greatest trial we have to suffer sometimes in the hours when our nervelessness is upon us, is to consent to bear the burden of our immortality. I can conceive that at certain times, and to certain temperaments, the thought of annihilation might be a real comfort. But the Christian world cannot endure it long. Hamlet plays with it, but cannot keep it. Either the dread of something after death; the chance of dreams in the sleep; or the nobler feeling, the desire for 'more life and fuller,' intervene, and we accept our immortal life with all its possible suffering rather than cease to be.

There is but one harbour of refuge from the stormy sea of these thoughts. It is belief in the fatherhood of God as revealed by Christ. Fatherhood implies education, and we can bear long years of struggle when we are simultaneously conscious of development and production. It is only unproductive struggle which wears out the will and consumes the heart, and God, if I may be permitted to use a homely metaphor, never admits crank-labour into His educating process. Nothing is wasted of all that He imposes or will impose on us. The end is always in view. Justice and love are training us, and all the secret of freedom from the torment of speculation on the future lies in faith in that truth. Again, Christ Himself had no uncertainty about the future. He was going to a Father. He is astonished at His disciples' sorrow for His departure, 'If ye loved me ye would rejoice, because I said I go to my Father.' He evidently believed that He had the secret of life, that He had solved its mystery, mystery of the future as well as of the present. After an existence which penetrated to the very depths of sorrow, He made death into life, and in our nature passed from earth triumphant as a conqueror.

If you would answer the riddle of existence, get into union with the spirit of this Man. 'Ascend in heart and mind' with Him into the higher life, and try if that will not heal the pain of speculation. Live above the world, above its petty maxims, above its low desires, above its foolish sneer, above its passion for the transient, above its selfish cry of 'Make your fortune.' For we shall never have any real feeling of eternal life till we have entered the temple of self-sacrifice, never any true conception of ever-growing perfection as long as we embrace the mortal as our only good, and cling to imperfection as our only hope. 'And with Him continually dwell!' Oh! to be able to do that—to live in His love, to breathe the air of His purity, to see and do the truth, to walk in justice, to make mercy the legitimate child of justice, to do nothing of ourselves, but all as we see the Father do; and to love this life in a Person whom we see moving in all around us, and feel moving in our own heart—this is the blessed life, indeed, for then as our deathful self is lost in love of God, so our true being is found in union with the self-giving Being of God.

It is then that faith in the life to come fills the heart, for the life itself has already begun to spring. It is then that speculation never brings despondency, for the spirit replies with conviction to the intellect. It is then that we can approach the exquisite dawnlight in which S. Paul and S. John lived, and, as our temperaments urge us, say with the aged saint, 'We know we shall be like Him, for we shall see Him as He is,' or with the aged warrior, 'It is a faithful saying, for if we be dead with Him, we shall also live with Him; if we suffer, we shall also reign with Him.'

[November 1, 1868.]

THE FESTIVAL OF ALL SAINTS.

Revelation vii. 9.

THIS is the festival of All Saints. Its origin in the Western Church is curious, partly as showing the way in which Pagan conceptions were taken up into Christianity, and partly as proving that so late as the seventh century the Romish See was still transforming the remnants of Paganism into Christian forms. It was in the year 608, when Boniface IV. became Pope, that he begged of the Greek emperor, Phocas, the gift of the Pantheon. Having received it, he dedicated it to Mary and all the martyrs. The dedication suggested the festival, and ever since, on November 1, the day on which it is said that the Pantheon was separated to Christianity, this festival has been observed in the Western Churches.

But though, at the moment, it was suggested by the idea of the Pantheon and its consecration, similar feast days existed already in both the Greek and Latin Church. It was in the same century that the imagination of men being greatly stirred by an outburst of interest in the Apocalypse, visions of the archangel Michael were continually seen by excited religious persons. Such a vision was seen at a particular church in Rome, and with the dedication of this church the feast of S. Michael

The Festival of All Saints. 291

and all Angels is connected. The origin of a feast may be ignoble, but the idea connected with it may be noble, and the idea of this feast is of such a character. It celebrates the existence of the Church triumphant; it is the memorial bond which unites in a common interest and a common work—the conquest of evil—the angelic host of heaven and the human host of Christian warriors upon earth.

The festival of All Saints is related in conception to, yet distinct from, the festival of All Angels. For while the latter speaks of angelic victory, the former speaks only of human victory, over evil. In the Greek Church, in which it was first introduced, it was celebrated as an octave to the feast of Pentecost, representing the idea that the collective force of all the saints against the evil of the world was due to the entrance of the Holy Spirit into human nature. In the Western Church the same thought was embodied, but the meaning seems to have taken a more objective form. It was considered to be the feast of the glorification of human nature by Christ.

Now what is it which glorifies human nature? It is expressed in the name of this festival. It is saintliness.

There are many things which gild the career of men and glorify their name. There is the glory which comes of daring courage or of calm endurance, such glory as fell to the French who charged, and to the English who stood still, upon the field of Waterloo. There is the glory of intellectual power, such glory as has given to the philosopher empire over the growth of human thought, to the scientific man empire over the world of nature. There is the glory of the imagination, such glory as rests on the memory of the artists who, penetrating to the heart of things, have revealed, not without a due reserve, the spiritual world which hides beneath the visible its own mysterious beauty. There is the glory of sympathy with humanity, such glory as falls upon those poets who, by expressing not only what is common to all men, but also that which is subtle and exquisite in particular men, have made life a hundred-fold more interesting by their creation of a new world of men; who have in all ages made men known to themselves, and given them, in so doing, aspiration and consolation; who have presented to the race the noble ideals which have exalted it.

But the greatest and the highest glory, the glory which is not confined to a few, but in the power of all, is the glory of holiness. There are many associations into which to enter was fame—companies of warriors, societies of science, bands of poets, circles of statesmen, orders of honour—but the most ancient, the most memorable, and the most continuous — continuous even for ever and ever—is the order of All the Saints.

For it is not only an earthly society; it does not belong to one nation alone; it does not seek its members only out of one age of history. It began with the beginning of the race. It has drawn its members out of every nation and kindred and tongue. It is existent in the world beyond the grave.

And being thus partly of heaven and partly of earth, it is divided into two parts with relation to its distinguishing glory—holiness. For those who belong to it in heaven have attained to saintliness; those who

The Festival of All Saints. 293

belong to it on earth are still contending towards saintliness. Their end is then the same, and in this unity of end, the company above and the company below are bound together into one. Theirs also is one Master, and they both live—the one in satisfied attainment, the other in aspiring effort—by love of His character and faith in His presence. Thus, though divided in degree and place, they are one in spirit.

We have now arrived at this idea — an innumerable multitude of diverse human spirits, of whom part are living in perfect glory of holiness in heaven, and part in imperfect glory of holiness on earth, bound together into one united polity by common love, common worship, and common dependence on the power of one King. This, in itself, is a sufficiently magnificent conception. But there is a further development of it. What is the constant, ceaseless work of this society? It is the overthrow of evil.

Is that work ever to cease? 'Yes,' answer some; 'it will cease when all the redeemed are gathered in, when the number of the elect is complete.' And where are the rest, we ask, the millions who have not reached your elect standard? 'They are in hell for ever' is the reply, 'deepening in evil: baffled revenge and hate, consuming and ruinous despair, growing darker and fiercer against God the good, from day to day of everlasting punishment.' Is that the cessation of God's work? Is that the result of the magnificent work of Christ? Is that the lame and impotent conclusion of the organization of the great society of the Church of Christ? Is that the end of the war against evil? Then I can only say that it seems no triumph at all to me, but ignominious defeat. Then good is not omnipotent, for it is impotent to root out evil. Then love is not lord of all, for it cannot conquer hatred. Then, indeed, we are not Christians who believe in perfect Good, but Manichæans, who believe in two rulers who divide between them a universe in which the evil ruler is with difficulty kept down by the power of the good ruler.

Where is the life, the happiness, the impulse in such a dreadful faith? What comfort is it to me that I am saved if half the world is lost? What blessedness have I in heaven if my brethren are for ever doomed to hell? It is no heaven to me. I have no union of spirit with its God. I feel as the old Frank warrior felt when he came to baptism. 'Where are my ancestors?' 'In hell for ever,' said the priest. 'Then I prefer to join them.' His answer has been recorded as an impiety; but for all that, men have sympathized with it and felt, as we feel now, that the spirit of Christ was more in the rude soldier than in the priest who stood beside him. For what did he say more than S. Paul?—'I could wish that myself were accursed from Christ, for my brethren, my kinsmen according to the flesh.'

Others answer, The battle against evil will cease when all the redeemed are gathered in and all the wicked annihilated. God will not punish evil men for ever, He will destroy them. Thousands of souls which have not reached the end of their existence shall be utterly blotted out, and God and good be all in all. They point to the analogy of nature, that out of fifty seeds it scarcely brings one to bear. But they forget that for the use of

The Festival of All Saints.

an analogy there must be some resemblance of relations between the things compared; and I should be glad to know what real analogy there is between a seed and a soul. They forget also the torture to a human soul which comes with the thought of the possibility of annihilation. They forget the ineradicable sense of immortality, of continued individuality, which clings to the heart of the basest and wickedest of the race. There is that within us—and it is one of those intuitions which, though they prove little, no wise man thinks meaningless if he believes in a God who has given ideas to the soul—there is that within us which prefers even the thought of torture to that of cessation of being. They forget that God is dishonoured when He confesses Himself incapable of redeeming the souls of men whose Father He has proclaimed Himself to be. In assuming fatherhood, He has assumed the duties of a father; and to destroy children because He can do nothing with them, to give up hope for them, is an idea I cannot connect with the Almighty Being who revealed Himself in Jesus Christ. If one soul perishes for ever, it is failure—evil has won the day.

This is not the true view of the cessation of evil. This is not the way in which the festival of All Saints shall finally be kept.

The war against evil which the Head of the Church and all the army of the saints are waging now will end, not when the victims of evil are damned or destroyed, but when the evil itself in them is consumed. In every soul of man, by the giving of joy or the giving of suffering, by a thousand means, each fitted to a thousand characters,

God will do His conquering work. Those who have already won the crown of saintliness are fellow-labourers with Him in the work of redemptive warfare. The power and the life of Christ are not only powerful and living upon earth—He is redeeming all in the other world. He continues to redeem.

For what has God done? He has conceived of the race as of one man, and He has incarnated that idea in Jesus Christ, the sinless image of humanity. That sinless image He will fulfil in the race whom the Saviour represented. All humanity shall be saintly, shall be Christ's, shall be God's, for Christ is God's. Then shall war be finished; then shall goodness be known to be that which it is always, triumphant; then shall man know that his experience of evil was but a shadow cast by goodness in the imperfect mirror of humanity; then a willing host shall bow the knee to God and thank Him for the suffering and the wrong which led them to the knowledge of the true life of self-surrender; then the holy Catholic Church, the Communion of saints, shall be perfect; then this festival of All Saints shall be kept by all the spirits who have ever taken life from the life of the heavenly Father.

This is the loftiest idea we can form of the completion of that everlasting society, the Church of Christ.

And now, having gained these conceptions of this grand society existing since the world began, destined to exist for ever, existing partly in peaceful work in heaven, partly in warfare and pain on earth; of which some on earth are members now in fact, of which all on earth are members now by right, of which all shall finally be saintly members; which possesses as its head and spirit the all-complete and holy humanity of Christ; we possess an idea to place opposite to that of the French philosopher, an idea which contains all the good which his contains, and which if I leave aside a hundred other tendernesses and beauties and humanities, in which his conception is deficient, speaks not as his does, only to the philosopher, but in comfort and ennobling thought to the poorest and the most ignorant, and passes on—not to say as he does that all the souls of men perish like the leaves which have fallen from the trees this year, and have no comfort save the comfort of the leaves, that they form the soil for future forests— but to say that none are lost, that all are gained, that all are developed, that not one subtle shred of character exists in any man which does not reach its end and have its use in the universe; that the ideal man is indeed no dream, but fulfilled in a nobler manner than the philosopher living apart from *common* life was capable of conceiving; fulfilled in the accomplished perfection of the whole race, without the loss of a single individual of the race. 'For we shall all come, in the unity of the faith and of the knowledge of the Son of God, unto the perfect (the full-grown) MAN.'

He who has grasped this overwhelming thought, too great for the intellect, not too great for the soul, has entered into a new life. His view of history is changed. He possesses a secret which resolves it into unity. His view of national relations takes a wider and firmer basis than that given by politicians. His view of inferior races cannot be that too generally held. They perish before our encroaching march, but, lost on earth, their education is continued in another world. His view of his fellow-men becomes large, generous, and tolerant. He cannot despair even of the worst and vilest. They are members of his society—evil, but being redeemed. Let him see one spark of goodness in the darkness of their life, and he cries, 'Ah! there is God. I see the spirit of Christ at work; let me show the Saviour who is with him to this miserable man.' And if his efforts are in vain he does not despair; no, he knows that God cannot fail; he says to himself, 'I shall not lose my brother, he too will be one of the assembly of the saints.' It is wonderful how life grows great in the illimitable atmosphere and landscape of this thought; how invigorating becomes the air of action; how deep our sympathy with, and yet how easy is our consolation for, all the misery and horrors with which we are encompassed; how time and its weariness, and space and its overwhelmingness, vanish away, and our life is lived in the eternal world, watching with faithful and enkindled eyes the mighty purposes of God moving onward like a sunlit river, whose banks are love and justice, to their fulfilment in the assimilation of all spirits to Himself.

In conclusion, let me grasp some of the principles of the life of this great society, and apply them to the minor society of the English nation. They will give us, especially at this time, when the relations of classes to one another in this country have begun to slowly alter under a new impulse, a few great lines of feeling and action by which to direct our lives.

First. In the Church of Christ, each true member is

an enthusiast in his work. His heart glows; his tongue cannot be basely silent, though often wisely silent. He feels inspired by the Spirit of God within him. He would rather die than be false to Christ. The thought of the battle against evil is never absent from his soul or from his active life. He sees in every business, in every office which he holds, in every position he sustains—as master or servant, as employer or workman—a field in which he may push forward, with Christ as his Friend, the interest and the progress of the accumulating Church of Christ.

Ought not that to be the feeling of the citizen towards the nation?—enthusiasm, not untaught and rude, but cultured by thought on great questions, and tempered by the experience of the past; enthusiasm so chastened by truthful love of country, that it can never degrade the man into a slave or a hireling of party; enthusiasm which will not permit the citizen to do, himself, one thing unworthy of the honourable past of England.

And this will free us from the political indifference which still belongs to many citizens. We shall have interest, not excitable and therefore fleeting, but deep and resolute, in all the important questions which the nation is now prepared to solve. We shall have a shame which will make the apathy of leisure or the retirement of comfort intolerable; we shall feel this so deeply for others, that it will lead us to bring to bear on those to whom we have given the franchise, but who have no political education, such a training as will awake them to the same sense of responsibility, and stir in them the same cultivated interest in the country as, I trust, we ourselves possess.

He who feels the enthusiasm of the Church of Christ ought above all men to be freed himself, and to free others, from political apathy.

Again. Both the Church of Christ and the English nation have a glorious past. The Christian and the Englishman are both the children of heroes. The freedom of both, in their several spheres, has been of that slow and dignified growth, and is of that firm, rooted character, which creates the reverence that makes love lasting. When the Christian is tempted to sin, when the Englishman is tempted to injure his country, both look round on the images of their spiritual ancestors and are shamed into penitence. 'Seeing,' we who belong to the communion of saints, 'that we are compassed about with so great a cloud of witnesses,' we run with patience the race that is set before us. And we who belong to the communion of the great English people, seeing we too are compassed about with so great a cloud of noble English witnesses, by whom the freedom we enjoy has been established, we also ought to run with patience (and the more liberal we are, the more we need a wise patience) in the path of national duty, looking indeed—and here the analogy melts into coincidence—looking to the true King of the nation, Christ, the Author of just laws, the Life, the Completer of the perfect State.

Again. In the vast society of which I speak each man lives for his brother, not for himself: he is freed from the weight of personal interests, he is freed from the burden of local selfishness, of class selfishness. He is

The Festival of All Saints. 301

above professional jealousies, above caste prejudices. For rich and poor meet together equal before God, peer and peasant kneel at the same table; those who do not understand each other's lives, and whose interests are opposed or different, worship in the same house and honour the same Master with a single voice. Men are united by common love to Christ.

I need not apply the analogy. I only ask that you should recognize as Englishmen the same principle. Do not permit class interests, local selfishness, the clashing elements of labour and capital, of aristocracy and democracy, of literary culture and middle-class Philistinism, to invalidate union for national welfare, to destroy that mutual tolerance of prejudices and position which may enable you and all to make of England one united body. For as the unity of the communion of saints is made by the pervading action of one spirit of love to Christ which ever, as it deepens, consumes the rancour of sects and the hatred of theology; so the unity of the English people will arise from the growth of a sacred love to the idea of the nation, which ever as it spreads and deepens will destroy, not different opinions, which are necessary, but the malice, impotence, and corruption of the party spirit which at once weakens and divides the nation. Social selfishness and party enmity will die.

Finally, there is one last lesson which the Christian Church teaches us. It denies not only local but also national selfishness. In it all national prejudices are broken down. S. Paul, the noblest example of the force of this principle, trampled under foot the Jewish exclusiveness, and became as the subject of Christ the citizen of the world. To him there was neither Jew nor Greek, Roman nor barbarian, Christ was all and in all. Humanity in the Man Christ Jesus—that was his nation.

The time has come in this age to carry out the same principle in the wide politics of the world. The time has come to regulate our relations with other nations by the words—which I for the moment make particular—Do unto other nations as ye would they should do unto you. The time has come when we should begin the attempt to sacrifice, when it seems just, English interests for the sake of the interests of the world. The time has come when it seems almost ridiculous to isolate ourselves and to talk of ourselves as the noblest and greatest nation in the world; ridiculous to ignore and to oppose the influences of other nations upon ourselves and on the race. The time has come when international self-sacrifice should replace international selfishness, and to us there should be neither Englishman nor Frenchman, German nor American, but the human race above all.

Then will political life be identical with Christian life, and love be all in all. 'But this is Utopia!' you exclaim. Yes, but what would life be without its ideals? It is only ideals which kindle continued action. What would this world be without our natural optimism? It would be a landscape without colour, uncheered by the beauty which, in creating hope, creates activity. True, we may never here on earth make the world and the Church coincident, never here celebrate the feast of All Saints; yet it has been the dream of all national inspiration, it has flowed out of the heart of every people, that a time will come at last when humanity, pervaded by the spirit of universal charity, shall make its very variousness conduce to unity, when there shall be many nations but one people, when the communion of all men shall be the communion of saints, and God at last, having taken all humanity into Himself, fulfil, in its last and highest sense, the fact and the promise of the Incarnation. For—the touch of Christ has made the whole world kin.

[September 29, 1867.]

ANGELIC LIFE AND ITS LESSONS.

Hebrews i. 7.

THE feast of S. Michael and All Angels, which falls this year upon a Sunday, suggests to us the subject of angelic life. It is a subject fraught with interest. For so much eager speculation has clustered round it that it cannot be devoid of some attraction to intelligent men; so much art and poetry have adorned it, so much religious life has mingled with it, that men either of poetic temperament or of spiritual minds can scarcely put it aside with indifference.

It is true there are many who deny the existence of any spiritual beings save God and man. The wide universe is to them a solitary land without inhabitants. There is but one oasis filled with living creatures. It is the earth on which we move; and we who have from century to century crawled from birth to death, and fretted out our little lives upon this speck of star-dust which sparkles amid a million million others upon the mighty plain of infinite space, we are the only living spirits. There is something pitiable in this impertinence. It is a drop of dew in the lonely cup of a gentian, which imagines itself to be all the water in the universe. It is the

Angelic Life and its Lessons. 305

summer midge which has never left its forest pool, dreaming that it and its companions are the only living creatures in earth or air.

There is no proof of the existence of other beings than ourselves, but there is also no proof of the contrary. Apart from revelation, we can think about the subject as we please. But it does seem incredible that we alone should represent in the universe the image of God; and if in one solitary star another race of beings dwell, if we concede the existence of a single spirit other than ourselves, we have allowed the principle; the angelic world of which the Bible speaks is possible to faith.

But we have fallen upon faithless times; and worse than the mediæval who saw the glint of the angel's wing in the dazzling of the noonday cloud, worse even than the Greek who peopled his woods with Deity, we see only in the cloud the storehouse of rain to ripen our corn, and in the woods a cover for our pheasants. Those who see more have small cheerfulness in the sight: neither the nymphs nor the angels haunt the hills to us. We do not hear in the cool of the day the voice of God in the trees of the garden. We gaze with sorrow on a world inanimate, and see in it only the reflection of our own unquiet heart. There is scarcely an unmixedly joyous description of nature in our modern poets. There is scarcely a picture of our great landscape artist which is not tinged with the passion of sorrow or the passion of death. We bring to bear upon the world of nature, not the spiritual eye, but a disintegrating and petty criticism. We do not let feeling have its way, but talk of harmonies of colour and proportion, and hunt after mere surface-beauty. We train the eye and not the heart, and we become victims of a sensualism of the eye, which renders the imagination gross, and of an insatiability of the eye, which, unable to rest and contemplate, comprehends the soul of nothing which we see. It is our sick craving for excitement — the superficiality of our worldly life—which we transfer to our relation to Nature. What wonder if Nature refuses to speak to us, and we ourselves are insensible to the wisdom, life, and spirit of the universe?

'The world is too much with us,' and God too little. We cannot see the life which moves around us through the dust of the death in which we live. He who dwells in the cabin of the visible cannot see the infinite world of the invisible through the clay-built walls. Our life with Nature has lost its beauty, its joy, its religion.

It was different with the ancient Jew, and with the Apostles and their followers. They lived in a world peopled with spiritual beings. They believed in invisible assistants, who were doing God's pleasure and sympathizing with His children. The hosts of heaven moved in myriads in the sky. The messengers of God went to and fro working His righteous will. The sons of God shouted for joy when the creation leaped to light. In every work of nature, in the summer rain and the winter frost, in the lifting of the billow on the sea and the growth of the flower on the plain, there were holy ones concerned who sang the hymn of continued creation to the Eternal Love. The very winds themselves were angels, and the flaming fires ministers of God. It was a happier and a grander world to live in then than now. We have more knowledge, yet less joy. We have more material power, yet less noble souls. Which of our poets could sing now, out of a full heart, the hundred and fourth Psalm?

It is too true to be strange, and yet what an insight does it give into the modern spirit that the impulse of praise has left us. Our religious utterances are all prayer. We want something for ourselves, or for others. We cannot get out of ourselves into the bright region of joy where praise mounts to heaven's gate like the morning song of the lark.

For this one day at least let us step backwards into that ancient time, and try to find out the principles which underlie the hints given to us in the Bible of angelic life in connection with God and with nature. The principles will be useful, even though we treat the stories as symbolical.

Take, first, the relation of God to angelic life.

The first thing we understand of the angels is that in distant eternities God created them. God gave of His own life to others, and filled His silence with living souls. Here we have the principle of the social life of God. We are too apt to picture Him as dwelling in solitary magnificence, like some Oriental king, unapproachable, self-sufficing, careless of the social life so dear to us, finding no pleasure in the love and praise of His children.

Long before man arose, the creation of angels denies this imagination. God did not wish to live alone. He gave Himself to others, and rejoiced in seeing Himself reflected even partially by others. He listened with pleasure to the song of joy which filled His universe, and received and gave back in ceaseless reciprocation the offered love of the spirits He had made.

And in that thought all social life on earth should be hallowed by being made like to that of God; we should be as gods and angels one to another, interchanging ever love and service. Is that—I put it to your conscience—is that the ideal which in society you strive to reach?

Again. The angelic creation reveals to us the very principle of God's proper life. He would not have a life which began and ended in Himself. His life was life in others. In giving of His life He lived. That autarkia, that self-sufficingness, which thinkers have bestowed on God, was not His perfect thought of being. Life did not consist of 'in Himself possessing His own desire.' His life consisted in giving of Himself away, and finding Himself in all things. I do not say God could not, but He would not, be alone.

And this is the deep principle of all being. That which *is*, is that which gives itself away. That which lives is that which lives in others. God would be dead were He to live for Himself alone, were He to cease to give; and we are dead when we live only to receive, when, folding the cloak of self around us, we cease to find our being in sacrifice of self.

I pass on to the relation of the angelic life to God.

It is described as a life of exalted praise. The angels are pictured as employed in ceaseless adoration. In the vision of Isaiah, in reciprocated song, they cry to one another, 'Holy, holy, holy is the Lord of hosts.' In the ears of the seer of Patmos they fall before the throne and worship, saying, ' Amen. Blessing and glory, and wisdom, and thanksgiving, and honour, and power, and might, be unto our God, for ever and ever.' In all Christian art they have been the embodiment of praise. In early painting, when art, being less self-conscious, was therefore more religious, the whole background of any picture which represented God or Christ in glory, is formed entirely of a multitude of adoring angels. Now, in the Bible this life of praise is represented as born of a deep consciousness of the holiness of God, and the child of this consciousness is awe, intense in love and veneration. The seraphim worshipped not because God was Almighty, but because He was holy, holy, holy, Lord God Almighty; and as they worshipped they covered their faces with their wings. Further, as this praise was excited by the holiness of God, so it was the mark of the personal holiness of the angels, for no living spirit can fix itself in adoration of the Holiest without becoming continually more like Him whom it contemplates and loves.

Here, then, we have a revelation of the life of heaven. Holiness deepening day by day; sacred love and awe increasing as the revelation of holiness advances, and the expression of these in ceaseless worship, ceaseless praise. And the worship is not admiration of God's power, but love of God's holiness ; and the praise is not singing of psalms and music of harps—these are but symbolical—it is the psalm of a life of loving service, the offering of a whole eternity of self-devoted activity to God; it is the music of a soul which, at harmony with God's life of sacrifice, is at harmony also with the inner soul of the universe.

The nearer, brethren, that you live to God here, the nearer you will approach the angelic life. Our state of imperfection is characterized by prayer, the state of perfection is characterized by praise; and it is curious to mark in the history of some of the noblest of God's saints, how, as they drew near the close of life and entered more into communion with the heavenly existence, prayer seems to be replaced by a sacred awe, and a deeper knowledge of holiness breaks forth into continual praise. I do not say we pray too much—God knows we pray too little—but our aspiration should picture to itself, not so much increased power of petition, as freedom from the necessity of petition, that oneness with Christ and the Father which is characterized by the words of Christ Himself, 'In that day ye shall ask me nothing.'

So far for angelic life in connection with God. We pass on to consider, as it is described in the Bible, angelic life in connection with nature.

The Hebrew religious feeling always retained some traces of its connection through Abraham with Chaldæa. The old pastoral faith which was born on the wide plains of the East, with a magnificent arch of sky above, in which the sun and moon and stars walked cloudless with what seemed the stately step of gods, was always breaking through the pure monotheism which God revealed to the patriarchs. Job mentions, as a possible temptation, the desire to kiss his hand

Angelic Life and its Lessons. 311

to the shining sun ; to adore the moon walking in her brightness. Warnings loud and deep against the star-worship pervade the Old Testament. But though the old worship was denounced in the revelation to the Hebrews, yet part of the idea of it remained in another form. The host of heaven were all but identified with the angels. The morning stars sang together, and all the sons of God shouted for joy. The fallen angel is called the day-star. God is said to call the host of heaven (an indiscriminate name for stars and angels) by their names, and to lead them forth by numbered phalanxes. In His sight the stars, considered as ruled by the angels, are not pure. And not only the ordering of the stars, but all manifestations of the forces of nature were, in the poetry of the Hebrews, directed by the angels.

Certain masters in science will smile at all this, and ask if that be philosophy? and I answer, No, not philosophy, but something higher—poetry; and as such, not disclosing the relations of phenomena, but revealing, through symbolic phrase, a principle. It matters very little whether the angels be the directing powers of the elements and their combinations or not; but it does make much matter to us as spiritual beings with what eyes we look upon the universe—as a living whole informed and supported by a living will, or as dead matter drifting on in obedience to dead laws. The latter view leaves us lonelier and sadder even than I have described our state at the beginning of this sermon, for it leaves us hopeless. The former makes arise before us dim possibilities of something wonderfully glorious beneath the mystery of nature. If it leaves us sorrowful, yet at least we do not sorrow as men without a hope. If the whole creation groaneth and travaileth in pain together, it is not to do so for ever; it is waiting for our redemption. Nay, it is redeemed, or rather, it never needed redemption. It is only when we come into contact with it that it groans and travails; it is only to us that it is fallen; it is only to us that it awaits redemption. It is only to our weak and purblind vision that its struggles seem to be struggles, and its pain pain. Were we at one with the spiritual universe of which it is to us the witness and the form, we should see its struggle as the easier grandeur of endeavour, and its agony as the ecstasy of love. Beneath the poetry of these descriptions of angelic life in connection with nature, lies the principle that the living and the spiritual underlie the dead and sensuous things which only appear to be. The mechanical universe which we behold with the eye of sense is not the actual universe—the actual universe is a spiritual life, in which we ought to live, and in union with which consists our only actual being.

But in the laws and processes of the apparent world we can discern at times the principles of the actual world it represents. We behold in the equivalence of that which we call force, not the dreadful circle of necessity always returning on itself, but the image of the perfect order in which God's living will expresses itself, and the real outward form of the unchanging identity of His life of love. This one living force of Love, giving of itself

Angelic Life and its Lessons. 313

to all things, is conditioned into different powers in the different forms of spiritual life; and stores itself up now in the strife and self-control, in the pain and passion, in the failure and the loss, in the shattered effort and the unaccomplished aspiration, which are the forms it takes in union with our weakness and our death.

Under these forms we see in man the potential force of God, which, when we are redeemed from death, shall be liberated as ecstasy, joy, righteousness, self-rule, self-sacrifice, and perfect peace.

These are the actual things which exist within the envelope of our weakness and death. They are also the actual things which exist in nature, and are nature; but we see them only through the glass of our defective being, and we see them all awry. The involuntary sacrifice of nature, for instance, suggests to us sorrow. It is in reality the joy of the world. The death of things gives us a sense of acute pain. It is in reality the expression of the world's intensest life. The true world is not the world which science investigates, nor the world which we see. But in discovering the principles of the phenomenal world, science points unconsciously to the related principles of the actual world, and in the way in which nature suggests to us pain and death and failure, we learn at last to find the truth that the pain and death and failure are in us, and that these things are in nature itself, joy and life and success. So do we grasp the truth of these old Hebrew sayings of the angels—that nature in essence, or rather, in that actual world of which it is the witness, is not inanimate, but living.

Then the universe becomes clothed in a more glorious form. 'The dead heavy mass which did but block up space is vanished, and in its place there flows forward, with the music of eternal waters, a stream of life and power and action' which issues from the source of all life—the living will of God. Then it happens that to us the whole course of nature, and each separate thing within it, give up to us the secrets they half conceal and half express. They speak not to intellect only or to feeling only, but to the entirety of our being. It is not, then, true to say that we receive but what we give, and that in our life alone doth nature live. That locks us up again in our self, and makes the universe dead again. We rise, on the contrary, out of our dead self, and mingle, a living spirit, with the living spiritual universe; and then, entering that region of pure insight at the gate of which science scorns to knock, and would knock in vain unless hand in hand with faith, we see in all the things which do appear the actual things of which they are the form. The winds do then indeed become His messengers, and the devouring flame His minister. The sun and stars and quiet sky have a wondrous story of solemn order and righteousness for our heart. The trees whisper and the lake murmurs at their feet the same secret of eternal life. There is in river, cloud, and mountain, in wood and plain and light, blending in their harmonies of colour and of form to create the landscape, a music so mystic and so sweet that, though the ear can never hear its song, the spirit thrills beneath its beauty. It is the inner universe, with its ten thousand voices,

Angelic Life and its Lessons. 315

praising God. In all the seeming sorrow and passion and tension of the world we see death as birth, the struggle of life with itself to assume a more glorious form; and asking ourselves what all this means to us, of what glorious work of God it is the witness, of what glorious hope it is the guarantee, we find for answer, that it is the love of God working out the redemption of the world; that the seeming death is life, the seeming pain joy, the seeming loss gain; that life given is life realized, that life in others is alone true being. All God's living spirits are doing within the sphere of His life a portion of this redeeming work. The angels do it perchance as He performs it, finding a perfect joy in sacrifice; we are doing it in agony, finding every sacrifice a pain, and yet learning through the very pain to realize the sacrifice as joy; giving up our life with strong crying and with tears, but strangely discovering that we have been led into life: till at last the secret smites upon our heart in an ineffable light which transfigures all our being, and looking up to where, upon the cross of Calvary, all humanity was sacrificed and all life given away in infinite love that the life of the world might be, we know at last in Him the mystery of the universe. We see the very Life itself in the love which, in giving His Son, gave Himself. We see in the entire sacrifice of the Son, not only the life of God, but that life as redeeming power; and in broken-hearted humility and joy we fall before His cross and pray, Lord God, my Saviour, take me up into Thy life; let me die with Thee into true being, let me feel the ecstasy of sacrifice, the rapture of life in others. Make my pain and sorrow part of Thy redemptive work, till, love having its perfect work in me, I dwell in God and God in me.

Then will praise be perfect, for in us love will be perfect; our voices, our unconscious aspiration, our whole life shall go forth in song to God as the river goes forth to seek the ocean. The perfect life will be perfect joy.

In all Christian ages there has been one symbol of this, in all ages in one way the human heart has expressed its joy and worship—in the harmonies of music and the sweetness of song. So deep is this feeling of the union of music and adoration, that in all the growth of natural things on earth, in the rising of the tree, the expanding of the flower, the swelling of the stream, and the beat of the ocean on its shores, men have seemed to hear the notes of a perfect music unfolding to a noble end.

The host of heaven was thought, not only by Jewish poets but by Grecian sages, to march to a music too grand to be audible to us, and the belief of the mediæval was embodied in these words :—

> There's not the smallest orb which thou behold'st
> But in his motion like an angel sings,
> Still quiring to the young-eyed cherubins.
> Such harmony is in immortal souls ;
> But while this muddy vesture of decay
> Doth grossly close us in, we cannot hear it.

The expression, then, of the angelic life is fitly said to be music. Therefore let music be ever honoured, ever chaste. Let those motions of the sense which it awakes

Angelic Life and its Lessons. 317

unite themselves to the deepest passion of humanity—the passion to be at one with God—and bear us upward into union with the mighty oratorio which all the universe sings, in the action and joy of sacrifice, to the ear of Eternal Love.*

---

* The idea which lies at the root of the latter half of this sermon I have derived from a book which has been of great value to me, *Life in Nature*, by James Hinton. As I am honoured by his friendship, he will not be displeased with this acknowledgment.

[October 6, 1867.]

ANGELIC LIFE IN CONNECTION WITH MAN.

Hebrews i. 14.

IN speaking last Sunday of the principles underlying the accounts given in the Bible of angelic life, we considered it in connection with God and in connection with nature. It remains to consider angelic life in connection with man.

Now there are many recorded appearances of angels in the Old Testament, from the time of Abraham onwards; some in visions, and others apparently intervening in the midst of daily life, such as the angels who came to visit Lot and Abraham. Those appearances which came to men in sleep we may put aside as presenting no difficulty. Persons brought up in the belief in angels will see angels in dreams and hear them speak. Only observe, that in saying this we do not deny the reality of the vision, nor the fact that it is sometimes a direct communication of God to the soul—the very usage of the word vision implying the unconscious belief of men that the soul *sees* sometimes in sleep or in trance into things pertaining to the soul, more clearly than it could see in the waking hours of the man. We only deny that the form of the vision—a being with wings, for example—necessarily answers to any reality

Angelic Life in connection with Man. 319

in the actual world. The existence of other spiritual beings than ourselves seems to me undeniable, but the appearance which any of those spiritual beings have taken, or may take, to a man in vision is entirely dependent on the ideas in which he has been educated. For example, a dying man sees a crowd of adoring angels round his bed, and hears the music of harps. In that vision, which has again and again occurred in this century, and which is just as real as the vision of Jacob on the hill, the thing which is actual is, that God is speaking in comfort to His servant's soul; but the form which God's communication takes is entirely conditioned by the paintings which the man has seen, and by the reading of the Apocalypse. This view is supported by the Bible itself. It is not till after the Israelites had seen the winged gods and animals of Egypt that the angels are represented as winged creatures. In the more archaic parts of Genesis the angel is never winged, but appears always in the form of a man. Therefore we come to this conclusion respecting the angelic visions recorded in the Bible—that the actual thing in them is that God speaks to men in visions, and that the merely phenomenal thing in them is the form in which the vision comes.

But we have to account for the other angelic appearances, those in which angels in the form of men came openly into the midst of waking life, talked, for example, and ate with Abraham, and drove Lot out of Sodom. What shall we say of these? Why, that they are poetical or mythical representations of some real occurrence, or of some spiritual truth. We find these stories always in the shadowy land of early history. As the world grows older, and we learn to discredit our senses more and more as giving us actual truth, these stories pass out of credit, so far as they claim an outward reality. Angelic beings do not appear now to our eyes, and yet I do not doubt that God speaks to us now as much as He did to Abraham, and saves men now from ruin as He saved Lot. And the Bible itself confirms this view. As we pass on from the early history of the Jewish nation to the later, the physical appearance of angels is succeeded by the visionary appearance of angels, the conversation at the tent-door by the visions of Isaiah and Ezekiel. It is the tendency of men in early times, when feeling is master of intellect, to represent spiritual impressions as sensuous impressions; indeed they *feel* so strongly that they *see*, and it is without the slightest want of truth that a patriarch would say that he heard God's voice speaking to him when in fact he had only received a vivid spiritual impression. The whole account of Abraham's intercession with the Lord is probably a poetic account of a real spiritual struggle in Abraham's soul, the embodiment in words of the questions and replies of a passionate prayer.

The first principle, then, contained in the stories is that God speaks directly to man.

We look upon these stories as isolated and præternatural. In this way we take all the comfort and reality out of the Bible. That book does not relate what God did once for men, but what God is always doing. Cling to the objective reality of these angelic appearances, and we are forced to admit that they do not occur now, and, in consequence, that God is farther from us than He was from Abraham; and the story, instead of giving us consolation, administers to us hopelessness. Cling to the uniqueness of these appearances, and what interest have they for us? What do we then care, why should we care, for what happened to Abraham when he was in doubt, or to Jacob when he left his tent? Unless we feel that these things can come home to us and occur to us in the nineteenth century, they have no more meaning to us than a fairy tale.

But putting aside the phenomenal in the stories as either mythical or seen in vision, and their form as conditioned by the beliefs of the time in which they are placed, and coming to the real truth beneath them, we claim them as representing in particular instances that which God is always doing. All these examples are of universal interpretation. If God spoke to Abraham, then, when he was in doubt, and vindicated His justice to His servant, He speaks to us now when the same terrible thought shakes us to our centre, that after all, perhaps, there is no eternal Right. We have but to go forth humbly into the evening solitude to confer with Him, and the answer comes we know not how. A voice speaks in our inmost soul. It is He who spoke to Abraham.

If God wrestled with Jacob till the dawn, at that dread crisis of his life when the old worldly crust of fourteen years broke up, and the fountains of the great deep of a human soul were unsealed that a new world of being might be made in him; He wrestles with us now, when our life comes to its Jabbok in the midnight, and the path divides to Heaven or to hell.

If in the wilderness, Hagar in the hour of her bitterest desolation found that the Omnipresent was beside her; we know now and for ever that wherever a mother bends in misery over her dying child, there is then with her God's never-failing Love. The child may die, but He is there waiting to take it to His fatherhood, and keep it for her coming. And when we read the terrible tales of heroic hearts left alone to die—those two of Franklin's crew found on the borders of the ice-bound bay beside the shattered boat, the New Testament lying between them—that hopeless crowd of human hearts on the deck of the ship 'London,' sinking slowly into the wild waters, without a chance—there rises along with the vision of the unavailing human effort and of the strong agony of men, the vision of a divine Presence, who, though He did not save from death, was there, never to leave them or forsake them after death.

These are the truths revealed to us by these angelic stories; not that God is far away, but that He is the Ever Near. No angels come to us! no celestial voices speak to us! Oh! believe it not. Every deep impression of the rightness of an action, every keen conviction of a truth, every inward cry for light and impulse onwards, are messengers, voices of God. Abraham, feeling these, would have said at once, 'I hear the voice of God; the Almighty One has spoken to me.' But we—partly blinded by the acrid atmosphere of faithlessness in which we live, partly led astray by the way in which the Bible history has been isolated into the region of a profitless supernaturalism, made unique and not representative—call these things conscientious scruples, intuitions, impulses; words meaningless to us, and the only province of which, when they are connected with the thought of a God, is to obscure the truth of a *living* God.

Brethren, God is here, around us, moving about our daily life, in us, stirring, speaking, acting in our hearts. That is what we want in this age, the conviction of a loving Father, in whom we live, and move, and have our being; without whom we ourselves, and all we do and think, are indeed 'such stuff as dreams are made of.' But when that conviction is attained, we recognize that all the Old Testament stories are written for our admonition, are told for us, are true of us.

'And God appeared unto Abraham, and said: I am the Almighty God; walk thou before me, and be thou perfect.' Has He never appeared to you? When you stepped from boyhood into youth, and sat alone in your rooms the first week in the University, looking forward in a moment of seriousness over your new career, realizing its temptations, or inspired by the atmosphere of the place to create and pursue an ideal—did no words shape themselves in your heart like those which the patriarch heard when he began an untrodden path in a new land? It was the very voice of Abraham's God.

Or, when oppressed with the multitudinous passions and thoughts of life, sick at soul of the vain show in which you walk, angry with those who dare to hope the best for the race, and despairing, when to your eyes the painted crust of life becomes transparent, and you see the unutterably woful and wicked stream of fire which flows beneath, bearing on its bosom the agony of men and women perishing—when you are driven like Elijah by these thoughts into the solitudes of nature, and hear, when the storm and earthquake have been hushed upon some mountain slope, a still small voice within your soul which whispers hope in the final issue, and a mystery of joy beneath the mystery of the pain of life, and then return to work and existence, calmed, you know not how, and with a hope for which you could give no reason—what is it which has done that work upon you? It is not a mere efflux from the heart of nature; it is God Himself repeating to you the experience and the lesson which Elijah learnt in the wild solitudes of Horeb.

O brethren! take these Old Testament stories to your hearts. Realize a living God, who penetrates with His presence and His action every moment of your being. In whatever light we view these accounts of angels, this they suggest at least. There is not a struggle of your soul which is not known to Him, not a crisis in your life which your Father does not hang over with intensest eagerness, waiting for the fitting moment to speak; sometimes smiting you down, that the simoom of a fiery temptation may pass over you without slaying your spiritual life: sometimes wrestling with your stubborn heart till the dawn break upon the horizon, and you demand with passionate eagerness, Who art Thou, Thou traveller unknown? Tell me, at last, Thy name, for now I know I cannot live till I possess Thee as my possession: sometimes knocking at the door, loud and long, till at last the sound is heard above the din of the world, the

Angelic Life in connection with Man. 325

applause of men, and the clank of gold. Oh! there is no moment, from the earliest dawn of reason to this last hour in this church, in which, if you would but open your eyes, you will not see His infinite love and watchful righteousness bending over you to upbraid you for your neglect, to punish you for your guilt, to sorrow for your cowardice, or to rejoice at your courage; to give you the sympathy of strength, and the life which is born of self-devotion.

And if this be true of our individual, so it is also true of our domestic, social, and national life. When the angel came to Manoah's altar, the truth was revealed that God takes interest in each man's home; that it should be pure and happy, a sacred altar of love, a school for sympathy and forbearance; a centre from which an impulse for wider work may spring, and whence self-sacrifice in daily trifles may swell into the self-sacrifice of a life for universal objects; a place where warriors may be trained for the army of Christ against the evil, a place where the heavenly life may be imaged forth by each living in the life of all. That was God's deep interest in old poetic times, and it is His deep interest now. Without that belief, there is a bitter taste of transiency in the sweet waters of home, an element of separation in the closest union; with that belief, home is secured as an everlasting possession, and is pervaded by the very spirit which unites God to the universe, and the universe to Him.

Nor is the related interference of angelic powers with social and national movements without a meaning to us now. If it tells us in the form of certain stories that

God was watching over and guiding Jewish society and Jewish national life, it tells us that God is watching over and directing English society and the English nation, every society and every nation. And God knows that we want here in England some belief of that sort to protect us from despair and the sloth and indifference which are born of despair. The apparent irreconcileability of the results of science with the faith which we hold most dear, not only with the worship of the heart in prayer, but even with the existence of God as a personal Will at all, have so confused and troubled us with a multitude of reasonings opposed to feelings, and of feelings opposed to phenomena, so troubled us with mysteries which we cannot solve without apparently flying in the face of truths on both sides of the questions, that more than two-thirds of the thinking men of England are wearied out, and, like men in mist upon a mountain, who can neither go backward nor forward without deeper perplexity, determine to leave all these things aside, and to resolve life into its simplest elements—eat and drink and do the work which each day says that they must do, search after truth which can be demonstrated, and leave the deep questions of life to solve themselves, if they are to be solved at all. These men, men who while hopeless are yet true, take refuge in a stern performance of their nearest duties, and they do them with a concealed fierceness and bitterness which is born of their hopelessness.

There are others, not strong but frivolous, not actual men but shadows of men, who take the dicta of the higher souls because it suits their desires, and whispering to themselves, 'There is no God, no hope for the world,' give themselves up to disregard for everything but self-amusement. Their motto is, though they keep it hidden—for a kind of spasmodic earnestness is the fashion—'Let us eat and drink, for to-morrow we die;' and their practice is to have the indifference of the Stoic without his morality, the irreverence of the Cynic without his austerity, and the life of the Epicurean without his enjoyment.

Between the thinkers and those who live for pleasure and fashion lies the great money-making, position-seeking body of society. The unbelief in God, which shows itself as hopelessness in one class of men, and as reckless enjoyment of the present followed by satiety in another, descends as a subtle influence upon the third class of persons I have mentioned; and among them has resulted in a curious relaxation of common morality, in a dulness of the social conscience. It manifests itself chiefly in an astonishing dishonesty in business life, and in a still more astonishing system of glossing over wickedness with specious excuses. The speculating banker who fails is not as guilty in the eyes of society as the robber who has carried off a few sovereigns, and struck down the owner; though the former has dragged hundreds with him into ruin, and the latter has only maimed a man.

The seducer who has torn from Eden an innocent girl, or betrayed the wife of his friend, can be still, and is still if he have power, rank, or wealth, received into society which would shrink with horror from touching the hand of the man who had revenged a similar wrong in the blood of the offender, and lay under sentence of death. Which of the two has committed the worse murder? I know who is guiltiest in the eyes of God. No one asks society to hang the seducer; but what sort of social morality is that which does not inflict any social punishment upon him?

The shopkeeper who daily poisons the poor, or who works his men to death to outsell his neighbour, or the tradesman who puts forth base wares at the price of good, or the shipowners who send forth on the coast of England more than four hundred rotten vessels every year, of which two hundred perish, are still received in their society as men who are getting on well in the world, and themselves can go to church, and take the Sacrament, and thank God they are not like the outcast crouching under the arch, or the miserable drunkard reeling home to a fever-haunted room, when, in the eyes of Almighty Justice, they are ten times as criminal, and all their gold is accursed, dark with the stains of human tears and the rust of the blood of men.

In face of these things there are some men who still dare to hope, and who point to the history of the Jewish nation as representative history. The same faithlessness, the same pleasure-hunting, the same dishonesty, the same wickedness, went on in the Jerusalem of Isaiah's time, and God rescued the nation from this abyss by judgment and by love. Therefore, till God is proved to be dead, we cannot let go our hopes for the nation, nor cease to labour, as if we *knew* that labour for God is incapable of failure. In the very determination of the thinkers, who have become infidel, to suffer no more shams, to look only at real things, to pursue after truth and truth alone, no matter if they lose all, there is an element of such new good in the future as seems to me quite incalculable. They have been living in a world of unrealities, and they have been talking and acting as if they were face to face with real beliefs. The first step to a true faith in God by which they can live, is to expose these unrealities relentlessly; and I, for my part, thank God for the rigid, unbending determination with which some men are now possessed to strip their souls naked of all merely conventional forms of truth, and to face the wilderness bitterly but bravely. Truth so sought will come; and as the true system of the universe arose only when the impossibility of past systems had been demonstrated, so a higher belief in God will spring out of the demonstration that past systems of theology, useful in their time, are incapable of meeting the difficulties and the problems of this age. The solution may be distant yet, for it seems to be true that we must pass through a phase of unbelief before we can step into a higher region of belief; but even in the unbelief there is a voice which forbids us to despair. What do we see in the religion of Positivism, the last intellectual phase of infidelity? We see, in spite of a rejection of immortality, unbounded hope for the progress of the race; a stern assertion of morality; a deep and universal sympathy for men, and eagerness to redeem them from physical evil and moral wrong; a sympathy for the race as a race which has never yet existed in society. These elements, which the Comtist sometimes forgets are directly derived from Christ's teaching, have been, it is true, not worked out in their universality by Christians who have an unchristian dislike to the word universal. We thank the Comtist for taking the ideas of Christ and showing to us how they may be expanded. We thank him especially for leavening the nominally unchristian and sceptical portion of society with these Christian ideas. I cannot but believe that the spirit of Christ's teaching, thus infused into men, even though it be only partially given, and mingled with so much error and with such a wretched practical mistake as the denial of the immortality of the personal soul, will descend through society to enkindle and wake the pleasure-hunter to a truer life, and to shame fashion out of its extravagance, and indifference into enthusiasm for the welfare of the race. Nor will dishonesty, and corruption, and public wickedness, and mere grasping of gain at the price of the lives of men and women, long bear up against a renovated public opinion.

And when God has thus brought by strange ways the body of English society into a more active life of self-sacrifice, a higher morality, and a wider love of the race, then I cannot but think that men will turn with new eyes to contemplate the life of Christ, and see in Him the true King of the new society; the real Teacher of all that is true in the religion of the Comtist; the highest enthusiast; the ideal of the true democrat and of the true aristocrat; the source of the bonds which alone can destroy national jealousies and national wars; the glorious proof and guarantee that humanity can become divine; the redeemer from, and the conqueror of evil; and the true leader of all the faithful souls of men in the battle against evil. For in Him alone, of all that ever lived upon this earth, was manifested that life of God which is the true life of the race, the life which is found negatively in absolute denial of self-life, positively in absolute giving of all that we are to form the life of others; a life which, here necessarily linked to suffering, is destined to become in the perfect society that which it is to God Himself, the very joy and ecstasy of being.

And now, to sweep back for a moment to our first subject, we have found a ground for the hope that the future society will be constituted as a host warring against evil, under the leadership of Christ. If that be so, we shall not be devoid of the sympathy, nor apart from the communion, of the other spiritual beings who may inhabit God's universe. Their life is no lazy dream, no indolent enjoyment. The spirit of the battle against evil is the spirit of their life. For 'there was war in heaven; Michael and his angels fought against the dragon.' When we read that stanza in the symbolic poem of the Apocalypse, our soul kindles. We have brother warriors, purer than we, who are waging the same great contest, and who watch us with faithful and sympathizing eyes. The hosts of earth and heaven are bound together by the comrade spirit, by a common indignation, by a common devotion to the same Leader. We can only conjecture why He has permitted evil, why He does not crush it; but it is enough for us, angels and men, that we have to fight against it. It is enough for us men to feel, as we do feel, that the more we throw ourselves into the war of Michael and the angels, the nobler becomes our nature, the keener our sense of a never-failing life, the more intimate our union with the natural home of the heart of man, the spirit of the perfect God.

ISAAC'S CHARACTER.

Genesis xxxv. 27—29.

THE lives of Abraham and Jacob are as attractive as the life of Isaac is apparently unattractive. The former has supplied materials for historians, preachers, and moralists, the latter has been left comparatively untouched. The reason of this is that the character of Isaac had few salient features. It had no great faults, it had no striking virtues; it was not boldly outlined like that of Abraham, which stands forth as if chiselled by Michael Angelo; it was not full of sharp and unexpected angles like that of Jacob; it is the quietest, smoothest, most silent character in the Old Testament. I might say that it was also the deepest, were it not that Isaac was weak, and the profoundest depths of character are due to strength of will.

And it is owing to this that there are so few remarkable events in the life of Isaac, for the remarkableness of events is created by the character which meets them. If Abraham's character had descended to his son, Isaac's history would have been a chequered one. Only see how Jacob's ambitious, scheming, pushing temperament made his life a continual scene of change.

Again, the character of Isaac was contemplative. Whatever were his spiritual struggles, they went on unseen in the hermitage of his own breast. None had ever sounded the depths of his feeling or his thought. He possessed the sadness which accompanies sensitiveness and reserve, and it is touching to feel how his life contradicted the meaning of his name. But it was no passionate melancholy. No bitter grief, no wild agony of wrestling with God, no moments of overwhelming doubt of God's justice passed over the quiet lake of Isaac's soul, brooding ever much upon itself. Such men make but little outward impression. The world does not care to read a character which does not express itself in action. Isaac's history has been neglected.

I make one more remark in introduction.

It seems to be a law that all national, social, and personal life should advance by alternate expansions and contractions. The wave of progress recedes before it rises higher on the strand. After a revolution, a few years of national repose occur before the people settle down into the new order; after a reformation, a general weariness of the subjects most insisted upon during the years of reform; after a crisis in a man's personal life, a period of stillness. Exhausted energies claim rest before they can recover sufficiently to push forward on a fresh career.

We meet this law, as we may call it, here. A great and new impulse had entered history when Abraham went forth to Canaan. Full of a sublime purpose, endowed with fiery energy and quickness of resolution, Abraham pushed the world forward. Pervading all his qualities was a deep and simple faith in God, which producing a stern sense of duty and an unquestioning obedience, knit

Isaac's Character. 335

together all his energies into a life for God, and made the impulse which he gave the world religious.

Now characters strong in action, and strong in suffering, seem to exhaust for a time the activity as well as the capability of pain possible to any family. There are but few instances where a great father has had a son who equalled him in greatness. The old power more often re-appears in Jacob than in Isaac. The spirit of Abraham's energy passed over his son to his son's son.

We ask, first, what were the circumstances which formed the character of Isaac.

He was an only son. Ishmael had been banished soon after his birth. He lived without any youthful companions. It was natural that he should become the sober, sensitive, silent child. The natural brightness and activity of a boy, when they are not drawn out by association with other children, are thrown inwards upon himself, and are transmuted into the activity only of reverie and the brightness only of delight in the visions which come to solitude.

Again, Isaac's parents were both very old. Thus an atmosphere of antique quiet hung around his life. There was in Abraham's tent, when the boy began to open his questioning eyes upon the world, an evening air of finished life, of silent waiting for the great change, of peaceful victory over trials, of calm repose upon the memory of an active past. This also subtly influenced the character of Isaac.

Again, these two old hearts lived for him alone. On him the pent-up parental love of many, many years was out-poured. His youth was sheltered as much as his childhood from the rough winds of life. Surrounded by the infinite delicacy of the experienced tenderness of old age —a tenderness doubly tender from the great shock it had suffered on Mount Gerizim—Isaac grew up to manhood.

So was moulded the man of thought and gentleness, while the man, like Jacob, of active and stormy life, was formed for his work by the struggle at home with Esau, was tried by the favouritism of his father, and sent out at last in loneliness to fight single-handed the battle of existence.

These, in brief, were the early influences which built up the character of Isaac. It is a character difficult to define, appearing far more from the absence than from the presence of things said and done; but we shall find his excellences and his faults exemplified in his life.

I take the excellences of his character first.

1. The first scene in which Isaac appears is on the ascent to Mount Gerizim. Both old man and young went up the slope alone. Isaac kept silence. Once only, as he laded himself with the fire and wood, did he question, quickly, 'Where is the lamb?' &c. He must have seen the trouble in his father's eyes, he must have noticed the constraint of manner, the signs of suppressed and mysterious sorrow, and there may have flashed upon his heart with a shock of horrible pain a thought familiar then to dwellers in Canaan, the thought of human sacrifice. Was Abraham victimless, because *he* was the victim? Yet he was still, and spoke no word. His trust in his father was entire. We read of no struggle, of no unmanly prayers, only of the submissive self-surrender in obedience unto

death, because what Abraham willed was also the will of Isaac.

In this he was a noble type indeed of Christ. Isaac, in the highest moment perhaps of his whole life, shadowed forth the perfect sacrifice of Him who was all that Isaac could not be.

Christian brethren, if you cannot in your life, as these old patriarchs did, typify Christ before He came, revealing glimpses of the perfect Man to come, you can make Him manifest now to men by setting your existence to the music of His Life. Oh! if God calls you, as He may, to give up youth, love, fame, noble prospects, as Abraham called on Isaac, then do so in Isaac's spirit—silent submission, unmurmuring obedience, deep faith that your Father loves you and knows best.

The next excellence of the character of Isaac was his tender constancy. It arose out of, or at least was deeply coloured by, the peculiar quietude of his temperament. It is exemplified in the story of his mother's death and of his marriage. He was forty years old when Sarah passed away. We should imagine that Isaac would not feel this loss much, for there could be little in common between a son and a mother separated by an interval of ninety years of age. But the habitudes of life to a man like Isaac are strong as iron chains, and the forcible severing of one of them makes him feel rudderless and adrift. His grief was not violent but deep, deep from the natural constancy of a silent heart. He could not bear the clamour of the encampment, it was intrusive; he could not bear the sight of the tent in the evening when his mother used to welcome him, for it made him

sadly conscious of a great want. Above all things, a
character like his demanded female sympathy. Deprived
of his mother's love, he wandered out to the fields
when the glow of the setting sun had reddened all the
sky, and drew into his soul calm from the peacefulness of
eventide. There he confided to the great Mother and to
God the sorrow which could not speak, the hopes which
thrilled him when he thought of Eliezer's mission. One
evening, as he walked, he saw the camels draw near from
the eastward; he turned, and found the answer to his
prayer in the sympathy which filled with tears the eyes of
Rebekah.

We are not told that he married a second wife. Of
all the patriarchs he alone had tender constancy enough
never to need any other solace than the first affection
of his manhood. He alone represented to the Jewish
nation the ideal of true marriage. He is the only
Hebrew in the Bible who appears to share in a more
northern type of character. Nay, there is, even in his
constancy to the memory of his mother and to his
wife, something of the coolness of a man whose passions were not capable of storm. There was no eastern
violence in his grief; nothing can be quieter than
the way he takes his marriage. Abraham seems to
manage the whole thing for him : he allows a servant
to choose his wife; he takes no visible interest in the
embassy to Haran. A man, apparently, who would
rather let events come and find him, and then be con-
tented with them, than one who would either seek for
events or lead them ; a man whose constancy was a natural
instinct rather than a virtue; who once put into any

position, such as marriage, would stay there and not feel the energy which might make the position so wearisome as to lead him to desire a change.

Of this kind also was his piety. It was as natural to him as to a woman to trust and love; not strongly, but constantly, sincerely. From his earliest years, through his still and dependent character, he received unquestioning his father's God and rested his heart upon the Lord. His trust became the habit of his soul. His days were knit each to each by natural piety. He had no doubt, no dark hours of passionate prayer, no fervent agony of soul. We may too much neglect him on account of this, for the strong man who has been brought close to God out of desperate struggle is more interesting, because apparently more heroic, than a tranquil man who has known the Heavenly Father from his youth. But we are much mistaken in our neglect. To have unquestioning faith is the highest blessedness of man, and many a poor woman and illiterate man who have never doubted, because they have never lived in the spirit of the world; never had any ecstasy in forgiveness because they have never sinned deeply, are far nearer Heaven than a man like Jacob. To have served God simply, calmly, unbrokenly, like Isaac, is indeed blessed. It is not without comfort and relief that we turn from the grandeur of Abraham's long life-contest, and from the slow, tempestuous, sorrowful growth of Jacob's religion, to the secluded, restful, continuous religious life of Isaac. Many a Jew, in after times, who could never have reached the height of Abraham's life, who could not sympathize with the burning force of Isaiah's heart, or with the impassioned sorrow of Jeremiah, must have looked back and found repose in contemplating the still valley of existence where the religion of Isaac worshipped and advanced. And many a Christian now, who perhaps thinks himself not so near to God as his friend, because he does not feel his struggle or his ecstasy of soul, may find in Isaac the prototype of his own life, and know that God is with him as He was with Isaac. It is true, it is a moment of rapture when one who has been worldly, sinful, thoughtless, like Jacob, finds his God at last; but it is more blessed still when a man can have, like Isaac, the thought that he has grown naturally, like a flower, from youth to manhood, into the likeness of the Heavenly Father.

We turn now to *the faults of the character of Isaa*

I have said of him that he was a man who would rather let events come and find him, than seek for or lead events. There had descended to him nothing of the lightning-like activity of Abraham, who, to rescue his relation and to vindicate a wrong, pursued all night in a forced march, surprised, and routed the army of the four kings. Isaac was slow, indifferent, inactive. We find this exemplified in the story of the wells. (Gen. xxvi. 18—22.)

There are times, and this was one of them, when war is necessary. Good, fair fighting is the only way to cut some knots and to settle some questions; and at such times the anything-for-peace party do this evil especially —they sacrifice the welfare of the future to their ease in the present.

This is exactly what Isaac was now doing. It was all-

Isaac's Character. 341

important for Abraham's family that they should be respected by the Canaanites. If they lost their reputation for bravery and for defence of their own rights, they would be treated as the weak are treated; one by one they would have perished, and the nation of Israel had never been. In these circumstances Isaac should not have given way.

But this is not Christian; we are told joyfully to suffer wrongs. I answer, first, that those were not Christian times; and secondly, that even if they had been so, the founder of a nation or the ruler of a tribe is not bound by the same rules of conduct as an Apostle, though he is bound by the same principles. Their work is different. If a settler in the backwoods were to allow Indians to cut his corn with impunity, it would not be long before his whole household would be slaughtered, and such a contempt created among the Indians for his fellow-settlers, that they in turn would suffer. There would be nothing Christian in that conduct; for though a man ought to forgive an injury, he must also defend public law; though he may give way on a personal point, as Abraham did to Lot, when no interests but his own were involved, he must not give way when the interests of others are engaged.

It is the mistake of such characters as Isaac, that they take a kind of pride in their willingness to forgive and their readiness to suffer wrong, and call this Christian, when in reality it is a want of power to feel a just indignation, and the desire to lead an undisturbed life, which are the reasons for their apparent self-surrender. The error of this impassiveness is great, for it entails misfortune on others who do feel acutely, and who have to bear the burden and heat of the injury. Isaac sat still in his tent while his herdsmen fought his battles for him; and when the noise became importunate upon his dainty meditation, gave way, left the place, and brought double trouble upon his people. All he wanted was tranquillity; he did not think of the comfort of others.

The same weakness, ending in selfishness, appears again in the history of Isaac's lie to Abimelech. Into the critical question about the repetition of the same story in Abraham's and Isaac's life, I do not enter. But looked at in contrast with Isaac's fearless silence when at the point of death under the knife of Abraham, this fear of being slain is curious as a mental problem.

The solution may be this. Isaac's character would lead him to acquiesce in the inevitable. Let him once know that death was certain, and he could die bravely; but he quailed before the imagination of death. So, provided he could escape from the haunting fear which, because it kept him in suspense, disturbed the even tenor of his life, he would not shrink from a lie, especially as it wore the aspect of a truth. Many of the greatest temptations of these sensitive and unpractical characters arise from the predominance of imagination over the will and the conscience. It is not only conscience which doth make cowards of us all. Isaac yielded to an imagined fear, and lied.

It is one of the melancholy results of a false view of Bible history and of inspiration that commentators are driven to immoral shifts and shuffling, in order to whiten over the dark spots in the lives of the Old Testament saints. We are told by one who should have known better, 'that Isaac did right to evade the difficulty as long as he could lawfully, and to wait and see if God would interpose.' This is quite miserable. A lie is a lie, and the lie of Isaac was a very shameful lie. It was the cowardice of involving his wife in possible dishonour that he might save his own life; it was throwing, by a deceit, the whole burden of a difficulty upon the shoulders of a woman.

Look at its results. Isaac had, so to speak, accredited deception within his household. The poison had been introduced which bore fruit in Rebekah's deceit and in Jacob's determined falsehood at a most solemn moment. From that time forth we seem also to feel, we know not why, that Rebekah's respect for her husband was destroyed. There is no longer any true community of interests or feeling between them. All goes wrong.

Brethren, no sin escapes its punishment; and a father's sin taints a household. Let fear drive you to swerve from honour; lie like Isaac to gain your point, if you will, but do not wonder afterwards if your son prefers his life to his honour, the 'blessing of prosperity' to the sacred rights of truth, to the welfare of a brother, and to the peace of a father's heart. It is your punishment, not arbitrary, but natural. Plant a lie in your life, and some bitter winter day you will have to eat its fruit.

In one other way the weakness which arose from Isaac's easiness of character manifested itself; in the division between his sons. He took no pains to harmonize Jacob and Esau with one another. He fell into the fault of meditative men, of men who live in their own world of thought; the fault of letting things take their course, lest interference should disturb him. Hence the curse of favouritism prevailed in his tent. Every one can see that Esau's character was a reaction from his father's, and for this very reason—that Isaac saw in his eldest son the qualities of daring and activity which he had not—he loved him most. He admired the bold hunter; he looked down on Jacob, who dwelt smoothly in the tent, in whom he saw his own faults modified or magnified. Hence arose a further division between Isaac and Rebekah. The woman adopted the cause of the neglected son, and practised with him against her husband and her eldest born. It is a sad spectacle. It is more; it is a solemn warning to the parents of this congregation. Look to it, I say, that laziness of contemplation and love of ease do not end in injustice, and injustice end in a household divided against itself; in an alienated wife, a son whose brave heart is turned to gall and revenge, another who goes forth into the world to cheat and shuffle and compromise, and only after long and weary pilgrimage to find rest at last in truth. It is wretched to think how many a home is ruined, as Isaac's was, by the fear of falsehood, sloth or favouritism, of a parent.

There is one more accusation usually made against Isaac—his love of savoury meat. But I do not speak of this so much as a fault as a natural consequence of his temperament and mode of life. An inactive man who has but little enjoyment in out-door exercise, or who, as we may suppose was the case with Isaac, allows himself to be so mastered by a physical misfortune, such as blindness, as always to keep his couch, very often becomes a slave to his appetites. Their gratification supplies him with the stimulus which an energetic man would derive from work. It is curious to see that Isaac seemed to have needed this stimulus prior to any mental exercise of foresight or will. This need, this pitiable love of savoury things, which seems never to have degenerated into gluttony, is quite in accordance with his general character. It only teaches us the great lesson that the body revenges itself for neglect of its laws. If we will not take healthy impulses from physical exercise towards the work of the brain and of the spirit, we must supply their place by unhealthy expedients, for man cannot live without some stimulus or other. We substitute our own way for God's way, we run counter to the universe, and we reap what we have sown in our body, and the body disturbs the mind, and the mind the spirit, and we are all unhinged. Let the man who spends a dreamy, sedentary, idle life beware lest he drop into a querulous old age, and end in becoming a mere lover of savoury meat.

Lastly. If the faults of Isaac were great, yet his excellences on the whole were greater. One sorrowful day, the day of his son's deceit, he saw what his weakness had done. He seems to me to have then looked in the face the fault of his whole character, and repented of it. I say this because I cannot otherwise account for the accession of strength which his character and the clear insight which his mind seem suddenly to have gained. It required strength of will to hold fast to the blessing he had pronounced on Jacob in spite of the passionate grief of his best-loved son. It required great insight, in spite of his own favouritism of the one and of the deceit of the other, to recognize beneath what was base in his younger son a higher character than that of Esau. From this moment I date the redemption of Isaac's character from his faults. He was left alone, and for many years we hear no more of the good old man. But we catch a last glimpse of him, and it is a happy one. To him, dwelling at Hebron, came his son Jacob, rich, blessed of God, with a goodly train of sons. And as Isaac saw the youths, he felt that the promise of Abraham's God was being fulfilled. He saw himself the father of many nations. His heart rejoiced in the future glory of his people.

Then came the last scene of this silent life. Beside his dying bed stood both his sons, reconciled to one another. His death united in love those whom his weakness and favouritism had separated. The scars of his life were healed. God was good to him, and gave him rest. Brightness was round the old man's head, and peace in the old man's heart, when death came tenderly and gathered Isaac to his fathers.

CLAY AND TAYLOR, PRINTERS, BUNGAY.

A LIST OF

C. KEGAN PAUL AND CO.'S
PUBLICATIONS.

7.81.

1, *Paternoster Square, London.*

A LIST OF
C. KEGAN PAUL AND CO.'S PUBLICATIONS.

ADAMS (F. O.), F.R.G.S.
The History of Japan. From the Earliest Period to the Present Time. New Edition, revised. 2 volumes. With Maps and Plans. Demy 8vo. Cloth, price 21s. each.

ADAMS (W. D.).
Lyrics of Love, from Shakespeare to Tennyson. Selected and arranged by. Fcap. 8vo. Cloth extra, gilt edges, price 3s. 6d.

ADAMSON (H. T.), B.D.
The Truth as it is in Jesus. Crown 8vo. Cloth, price 8s. 6d.

The Three Sevens. Crown 8vo. Cloth, price 5s. 6d.

A. K. H. B.
From a Quiet Place. A New Volume of Sermons. Crown 8vo. Cloth, price 5s.

ALBERT (Mary).
Holland and her Heroes to the year 1585. An Adaptation from Motley's "Rise of the Dutch Republic." Small crown 8vo. Cloth, price, 4s. 6d.

ALLEN (Rev. R.), M.A.
Abraham; his Life, Times, and Travels, 3,800 years ago. Second Edition. With Map. Post 8vo. Cloth, price 6s.

ALLEN (Grant), B.A.
Physiological Æsthetics. Large post 8vo. 9s.

ALLIES (T. W.), M.A.
Per Crucem ad Lucem. The Result of a Life. 2 vols. Demy 8vo. Cloth, price 25s.

A Life's Decision. Crown 8vo. Cloth, price 7s. 6d.

AMATEUR.
A Few Lyrics. Small crown 8vo. Cloth, price 2s.

ANDERSON (Col. R. P.).
Victories and Defeats. An Attempt to explain the Causes which have led to them. An Officer's Manual. Demy 8vo. Cloth, price 14s.

ANDERSON (R. C.), C.E.
Tables for Facilitating the Calculation of every Detail in connection with Earthen and Masonry Dams. Royal 8vo. Cloth, price £2 2s.

Antiope. A Tragedy. Large crown 8vo. Cloth, price 6s.

ARCHER (Thomas).
About my Father's Business. Work amidst the Sick, the Sad, and the Sorrowing. Crown 8vo. Cloth, price 2s. 6d.

ARMSTRONG (Richard A.), B.A.
Latter-Day Teachers. Six Lectures. Small crown 8vo. Cloth, price 2s. 6d.

Army of the North German Confederation.
A Brief Description of its Organization, of the Different Branches of the Service and their *rôle* in War, of its Mode of Fighting, &c. &c. Translated from the Corrected Edition, by permission of the Author, by Colonel Edward Newdigate. Demy 8vo. Cloth, price 5s.

ARNOLD (Arthur).
Social Politics. Demy 8vo. Cloth, price 14s.

Free Land. Crown 8vo. Cloth, price 6s.

A List of C. Kegan Paul & Co.'s Publications. 3

AUBERTIN (J. J.).
Camoens' Lusiads. Portuguese Text, with Translation by. With Map and Portraits. 2 vols. Demy 8vo. Price 30s.

Seventy Sonnets of Camoens'. Portuguese text and translation, with some original poems. Dedicated to Captain Richard F. Burton. Printed on hand-made paper. Cloth, bevelled boards, gilt top, price 7s. 6d.

Aunt Mary's Bran Pie. By the author of "St. Olave's." Illustrated. Cloth, price 3s. 6d.

AVIA.
The Odyssey of Homer Done into English Verse. Fcap. 4to. Cloth, price 15s.

BADGER (George Perry), D.C.L.
An English-Arabic Lexicon. In which the equivalents for English words and idiomatic sentences are rendered into literary and colloquial Arabic. Royal 4to. Cloth, price £9 9s.

BAGEHOT (Walter).
Some Articles on the Depreciation of Silver, and Topics connected with it. Demy 8vo. Price 5s.

The English Constitution. A New Edition, Revised and Corrected, with an Introductory Dissertation on Recent Changes and Events. Crown 8vo. Cloth, price 7s. 6d.

Lombard Street. A Description of the Money Market. Seventh Edition. Crown 8vo. Cloth, price 7s. 6d.

BAGOT (Alan).
Accidents in Mines: their Causes and Prevention. Crown 8vo. Cloth, price 6s.

BAKER (Sir Sherston, Bart.).
Halleck's International Law; or Rules Regulating the Intercourse of States in Peace and War. A New Edition, Revised, with Notes and Cases. 2 vols. Demy 8vo. Cloth, price 38s.

BAKER (Sir Sherston, Bart.)—
continued.
The Laws relating to Quarantine. Crown 8vo. Cloth, price 12s. 6d.

BALDWIN (Capt. J. H.), F.Z.S.
The Large and Small Game of Bengal and the North-Western Provinces of India. 4to. With numerous Illustrations. Second Edition. Cloth, price 21s.

BANKS (Mrs. G. L.).
God's Providence House. New Edition. Crown 8vo. Cloth, price 3s. 6d.

Ripples and Breakers. Poems. Square 8vo. Cloth, price 5s.

BARLEE (Ellen).
Locked Out: a Tale of the Strike. With a Frontispiece. Royal 16mo. Cloth, price 1s. 6d.

BARNES (William).
An Outline of English Speechcraft. Crown 8vo. Cloth, price 4s.

Poems of Rural Life, in the Dorset Dialect. New Edition, complete in 1 vol. Crown 8vo. Cloth, price 8s. 6d.

Outlines of Redecraft (Logic). With English Wording. Crown 8vo. Cloth, price 3s.

BARTLEY (George C. T.).
Domestic Economy: Thrift in Every Day Life. Taught in Dialogues suitable for Children of all ages. Small crown 8vo. Cloth, limp, 2s.

BAUR (Ferdinand), Dr. Ph.
A Philological Introduction to Greek and Latin for Students. Translated and adapted from the German of. By C. KEGAN PAUL, M.A. Oxon., and the Rev. E. D. STONE, M.A., late Fellow of King's College, Cambridge, and Assistant Master at Eton. Second and revised edition. Crown 8vo. Cloth, price 6s.

BAYNES (Rev. Canon R. H.).
At the Communion Time. A Manual for Holy Communion. With a preface by the Right Rev.

BAYNES (Rev. Canon R. H.)—*continued.*
the Lord Bishop of Derry and Raphoe. Cloth, price 1s. 6d.
⁎ Can also be had bound in French morocco, price 2s. 6d.; Persian morocco, price 3s.; Calf, or Turkey morocco, price 3s. 6d.

BELLINGHAM (Henry), Barrister-at-Law.
Social Aspects of Catholicism and Protestantism in their Civil Bearing upon Nations. Translated and adapted from the French of M. le Baron de Haulleville. With a Preface by His Eminence Cardinal Manning. Second and cheaper edition. Crown 8vo. Cloth, price 3s. 6d.

BENNETT (Dr. W. C.).
Narrative Poems & Ballads. Fcap. 8vo. Sewed in Coloured Wrapper, price 1s.

Songs for Sailors. Dedicated by Special Request to H. R. H. the Duke of Edinburgh. With Steel Portrait and Illustrations. Crown 8vo. Cloth, price 3s. 6d.
An Edition in Illustrated Paper Covers, price 1s.

Songs of a Song Writer. Crown 8vo. Cloth, price 6s.

BENT (J. Theodore).
Genoa. How the Republic Rose and Fell. With 18 Illustrations. Demy 8vo. Cloth, price 18s.

BETHAM - EDWARDS (Miss M.).
Kitty. With a Frontispiece. Crown 8vo. Cloth, price 6s.

BEVINGTON (L. S.).
Key Notes. Small crown 8vo. Cloth, price 5s.

Blue Roses; or, Helen Malinofska's Marriage. By the Author of "Véra." 2 vols. Fifth Edition. Cloth, gilt tops, 12s.
⁎ Also a Cheaper Edition in 1 vol. With Frontispiece. Crown 8vo. Cloth, price 6s.

BLUME (Major W.).
The Operations of the German Armies in France, from Sedan to the end of the war of 1870-

BLUME (Major W.)—*continued.*
71. With Map. From the Journals of the Head-quarters Staff. Translated by the late E. M. Jones, Maj. 20th Foot, Prof. of Mil. Hist., Sandhurst. Demy 8vo. Cloth, price 9s.

BOGUSLAWSKI (Capt. A. von).
Tactical Deductions from the War of 1870-71. Translated by Colonel Sir Lumley Graham, Bart., late 18th (Royal Irish) Regiment. Third Edition, Revised and Corrected. Demy 8vo. Cloth, price 7s.

BONWICK (J.), F.R.G.S.
Egyptian Belief and Modern Thought. Large post 8vo. Cloth, price 10s. 6d.

Pyramid Facts and Fancies. Crown 8vo. Cloth, price 5s.

The Tasmanian Lily. With Frontispiece. Crown 8vo. Cloth, price 5s.

Mike Howe, the Bushranger of Van Diemen's Land. With Frontispiece. New and cheaper edition. Crown 8vo. Cloth, price 3s. 6d.

BOWEN (H. C.), M. A.
English Grammar for Beginners. Fcap. 8vo. Cloth, price 1s.

Studies in English, for the use of Modern Schools. Small crown 8vo. Cloth, price 1s. 6d.

Simple English Poems. English Literature for Junior Classes. In Four Parts. Parts I. and II., price 6d. each, now ready.

BOWRING (Sir John).
Autobiographical Recollections. With Memoir by Lewin B. Bowring. Demy 8vo. Price 14s.

Brave Men's Footsteps. By the Editor of "Men who have Risen." A Book of Example and Anecdote for Young People. With Four Illustrations by C. Doyle. Sixth Edition. Crown 8vo. Cloth, price 3s. 6d.

BRIALMONT (Col. A.).
Hasty Intrenchments. Translated by Lieut. Charles A. Empson, R. A. With Nine Plates. Demy 8vo. Cloth, price 6s.

BRIDGETT (Rev. J. E.).
History of the Holy Eucharist in Great Britain. 2 vols., demy 8vo. Cloth, price 18s.

BRODRICK (The Hon. G. C.).
Political Studies. Demy 8vo. Cloth, price 14s.

BROOKE (Rev. S. A.), M. A.
The Late Rev. F. W. Robertson, M.A., Life and Letters of. Edited by.
I. Uniform with the Sermons. 2 vols. With Steel Portrait. Price 7s. 6d.
II. Library Edition. 8vo. With Portrait. Price 12s.
III. A Popular Edition, in 1 vol. 8vo. Price 6s.

The Spirit of the Christian Life. A New Volume of Sermons. Crown 8vo. Cloth, price 7s. 6d.

Theology in the English Poets. — COWPER, COLERIDGE, WORDSWORTH, and BURNS. Fourth and Cheaper Edition. Post 8vo. Cloth, price 5s.

Christ in Modern Life. Fifteenth and Cheaper Edition. Crown 8vo. Cloth, price 5s.

Sermons. First Series. Eleventh Edition. Crown 8vo. Cloth, price 6s.

Sermons. Second Series. Fourth Edition. Crown 8vo. Cloth, price 7s.

The Fight of Faith. Sermons preached on various occasions. Fifth Edition. Crown 8vo. Cloth, price 7s. 6d.

BROOKE (W. G.), M. A.
The Public Worship Regulation Act. With a Classified Statement of its Provisions, Notes, and Index. Third Edition, Revised and Corrected. Crown 8vo. Cloth, price 3s. 6d.

Six Privy Council Judgments—1850-1872. Annotated by. Third Edition. Crown 8vo. Cloth, price 9s.

BROUN (J. A.).
Magnetic Observations at Trevandrum and Augustia Malley. Vol. I. 4to. Cloth, price 63s.
The Report from above, separately sewed, price 21s.

BROWN (Rev. J. Baldwin).
The Higher Life. Its Reality, Experience, and Destiny. Fifth and Cheaper Edition. Crown 8vo. Cloth, price 5s.

Doctrine of Annihilation in the Light of the Gospel of Love. Five Discourses. Third Edition. Crown 8vo. Cloth, price 2s. 6d.

The Christian Policy of Life. A Book for Young Men of Business. New and Cheaper Edition. Crown 8vo. Cloth, price 3s. 6d.

BROWN (J. Croumbie), LL.D.
Reboisement in France; or, Records of the Replanting of the Alps, the Cevennes, and the Pyrenees with Trees, Herbage, and Bush. Demy 8vo. Cloth, price 12s. 6d.

The Hydrology of Southern Africa. Demy 8vo. Cloth, price 10s. 6d.

BROWNE (W. R.).
The Inspiration of the New Testament. With a Preface by the Rev. J. P. NORRIS, D.D. Fcap. 8vo. Cloth, price 2s. 6d.

BRYANT (W. C.)
Poems. Red-line Edition. With 24 Illustrations and Portrait of the Author. Crown 8vo. Cloth extra, price 7s. 6d.
A Cheaper Edition, with Frontispiece. Small crown 8vo. Cloth, price 3s. 6d.

BURCKHARDT (Jacob).
The Civilization of the Period of the Renaissance in Italy. Authorized translation, by S. G. C. Middlemore. 2 vols. Demy 8vo. Cloth, price 24s.

BURTON (Mrs. Richard).
The Inner Life of Syria, Palestine, and the Holy Land. With Maps, Photographs, and Coloured Plates. 2 vols. Second Edition. Demy 8vo. Cloth, price 24s.
*** Also a Cheaper Edition in one volume. Large post 8vo. Cloth, price 10s. 6d.

BURTON (Capt. Richard F.).
The Gold Mines of Midian and the Ruined Midianite Cities. A Fortnight's Tour in

BURTON (Capt. Richard F.)— *continued.*
North Western Arabia. With numerous Illustrations. Second Edition. Demy 8vo. Cloth, price 18s.
The Land of Midian Revisited. With numerous illustrations on wood and by Chromolithography. 2 vols. Demy 8vo. Cloth, price 32s.

BUSBECQ (Ogier Ghiselin de).
His Life and Letters. By Charles Thornton Forster, M.D. and F. H. Blackburne Daniell, M.D. 2 vols. With Frontispieces. Demy 8vo. Cloth, price 24s.

BUTLER (Alfred J.).
Amaranth and Asphodel. Songs from the Greek Anthology.— I. Songs of the Love of Women. II. Songs of the Love of Nature. III. Songs of Death. IV. Songs of Hereafter. Small crown 8vo. Cloth, price 2s.

BYRNNE (E. Fairfax).
Milicent. A Poem. Small crown 8vo. Cloth, price 6s.

CALDERON.
Calderon's Dramas: The Wonder-Working Magician—Life is a Dream—The Purgatory of St. Patrick. Translated by Denis Florence MacCarthy. Post 8vo. Cloth, price 10s.

CANDLER (H.).
The Groundwork of Belief. Crown 8vo. Cloth, price 7s.

CARPENTER (W. B.), M.D.
The Principles of Mental Physiology. With their Applications to the Training and Discipline of the Mind, and the Study of its Morbid Conditions. Illustrated. Fifth Edition. 8vo. Cloth, price 12s.

CARPENTER (Dr. Philip P.).
His Life and Work. Edited by his brother, Russell Lant Carpenter. With portrait and vignette. Second Edition. Crown 8vo. Cloth, price 7s. 6d.

CAVALRY OFFICER.
Notes on Cavalry Tactics, Organization, &c. With Diagrams Demy 8vo. Cloth, price 12s.

CERVANTES.
The Ingenious Knight Don Quixote de la Mancha. A New Translation from the Originals of 1605 and 1608. By A. J. Duffield. With Notes. 3 vols. demy 8vo. Cloth, price 42s.

CHAPMAN (Hon. Mrs. E. W.).
A Constant Heart. A Story. 2 vols. Cloth, gilt tops, price 12s.

CHEYNE (Rev. T. K.).
The Prophecies of Isaiah. Translated, with Critical Notes and Dissertations by. Two vols., demy 8vo. Cloth, price 25s.

Children's Toys, and some Elementary Lessons in General Knowledge which they teach. Illustrated. Crown 8vo. Cloth, price 5s.

Clairaut's Elements of Geometry. Translated by Dr. Kaines, with 145 figures. Crown 8vo. Cloth, price 4s. 6d.

CLARKE (Mary Cowden).
Honey from the Weed. Crown 8vo. Cloth, price 7s.

CLAYDEN (P. W.).
England under Lord Beaconsfield. The Political History of the Last Six Years, from the end of 1873 to the beginning of 1880. Second Edition. With Index, and Continuation to March, 1880. Demy 8vo. Cloth, price 16s.

CLERY (C.), Lieut.-Col.
Minor Tactics. With 26 Maps and Plans. Fifth and Revised Edition. Demy 8vo. Cloth, price 16s.

CLODD (Edward), F.R.A.S.
The Childhood of the World: a Simple Account of Man in Early Times. Sixth Edition. Crown 8vo. Cloth, price 3s.
A Special Edition for Schools. Price 1s.

The Childhood of Religions. Including a Simple Account of the Birth and Growth of Myths and Legends. Third Thousand. Crown 8vo. Cloth, price 5s.
A Special Edition for Schools. Price 1s. 6d.

CLODD (Edward), F.R.A.S.—*continued.*
Jesus of Nazareth. With a brief Sketch of Jewish History to the Time of His Birth. Small crown 8vo. Cloth, price 6s.

COGHLAN (J. Cole), D.D.
The Modern Pharisee and other Sermons. Edited by the Very Rev. A. H. Dickinson, D.D., Dean of Chapel Royal, Dublin. New and cheaper edition. Crown 8vo. Cloth, price 7s. 6d.

COLERIDGE (Sara).
Pretty Lessons in Verse for Good Children, with some Lessons in Latin, in Easy Rhyme. A New Edition. Illustrated. Fcap. 8vo. Cloth, price 3s. 6d.

Phantasmion. A Fairy Tale. With an Introductory Preface by the Right Hon. Lord Coleridge, of Ottery St. Mary. A New Edition. Illustrated. Crown 8vo. Cloth, price 7s. 6d.

Memoir and Letters of Sara Coleridge. Edited by her Daughter. Cheap Edition. With one Portrait. Cloth, price 7s. 6d.

COLLINS (Mortimer).
The Secret of Long Life. Small crown 8vo. Cloth, price 3s. 6d.

Inn of Strange Meetings, and other Poems. Crown 8vo. Cloth, price 5s.

COLOMB (Colonel).
The Cardinal Archbishop. A Spanish Legend in twenty-nine Cancions. Small crown 8vo. Cloth, price 5s.

CONNELL (A. K.).
Discontent and Danger in India. Small crown 8vo. Cloth, price 3s. 6d.

CONWAY (Hugh).
A Life's Idylls. Small crown 8vo. Cloth, price 3s. 6d.

COOKE (Prof. J. P.)
Scientific Culture. Crown 8vo. Cloth, price 1s.

COOPER (H. J.).
The Art of Furnishing on Rational and Æsthetic Principles. New and Cheaper Edition. Fcap. 8vo. Cloth, price 1s. 6d.

COPPÉE (François).
L'Exilée. Done into English Verse with the sanction of the Author by I. O. L. Crown 8vo. Vellum, price 5s.

CORFIELD (Prof.), M.D.
Health. Crown 8vo. Cloth, price 6s.

CORY (William).
A Guide to Modern English History. Part I. MDCCCXV.—MDCCCXXX. Demy 8vo. Cloth, price 9s.

COURTNEY (W. L).
The Metaphysics of John Stuart Mill. Crown 8vo. Cloth, price 5s. 6d.

COWAN (Rev. William).
Poems : Chiefly Sacred, including Translations from some Ancient Latin Hymns. Fcap. 8vo. Cloth, price 5s.

COX (Rev. Sir G. W.), Bart.
A History of Greece from the Earliest Period to the end of the Persian War. New Edition. 2 vols. Demy 8vo. Cloth, price 36s.

The Mythology of the Aryan Nations. New Edition. 2 vols. Demy 8vo. Cloth, price 28s.

A General History of Greece from the Earliest Period to the Death of Alexander the Great, with a sketch of the subsequent History to the present time. New Edition. Crown 8vo. Cloth, price 7s. 6d.

Tales of Ancient Greece. New Edition. Small crown 8vo Cloth, price 6s.

School History of Greece. With Maps. New Edition. Fcap 8vo. Cloth, price 3s. 6d.

The Great Persian War from the Histories of Herodotus. New Edition. Fcap. 8vo. Cloth, price 3s. 6d.

A Manual of Mythology in the form of Question and Answer New Edition. Fcap. 8vo. Cloth, price 3s.

An Introduction to the Science of Comparative Mythology and Folk-Lore. Large crown 8vo. Cloth, price 9s.

COX (Rev. Sir G. W.), Bart., M.A., and EUSTACE HINTON JONES.
Popular Romances of the Middle Ages. Second Edition in one volume. Crown 8vo. Cloth, price 6s.

COX (Rev. Samuel).
A Commentary on the Book of Job. With a Translation. Demy 8vo. Cloth, price 15s.

Salvator Mundi; or, Is Christ the Saviour of all Men? Sixth Edition. Crown 8vo. Cloth, price 5s.

The Genesis of Evil, and other Sermons, mainly Expository. Second Edition. Crown 8vo. Cloth, price 6s.

CRAUFURD (A. H.).
Seeking for Light: Sermons. Crown 8vo. Cloth, price 5s.

CRAVEN (Mrs.).
A Year's Meditations. Crown 8vo. Cloth, price 6s.

CRAWFURD (Oswald).
Portugal, Old and New. With Illustrations and Maps. Demy 8vo. Cloth, price 16s.

CRESSWELL (Mrs. G.).
The King's Banner. Drama in Four Acts. Five Illustrations. 4to. Cloth, price 10s. 6d.

CROZIER (John Beattie), M.B.
The Religion of the Future. Crown 8vo. Cloth, price 6s.

DALTON (John Neale), M.A., R.N.
Sermons to Naval Cadets. Preached on board H.M.S. "Britannia." Second Edition. Small crown 8vo. Cloth, price 3s. 6d.

D'ANVERS (N. R.).
Parted. A Tale of Clouds and Sunshine. With 4 Illustrations. Extra Fcap. 8vo. Cloth, price 3s. 6d.

Little Minnie's Troubles. An Every-day Chronicle. With Four Illustrations by W. H. Hughes. Fcap. Cloth, price 3s. 6d.

D'ANVERS (N. R)—*continued.*

Pixie's Adventures; or, the Tale of a Terrier. With 21 Illustrations. 16mo. Cloth, price 4s. 6d.

Nanny's Adventures; or, the Tale of a Goat. With 12 Illustrations. 16mo. Cloth, price 4s. 6d.

DAVIDSON (Rev. Samuel), D.D., LL.D.
The New Testament, translated from the Latest Greek Text of Tischendorf. A New and thoroughly Revised Edition. Post 8vo. Cloth, price 10s. 6d.

Canon of the Bible: Its Formation, History, and Fluctuations. Third Edition, revised and enlarged. Small crown 8vo. Cloth, price 5s.

DAVIES (G. Christopher).
Rambles and Adventures of Our School Field Club. With Four Illustrations. Crown 8vo. Cloth, price 5s.

DAVIES (Rev. J. L.), M.A.
Theology and Morality. Essays on Questions of Belief and Practice. Crown 8vo. Cloth, price 7s. 6d.

DAVIES (T. Hart.).
Catullus. Translated into English Verse. Crown 8vo. Cloth, price 6s.

DAWSON (George), M.A.
Prayers, with a Discourse on Prayer. Edited by his Wife. Fifth Edition, Crown 8vo. Price 6s.

Sermons on Disputed Points and Special Occasions. Edited by his Wife. Third Edition. Crown 8vo. Cloth, price 6s.

Sermons on Daily Life and Duty. Edited by his Wife. Second Edition. Crown 8vo. Cloth, price 6s.

DE L'HOSTE (Col. E. P.).
The Desert Pastor, Jean Jarousseau. Translated from the French of Eugène Pelletan. With a Frontispiece. New Edition. Fcap. 8vo. Cloth, price 3s. 6d.

DE REDCLIFFE (Viscount Stratford), P.C., K.G., G.C.B.
Why am I a Christian? Fifth Edition. Crown 8vo. Cloth, price 3s.

DESPREZ (Philip S.).
Daniel and John; or, the Apocalypse of the Old and that of the New Testament. Demy 8vo. Cloth, price 12s.

DE TOCQUEVILLE (A.).
Correspondence and Conversations of, with Nassau William Senior, from 1834 to 1859. Edited by M. C. M. Simpson. 2 vols. Post 8vo. Cloth, price 21s.

DE VERE (Aubrey).
Legends of the Saxon Saints. Small crown 8vo. Cloth, price 6s.

Alexander the Great. A Dramatic Poem. Small crown 8vo. Cloth, price 5s.

The Infant Bridal, and other Poems. A New and Enlarged Edition. Fcap. 8vo. Cloth, price 7s. 6d.

The Legends of St. Patrick, and other Poems. Small crown 8vo. Cloth, price 5s.

St. Thomas of Canterbury. A Dramatic Poem. Large fcap. 8vo. Cloth, price 5s.

Antar and Zara: an Eastern Romance. INISFAIL, and other Poems, Meditative and Lyrical. Fcap. 8vo. Price 6s.

The Fall of Rora, the Search after Proserpine, and other Poems, Meditative and Lyrical. Fcap. 8vo. Price 6s.

DOBELL (Mrs. Horace).
Ethelstone, Eveline, and other Poems. Crown 8vo. Cloth, price 6s.

DOBSON (Austin).
Vignettes in Rhyme and Vers de Société. Third Edition. Fcap. 8vo. Cloth, price 5s.

Proverbs in Porcelain. By the Author of "Vignettes in Rhyme." Second Edition. Crown 8vo. 6s.

Dorothy. A Country Story in Elegiac Verse. With Preface. Demy 8vo. Cloth, price 5s.

DOWDEN (Edward), LL.D.
Shakspere: a Critical Study of his Mind and Art. Fifth Edition. Large post 8vo. Cloth, price 12s.

Studies in Literature, 1789-1877. Large post 8vo. Cloth, price 12s.

Poems. Second Edition. Fcap. 8vo. Cloth, price 5s.

DOWNTON (Rev. H.), M.A.
Hymns and Verses. Original and Translated. Small crown 8vo. Cloth, price 3s. 6d.

DREWRY (G. O.), M.D.
The Common-Sense Management of the Stomach. Fifth Edition. Fcap. 8vo. Cloth, price 2s. 6d.

DREWRY (G. O.), M.D., and BARTLETT (H. C.), Ph.D., F.C.S.
Cup and Platter: or, Notes on Food and its Effects. New and cheaper Edition. Small 8vo. Cloth, price 1s. 6d.

DRUMMOND (Miss).
Tripps Buildings. A Study from Life, with Frontispiece. Small crown 8vo. Cloth, price 3s. 6d.

DUFFIELD (A. J.).
Don Quixote. His Critics and Commentators. With a Brief Account of the Minor Works of Miguel de Cervantes Saavedra, and a statement of the end and aim of the greatest of them all. A Handy Book for General Readers. Crown 8vo. Cloth, price 3s. 6d.

DU MONCEL (Count).
The Telephone, the Microphone, and the Phonograph. With 74 Illustrations. Small crown 8vo. Cloth, price 5s.

DUTT (Toru).
A Sheaf Gleaned in French Fields. New Edition, with Portrait. Demy 8vo. Cloth, price 10s. 6d.

A 2

DU VERNOIS (Col. von Verdy).
Studies in leading Troops. An authorized and accurate Translation by Lieutenant H. J. T. Hildyard, 71st Foot. Parts I. and II. Demy 8vo. Cloth, price 7s.

EDEN (Frederick).
The Nile without a Dragoman. Second Edition. Crown 8vo. Cloth, price 7s. 6d.

EDGEWORTH (F. Y.).
Mathematical Psychics: an Essay on the Application of Mathematics to Social Science. Demy 8vo. Cloth, price 7s. 6d.

EDIS (Robert W.).
Decoration and Furniture of Town Houses. A series of Cantor Lectures delivered before the Society of Arts, 1880. Amplified and enlarged, with 29 full-page Illustrations and numerous sketches. Second Edition. Square 8vo. Cloth, price 12s. 6d.

EDMONDS (Herbert).
Well Spent Lives: a Series of Modern Biographies. Crown 8vo. Price 5s.

Educational Code of the Prussian Nation, in its Present Form. In accordance with the Decisions of the Common Provincial Law, and with those of Recent Legislation. Crown 8vo. Cloth, price 2s. 6d.

EDWARDS (Rev. Basil).
Minor Chords; or, Songs for the Suffering: a Volume of Verse. Fcap. 8vo. Cloth, price 3s. 6d.; paper, price 2s. 6d.

ELLIOT (Lady Charlotte).
Medusa and other Poems. Crown 8vo. Cloth, price 6s.

ELLIOTT (Ebenezer), The Corn-Law Rhymer.
Poems. Edited by his Son, the Rev. Edwin Elliott, of St. John's, Antigua. 2 vols. Crown 8vo. Cloth, price 18s.

ELSDALE (Henry).
Studies in Tennyson's Idylls. Crown 8vo. Cloth, price 5s.

ELYOT (Sir Thomas).
The Boke named the Gouernour. Edited from the First Edition of 1531 by Henry Herbert Stephen Croft, M.A., Barrister-at-Law. With Portraits of Sir Thomas and Lady Elyot, copied by permission of her Majesty from Holbein's Original Drawings at Windsor Castle. 2 vols. fcap. 4to. Cloth, price 50s.

Epic of Hades (The).
By the author of "Songs of Two Worlds." Twelfth Edition. Fcap. 8vo. Cloth, price 7s. 6d.
∗ Also an Illustrated Edition with seventeen full-page designs in photomezzotint by GEORGE R. CHAPMAN. 4to. Cloth, extra gilt leaves, price 25s, and a Large Paper Edition, with portrait, price 10s. 6d.

EVANS (Anne).
Poems and Music. With Memorial Preface by Ann Thackeray Ritchie. Large crown 8vo. Cloth, price 7s. 6d.

EVANS (Mark).
The Gospel of Home Life. Crown 8vo. Cloth, price 4s. 6d.

The Story of our Father's Love, told to Children. Fourth and Cheaper Edition. With Four Illustrations. Fcap. 8vo. Cloth, price 1s. 6d.

A Book of Common Prayer and Worship for Household Use, compiled exclusively from the Holy Scriptures. New and Cheaper Edition. Fcap. 8vo. Cloth, price 1s.

The King's Story Book. In three parts. Fcap. 8vo. Cloth, price 1s. 6d. each.
∗ Parts I. and II., with eight illustrations and two Picture Maps, now ready.

EX-CIVILIAN.
Life in the Mofussil; or, Civilian Life in Lower Bengal. 2 vols. Large post 8vo. Price 14s.

FARQUHARSON (M.).
I. Elsie Dinsmore. Crown 8vo. Cloth, price 3s. 6d.

FARQUHARSON (M.)—*continued.*

II. **Elsie's Girlhood.** Crown 8vo. Cloth, price 3s. 6d.

III. **Elsie's Holidays at Roselands.** Crown 8vo. Cloth, price 3s. 6d.

FELKIN (H. M.).
Technical Education in a Saxon Town. Published for the City and Guilds of London Institute for the Advancement of Technical Education. Demy 8vo. Cloth, price 2s.

FIELD (Horace), B.A. Lond.
The Ultimate Triumph of Christianity. Small crown 8vo. Cloth, price 3s. 6d.

FINN (the late James), M.R.A.S.
Stirring Times; or, Records from Jerusalem Consular Chronicles of 1853 to 1856. Edited and Compiled by his Widow. With a Preface by the Viscountess STRANGFORD. 2 vols. Demy 8vo. Price 30s.

FLOREDICE (W. H.).
A Month among the Mere Irish. Small crown 8vo. Cloth, price 5s.

Folkestone Ritual Case (The). The Argument, Proceedings, Judgment, and Report, revised by the several Counsel engaged. Demy 8vo. Cloth, price 25s.

FORMBY (Rev. Henry).
Ancient Rome and its Connection with the Christian Religion: an Outline of the History of the City from its First Foundation down to the Erection of the Chair of St. Peter, A.D. 42-47. With numerous Illustrations of Ancient Monuments, Sculpture, and Coinage, and of the Antiquities of the Christian Catacombs. Royal 4to. Cloth extra, price 50s. Roxburgh, half-morocco, price 52s. 6d.

FOWLE (Rev. T. W.), M.A.
The Reconciliation of Religion and Science. Being Essays on Immortality, Inspiration, Miracles, and the Being of Christ. Demy 8vo. Cloth, price 10s. 6d.

The Divine Legation of Christ. Crown 8vo. Cloth, price 7s.

FRASER (Donald).
Exchange Tables of Sterling and Indian Rupee Currency, upon a new and extended system, embracing Values from One Farthing to One Hundred Thousand Pounds, and at Rates progressing, in Sixteenths of a Penny, from 1s. 9d. to 2s. 3d. per Rupee. Royal 8vo. Cloth, price 10s. 6d.

FRISWELL (J. Hain).
The Better Self. Essays for Home Life. Crown 8vo. Cloth, price 6s.

One of Two; or, **A Left-Handed Bride.** With a Frontispiece. Crown 8vo. Cloth, price 3s. 6d.

GARDINER (Samuel R.) and J. BASS MULLINGER, M.A.
Introduction to the Study of English History. Large crown 8vo. Cloth, price 9s.

GARDNER (J.), M.D.
Longevity: The Means of Prolonging Life after Middle Age. Fourth Edition, Revised and Enlarged. Small crown 8vo. Cloth, price 4s.

GARRETT (E.).
By Still Waters. A Story for Quiet Hours. With Seven Illustrations. Crown 8vo. Cloth, price 6s.

GEBLER (Karl Von).
Galileo Galilei and the Roman Curia, from Authentic Sources. Translated with the sanction of the Author, by Mrs. GEORGE STURGE. Demy 8vo. Cloth, price 12s.

GEDDES (James).
History of the Administration of John de Witt, Grand Pensionary of Holland. Vol. I. 1623—1654. Demy 8vo., with Portrait. Cloth, price 15s.

GEORGE (Henry).
Progress and Poverty. An Inquiry into the Cause of Industrial Depressions and of Increase of Want with Increase of Wealth. The Remedy. Post 8vo. Cloth, price 7s. 6d.

GILBERT (Mrs.).
Autobiography and other Memorials. Edited by Josiah

GILBERT (Mrs.)—*continued*.
Gilbert. Third Edition. With Portrait and several Wood Engravings. Crown 8vo. Cloth, price 7s. 6d.

GLOVER (F.), M.A.
Exempla Latina. A First Construing Book with Short Notes, Lexicon, and an Introduction to the Analysis of Sentences. Fcap. 8vo. Cloth, price 2s.

GODWIN (William).
William Godwin: His Friends and Contemporaries. With Portraits and Facsimiles of the handwriting of Godwin and his Wife. By C. Kegan Paul. 2 vols. Demy 8vo. Cloth, price 28s.

The Genius of Christianity Unveiled. Being Essays never before published. Edited, with a Preface, by C. Kegan Paul. Crown 8vo. Cloth, price 7s. 6d.

GOETZE (Capt. A. von).
Operations of the German Engineers during the War of 1870-1871. Published by Authority, and in accordance with Official Documents. Translated from the German by Colonel G. Graham, V.C., C.B., R.E. With 6 large Maps. Demy 8vo. Cloth, price 21s.

GOLDSMID (Sir Francis Henry).
Memoir of. With Portrait. Crown 8vo. Cloth, price 5s.

GOODENOUGH (Commodore J. G.), R.N., C.B., C.M.G.
Memoir of, with Extracts from his Letters and Journals. Edited by his Widow. With Steel Engraved Portrait. Square 8vo. Cloth, 5s.
⁎ Also a Library Edition with Maps, Woodcuts, and Steel Engraved Portrait. Square post 8vo. Cloth, price 14s.

GOSSE (Edmund W.).
Studies in the Literature of Northern Europe. With a Frontispiece designed and etched by Alma Tadema. Large post 8vo. Cloth, price 12s.

New Poems. Crown 8vo. Cloth, price 7s. 6d.

GOULD (Rev. S. Baring), M.A.
Germany, Present and Past. 2 Vols. Demy 8vo. Cloth, price 21s.
The Vicar of Morwenstow: a Memoir of the Rev. R. S. Hawker. With Portrait. Third Edition, revised. Square post 8vo. Cloth, 10s. 6d.

GRAHAM (William), M.A.
The Creed of Science : Religious, Moral, and Social. Demy 8vo. Cloth, price 12s.

GREENOUGH (Mrs. Richard).
Mary Magdalene : A Poem. Large post 8vo. Parchment antique, price 6s.

GRIFFITH (Thomas), A.M.
The Gospel of the Divine Life. A Study of the Fourth Evangelist. Demy 8vo. Cloth, price 14s.

GRIMLEY (Rev. H. N.), M.A.
Tremadoc Sermons, chiefly on the SPIRITUAL BODY, the UNSEEN WORLD, and the DIVINE HUMANITY. Second Edition. Crown 8vo. Cloth, price 6s.

GRÜNER (M. L.).
Studies of Blast Furnace Phenomena. Translated by L. D. B. Gordon, F.R.S.E., F.G.S. Demy 8vo. Cloth, price 7s. 6d.

GURNEY (Rev. Archer).
Words of Faith and Cheer. A Mission of Instruction and Suggestion. Crown 8vo. Cloth, price 6s.

Gwen : A Drama in Monologue. By the Author of the "Epic of Hades." Second Edition. Fcap. 8vo. Cloth, price 5s.

HAECKEL (Prof. Ernst).
The History of Creation. Translation revised by Professor E. Ray Lankester, M.A., F.R.S. With Coloured Plates and Genealogical Trees of the various groups of both plants and animals. 2 vols. Second Edition. Post 8vo. Cloth, price 32s.

The History of the Evolution of Man. With numerous Illustrations. 2 vols. Large post 8vo. Cloth, price 32s.

Freedom in Science and Teaching. From the German of

HAECKEL (Prof. Ernst) — *continued.*
Ernst Haeckel, with a Prefatory Note by T. H. Huxley, F.R.S. Crown 8vo. Cloth, price 5*s.*

HALF-CROWN SERIES.
Sister Dora: a Biography. By Margaret Lonsdale.
True Words for Brave Men. A Book for Soldiers and Sailors. By the late Charles Kingsley.
An Inland Voyage. By R. L. Stevenson.
Travels with a Donkey. By R. L. Stevenson.
A Nook in the Apennines. By Leader Scott.
Notes of Travel. Being Extracts from the Journals of Count Von Moltke.
Letters from Russia. By Count Von Moltke.
English Sonnets. Collected and Arranged by J. Dennis.
Lyrics of Love from Shakespeare to Tennyson. Selected and Arranged by W. D. Adams.
London Lyrics. By Frederick Locker.
Home Songs for Quiet Hours. By the Rev. Canon R. H. Baynes.

Halleck's International Law; or, Rules Regulating the Intercourse of States in Peace and War. A New Edition, revised, with Notes and Cases. By Sir Sherston Baker, Bart. 2 vols. Demy 8vo. Cloth, price 38*s.*

HARDY (Thomas).
A Pair of Blue Eyes. New Edition. With Frontispiece. Crown 8vo. Cloth, price 6*s.*
The Return of the Native. New Edition. With Frontispiece. Crown 8vo. Cloth, price 6*s.*

HARRISON (Lieut.-Col. R.).
The Officer's Memorandum Book for Peace and War. Third Edition. Oblong 32mo. roan, with pencil, price 3*s.* 6*d.*

HARTINGTON (The Right Hon. the Marquis of), M.P.
Election Speeches in 1879 and 1880. With Address to the Electors of North-East Lancashire. Crown 8vo. Cloth, price 3*s.* 6*d.*

HAWEIS (Rev. H. R.), M.A.
Arrows in the Air. Crown 8vo. Second Edition. Cloth, price 6*s.*
Current Coin. Materialism—The Devil—Crime—Drunkenness—Pauperism—Emotion—Recreation—The Sabbath. Third Edition. Crown 8vo. Cloth, price 6*s.*
Speech in Season. Fourth Edition. Crown 8vo. Cloth, price 9*s.*
Thoughts for the Times. Eleventh Edition. Crown 8vo. Cloth, price 7*s.* 6*d.*
Unsectarian Family Prayers. New and Cheaper Edition. Fcap. 8vo. Cloth, price 1*s.* 6*d.*

HAWKER (Robert Stephen).
The Poetical Works of. Now first collected and arranged with a prefatory notice by J. G. Godwin. With Portrait. Crown 8vo. Cloth, price 12*s.*

HAWKINS (Edwards Comerford).
Spirit and Form. Sermons preached in the parish church of Leatherhead. Crown 8vo. Cloth, price 6*s.*

HAWTREY (Edward M.).
Corydalis. A Story of the Sicilian Expedition. Small crown 8vo. Cloth, price 3*s.* 6*d.*

HAYES (A. H.).
New Colorado and the Santa Fé Trail. With map and 60 Illustrations. Crown 8vo. Cloth, price 9*s.*

HEIDENHAIN (Rudolf), M.D.
Animal Magnetism. Physiological Observations. Translated from the Fourth German Edition, by L. C. Wooldridge. With a Preface by G. R. Romanes, F.R.S. Crown 8vo. Cloth, price 2*s.* 6*d.*

HELLWALD (Baron F. von).
The Russians in Central Asia. A Critical Examination, down to the present time, of the

HELLWALD (Baron F. von)—*continued*.
Geography and History of Central Asia. Translated by Lieut.-Col. Theodore Wirgman, LL.B. Large post 8vo. With Map. Cloth, price 12s.

HELVIG (Major H.).
The Operations of the Bavarian Army Corps. Translated by Captain G. S. Schwabe. With Five large Maps. In 2 vols. Demy 8vo. Cloth, price 24s.

Tactical Examples: Vol. I. The Battalion, price 15s. Vol. II. The Regiment and Brigade, price 10s. 6d. Translated from the German by Col. Sir Lumley Graham. With numerous Diagrams. Demy 8vo. Cloth.

HERFORD (Brooke).
The Story of Religion in England. A Book for Young Folk. Crown 8vo. Cloth, price 5s.

HINTON (James).
Life and Letters of. Edited by Ellice Hopkins, with an Introduction by Sir W. W. Gull, Bart., and Portrait engraved on Steel by C. H. Jeens. Second Edition. Crown 8vo. Cloth, 8s. 6d.

Chapters on the Art of Thinking, and other Essays. With an Introduction by Shadworth Hodgson. Edited by C. H. Hinton. Crown 8vo. Cloth, price 8s. 6d.

The Place of the Physician. To which is added ESSAYS ON THE LAW OF HUMAN LIFE, AND ON THE RELATION BETWEEN ORGANIC AND INORGANIC WORLDS. Second Edition. Crown 8vo. Cloth, price 3s. 6d.

Physiology for Practical Use. By various Writers. With 50 Illustrations. Third and cheaper edition. Crown 8vo. Cloth, price 5s.

An Atlas of Diseases of the Membrana Tympani. With Descriptive Text. Post 8vo. Price £6 6s.

The Questions of Aural Surgery. With Illustrations. 2 vols. Post 8vo. Cloth, price 12s. 6d.

The Mystery of Pain. New Edition. Fcap. 8vo. Cloth limp, 1s.

HOCKLEY (W. B.).
Tales of the Zenana; or, A Nuwab's Leisure Hours. By the Author of "Pandurang Hari." With a Preface by Lord Stanley of Alderley. 2 vols. Crown 8vo. Cloth, price 21s.

Pandurang Hari; or, Memoirs of a Hindoo. A Tale of Mahratta Life sixty years ago. With a Preface by Sir H. Bartle E. Frere, G. C. S. I., &c. New and Cheaper Edition. Crown 8vo. Cloth, price 6s.

HOFFBAUER (Capt.).
The German Artillery in the Battles near Metz. Based on the official reports of the German Artillery. Translated by Capt. E. O. Hollist. With Map and Plans. Demy 8vo. Cloth, price 21s.

HOLMES (E. G. A.).
Poems. First and Second Series. Fcap. 8vo. Cloth, price 5s. each.

HOOPER (Mary).
Little Dinners: How to Serve them with Elegance and Economy. Thirteenth Edition. Crown 8vo. Cloth, price 5s.

Cookery for Invalids, Persons of Delicate Digestion, and Children. Crown 8vo. Cloth, price 3s. 6d.

Every-Day Meals. Being Economical and Wholesome Recipes for Breakfast, Luncheon, and Supper. Second Edition. Crown 8vo. Cloth, price 5s.

HOOPER (Mrs. G.).
The House of Raby. With a Frontispiece. Crown 8vo. Cloth, price 3s. 6d.

HOPKINS (Ellice).
Life and Letters of James Hinton, with an Introduction by Sir W. W. Gull, Bart., and Portrait engraved on Steel by C. H. Jeens. Second Edition. Crown 8vo. Cloth price 8s. 6d.

HOPKINS (M.).
The Port of Refuge; or, Counsel and Aid to Shipmasters in Difficulty, Doubt, or Distress. Crown 8vo. Second and Revised Edition. Cloth, price 6s.

HORNER (The Misses).
Walks in Florence. A New and thoroughly Revised Edition. 2 vols. Crown 8vo. Cloth limp. With Illustrations.
Vol. I.—Churches, Streets, and Palaces. 10s. 6d. Vol. II.—Public Galleries and Museums. 5s.

Household Readings on Prophecy. By a Layman. Small crown 8vo. Cloth, price 3s. 6d.

HULL (Edmund C. P.).
The European in India. With a MEDICAL GUIDE FOR ANGLO-INDIANS. By R. R. S. Mair, M.D., F.R.C.S.E. Third Edition, Revised and Corrected. Post 8vo. Cloth, price 6s.

HUTCHISON (Lieut.-Col. F. J.), and Capt. G. H. MACGREGOR.
Military Sketching and Reconnaissance. With Fifteen Plates. Second edition. Small 8vo. Cloth, price 6s.
The first Volume of Military Handbooks for Regimental Officers. Edited by Lieut.-Col. C. B. BRACKENBURY, R.A., A.A.G.

HUTTON (Arthur), M.A.
The Anglican Ministry. Its Nature and Value in relation to the Catholic Priesthood. With a Preface by his Eminence Cardinal Newman. Demy 8vo. Cloth, price 14s.

INCHBOLD (J. W.).
Annus Amoris. Sonnets. Fcap. 8vo. Cloth, price 4s. 6d.

INGELOW (Jean).
Off the Skelligs. A Novel. With Frontispiece. Second Edition. Crown 8vo. Cloth, price 6s.

The Little Wonder-horn. A Second Series of "Stories Told to a Child." With Fifteen Illustrations. Small 8vo. Cloth, price 2s. 6d.

Indian Bishoprics. By an Indian Churchman. Demy 8vo. 6d.

International Scientific Series (The).
I. Forms of Water: A Familiar Exposition of the Origin and Phenomena of Glaciers. By J. Tyndall, LL.D., F.R.S. With 25 Illustrations. Seventh Edition. Crown 8vo. Cloth, price 5s.

International Scientific Series (The)—*continued.*
II. Physics and Politics; or, Thoughts on the Application of the Principles of "Natural Selection" and "Inheritance" to Political Society. By Walter Bagehot. Fifth Edition. Crown 8vo. Cloth, price 4s.

III. Foods. By Edward Smith, M.D., &c. With numerous Illustrations. Seventh Edition. Crown 8vo. Cloth, price 5s.

IV. Mind and Body: The Theories of their Relation. By Alexander Bain, LL.D. With Four Illustrations. Tenth Edition. Crown 8vo. Cloth, price 4s.

V. The Study of Sociology. By Herbert Spencer. Tenth Edition. Crown 8vo. Cloth, price 5s.

VI. On the Conservation of Energy. By Balfour Stewart, LL.D., &c. With 14 Illustrations. Fifth Edition. Crown 8vo. Cloth, price 5s.

VII. Animal Locomotion; or, Walking, Swimming, and Flying. By J. B. Pettigrew, M.D., &c. With 130 Illustrations. Second Edition. Crown 8vo. Cloth, price 5s.

VIII. Responsibility in Mental Disease. By Henry Maudsley, M.D. Third Edition. Crown 8vo. Cloth, price 5s.

IX. The New Chemistry. By Professor J. P. Cooke. With 31 Illustrations. Fifth Edition. Crown 8vo. Cloth, price 5s.

X. The Science of Law. By Prof. Sheldon Amos. Fourth Edition. Crown 8vo. Cloth, price 5s.

XI. Animal Mechanism. A Treatise on Terrestrial and Aerial Locomotion. By Prof. E. J. Marey. With 117 Illustrations. Second Edition. Crown 8vo. Cloth, price 5s.

XII. The Doctrine of Descent and Darwinism. By Prof. Osca Schmidt. With 26 Illustrations. Fourth Edition. Crown 8vo. Cloth, price 5s.

XIII. The History of the Conflict between Religion and Science. By J. W. Draper, M.D., LL.D. Fifteenth Edition. Crown 8vo. Cloth, price 5s.

International Scientific Series (The)—*continued.*

XIV. **Fungi**; their Nature, Influences, Uses, &c. By M. C. Cooke, LL.D. Edited by the Rev. M. J. Berkeley, F.L.S. With numerous Illustrations. Second Edition. Crown 8vo. Cloth, price 5s.

XV. **The Chemical Effects of Light and Photography.** By Dr. Hermann Vogel. With 100 Illustrations. Third and Revised Edition. Crown 8vo. Cloth, price 5s.

XVI. **The Life and Growth of Language.** By Prof. William Dwight Whitney. Third Edition. Crown 8vo. Cloth, price 5s.

XVII. **Money and the Mechanism of Exchange.** By W. Stanley Jevons, F.R.S. Fourth Edition. Crown 8vo. Cloth, price 5s.

XVIII. **The Nature of Light:** With a General Account of Physical Optics. By Dr. Eugene Lommel. With 188 Illustrations and a table of Spectra in Chromo-lithography. Third Edition. Crown 8vo. Cloth, price 5s.

XIX. **Animal Parasites and Messmates.** By M. Van Beneden. With 83 Illustrations. Second Edition. Crown 8vo. Cloth, price 5s.

XX. **Fermentation.** By Prof. Schützenberger. With 28 Illustrations. Third Edition. Crown 8vo. Cloth, price 5s.

XXI. **The Five Senses of Man.** By Prof. Bernstein. With 91 Illustrations. Second Edition. Crown 8vo. Cloth, price 5s.

XXII. **The Theory of Sound in its Relation to Music.** By Prof. Pietro Blaserna. With numerous Illustrations. Second Edition. Crown 8vo. Cloth, price 5s.

XXIII. **Studies in Spectrum Analysis.** By J. Norman Lockyer, F.R.S. With six photographic Illustrations of Spectra, and numerous engravings on wood. Crown 8vo. Second Edition. Cloth, price 6s. 6d.

XXIV. **A History of the Growth of the Steam Engine.** By Prof. R. H. Thurston. With numerous Illustrations. Second Edition. Crown 8vo. Cloth, price 6s. 6d.

XXV. **Education as a Science.** By Alexander Bain, LL.D. Third Edition. Crown 8vo. Cloth, price 5s.

International Scientific Series (The)—*continued.*

XXVI. **The Human Species.** By Prof. A. de Quatrefages. Third Edition. Crown 8vo. Cloth, price 5s.

XXVII. **Modern Chromatics.** With Applications to Art and Industry, by Ogden N. Rood. Second Edition. With 130 original Illustrations. Crown 8vo. Cloth, price 5s.

XXVIII. **The Crayfish**: an Introduction to the Study of Zoology. By Prof. T. H. Huxley. Third edition. With eighty-two Illustrations. Crown 8vo. Cloth, price 5s.

XXIX. **The Brain as an Organ of Mind.** By H. Charlton Bastian, M.D. With numerous Illustrations. Second Edition. Crown 8vo. Cloth, price 5s.

XXX. **The Atomic Theory.** By Prof. Ad. Wurtz. Translated by E. Clemin-Shaw. Second Edition. Crown 8vo. Cloth, price 5s.

XXXI. **The Natural Conditions of Existence as they affect Animal Life.** By Karl Semper. Second Edition. Crown 8vo. Cloth, price 5s.

XXXII. **General Physiology of Muscles and Nerves.** By Prof. J. Rosenthal. Second Edition, with illustrations. Crown 8vo. Cloth, price 5s.

XXXIII. **Sight**: an Exposition of the Principles of Monocular and Binocular Vision. By Joseph Le Conte, LL.D. With 132 illustrations. Crown 8vo. Cloth, price 5s.

XXXIV. **Illusions**: A Psychological Study. By James Sully. Crown 8vo. Cloth, price 5s.

XXXV. **Volcanoes**: What they are and What they Teach. By Prof. J. W. Judd, F.R.S. With 92 Illustrations on Wood. Crown 8vo. Cloth, price 5s.

JENKINS (E.) and RAYMOND (J.).
The Architect's Legal Handbook. Third Edition Revised. Crown 8vo. Cloth, price 6s.

JENKINS (Rev. R. C.), M.A.
The Privilege of Peter and the Claims of the Roman Church confronted with the Scriptures, the Councils, and the Testimony of the Popes themselves. Fcap. 8vo. Cloth, price 3s. 6d.

JENNINGS (Mrs. Vaughan).
Rahel: Her Life and Letters. With a Portrait from the Painting by Daffinger. Square post 8vo. Cloth, price 7s. 6d.

Jeroveam's Wife and other Poems. Fcap. 8vo. Cloth, price 3s. 6d.

JOEL (L.).
A Consul's Manual and Shipowner's and Shipmaster's Practical Guide in their Transactions Abroad. With Definitions of Nautical, Mercantile, and Legal Terms; a Glossary of Mercantile Terms in English, French, German, Italian, and Spanish. Tables of the Money, Weights, and Measures of the Principal Commercial Nations and their Equivalents in British Standards; and Forms of Consular and Notarial Acts. Demy 8vo. Cloth, price 12s.

JOHNSON (Virginia W.).
The Catskill Mountains. Illustrated by Alfred Fredericks. Cloth, price 5s.

JOHNSTONE (C. F.), M.A.
Historical Abstracts. Being Outlines of the History of some of the less-known States of Europe. Crown 8vo. Cloth, price 7s. 6d.

JONES (Lucy).
Puddings and Sweets. Being Three Hundred and Sixty-Five Receipts approved by Experience. Crown 8vo., price 2s. 6d.

JOYCE (P. W.), LL.D., &c.
Old Celtic Romances. Translated from the Gaelic by. Crown 8vo. Cloth, price 7s. 6d.

KAUFMANN (Rev. M.), B.A.
Utopias; or, Schemes of Social Improvement, from Sir Thomas More to Karl Marx. Crown 8vo. Cloth, price 5s.

Socialism: Its Nature, its Dangers, and its Remedies considered. Crown 8vo. Cloth, price 7s. 6d.

KAY (Joseph), M.A., Q.C.
Free Trade in Land. Edited by his Widow. With Preface by the Right Hon. John Bright, M. P. Sixth Edition. Crown 8vo. Cloth, price 5s.

KENT (Carolo).
Carona Catholica ad Petri successoris Pedes Oblata. De Summi Pontificis Leonis XIII. Assumptione Epiggramma. In Quinquaginta Linguis. Fcap. 4to. Cloth, price 15s.

KER (David).
The Boy Slave in Bokhara. A Tale of Central Asia. With Illustrations. Crown 8vo. Cloth, price 3s. 6d.

The Wild Horseman of the Pampas. Illustrated. Crown 8vo. Cloth, price 3s. 6d.

KERNER (Dr. A.), Professor of Botany in the University of Innsbruck.

Flowers and their Unbidden Guests. Translation edited by W. OGLE, M.A., M.D., and a prefatory letter by C. Darwin, F.R.S. With Illustrations. Sq. 8vo. Cloth, price 9s.

KIDD (Joseph), M.D.
The Laws of Therapeutics, or, the Science and Art of Medicine. Second Edition. Crown 8vo. Cloth, price 6s.

KINAHAN (G. Henry), M.R.I.A., &c., of her Majesty's Geological Survey.
Manual of the Geology of Ireland. With 8 Plates, 26 Woodcuts, and a Map of Ireland, geologically coloured. Square 8vo. Cloth, price 15s.

KING (Mrs. Hamilton).
The Disciples. Fourth Edition, with Portrait and Notes. Crown 8vo. Cloth, price 7s. 6d.

Aspromonte, and other Poems. Second Edition. Fcap. 8vo. Cloth, price 4s. 6d.

KING (Edward).
Echoes from the Orient. With Miscellaneous Poems. Small crown 8vo. Cloth, price 3s. 6d.

KINGSLEY (Charles), M.A.
Letters and Memories of his Life. Edited by his WIFE. With 2 Steel engraved Portraits and numerous Illustrations on Wood, and a Facsimile of his Handwriting.

KINGSLEY (Charles), M.A.—*continued.*
Thirteenth Edition. 2 vols. Demy 8vo. Cloth, price 36s.
*** Also the ninth Cabinet Edition in 2 vols. Crown 8vo. Cloth, price 12s.
All Saints' Day and other Sermons. Second Edition. Crown 8vo. Cloth, 7s. 6d.
True Words for Brave Men: a Book for Soldiers' and Sailors' Libraries. Eighth Edition. Crown 8vo. Cloth, price 2s. 6d.

KNIGHT (Professor W.).
Studies in Philosophy and Literature. Large post 8vo. Cloth, price 7s. 6d.

KNOX (Alexander A.).
The New Playground: or, Wanderings in Algeria. Large crown 8vo. Cloth, price 10s. 6d.

LACORDAIRE (Rev. Père).
Life: Conferences delivered at Toulouse. A New and Cheaper Edition. Crown 8vo. Cloth, price 3s. 6d.

LAIRD-CLOWES (W.).
Love's Rebellion: a Poem. Fcap. 8vo. Cloth, price 3s. 6d.

LAMONT (Martha MacDonald).
The Gladiator: A Life under the Roman Empire in the beginning of the Third Century. With four Illustrations by H. M. Paget. Extra fcap. 8vo. Cloth, price 3s. 6d.

LANG (A.).
XXXII Ballades in Blue China. Elzevir. 8vo. Parchment, price 5s.

LAYMANN (Capt.).
The Frontal Attack of Infantry. Translated by Colonel Edward Newdigate. Crown 8vo. Cloth, price 2s. 6d.

LEANDER (Richard).
Fantastic Stories. Translated from the German by Paulina B. Granville. With Eight full-page Illustrations by M. E. Fraser-Tytler. Crown 8vo. Cloth, price 5s.

LEE (Rev. F. G.), D.C.L.
The Other World; or, Glimpses of the Supernatural. 2 vols. A New Edition. Crown 8vo. Cloth, price 15s.

LEE (Holme).
Her Title of Honour. A Book for Girls. New Edition. With a Frontispiece. Crown 8vo. Cloth, price 5s.

LEIGH (Arran and Isla).
Bellerophôn. Small crown 8vo. Cloth, price 5s.

LEIGHTON (Robert).
Records and other Poems. With Portrait. Small crown 8vo. Cloth, price 7s. 6d.

LEWIS (Edward Dillon).
A Draft Code of Criminal Law and Procedure. Demy 8vo. Cloth, price 21s.

LEWIS (Mary A.).
A Rat with Three Tales. New and cheaper edition. With Four Illustrations by Catherine F. Frere. Crown 8vo. Cloth, price 3s. 6d.

LINDSAY (W. Lauder), M.D., &c.
Mind in the Lower Animals in Health and Disease. 2 vols. Demy 8vo. Cloth, price 32s.

LLOYD (Francis) and Charles Tebbitt.
Extension of Empire Weakness? Deficits Ruin? With a Practical Scheme for the Reconstruction of Asiatic Turkey. Small crown 8vo. Cloth, price 3s. 6d.

LOCKER (F.).
London Lyrics. A New and Revised Edition, with Additions and a Portrait of the Author. Crown 8vo. Cloth, elegant, price 6s.

LOKI.
The New Werther. Small crown 8vo. Cloth, price 2s. 6d.

LORIMER (Peter), D.D.
John Knox and the Church of England: His Work in her Pulpit, and his Influence upon her Liturgy, Articles, and Parties. Demy 8vo. Cloth, price 12s.
John Wiclif and his English Precursors, by Gerhard Victor Lechler. Translated from the German, with additional Notes. 2 vols. Demy 8vo. Cloth, price 21s.
Love's Gamut and other Poems. Small crown 8vo. Cloth, price 3s. 6d.

Love Sonnets of Proteus. With frontispiece by the Author. Elzevir 8vo. Cloth, price 5s.

LOWNDES (Henry).
Poems and Translations. Crown 8vo. Cloth, price 6s.

LUMSDEN (Lieut.-Col. H. W.).
Beowulf. An Old English Poem. Translated into modern rhymes. Small crown 8vo. Cloth, price 5s.

MAC CLINTOCK (L.).
Sir Spangle and the Dingy Hen. Illustrated. Square crown 8vo., price 2s. 6d.

MACDONALD (G.).
Malcolm. With Portrait of the Author engraved on Steel. Fourth Edition. Crown 8vo. Price 6s.
The Marquis of Lossie. Second Edition. Crown 8vo. Cloth, price 6s.
St. George and St. Michael. Second Edition. Crown 8vo. Cloth, 6s.

MACKENNA (S. J.).
Plucky Fellows. A Book for Boys. With Six Illustrations. Fourth Edition. Crown 8vo. Cloth, price 3s. 6d.
At School with an Old Dragoon. With Six Illustrations. Second Edition. Crown 8vo. Cloth, price 5s.

MACLACHLAN (Mrs.).
Notes and Extracts on Everlasting Punishment and Eternal Life, according to Literal Interpretation. Small crown 8vo. Cloth, price 3s. 6d.

MACLEAN (Charles Donald).
Latin and Greek Verse Translations. Small crown 8vo. Cloth, price 2s.

MACNAUGHT (Rev. John).
Cœna Domini: An Essay on the Lord's Supper, its Primitive Institution, Apostolic Uses, and Subsequent History. Demy 8vo. Cloth, price 14s.

MAGNUS (Mrs.).
About the Jews since Bible Times. From the Babylonian exile till the English Exodus. Small crown 8vo. Cloth, price 5s.

MAGNUSSON (Eirikr), M.A., and PALMER (E.H.), M.A.
Johan Ludvig Runeberg's Lyrical Songs, Idylls and Epigrams. Fcap. 8vo. Cloth, price 5s.

MAIR (R. S.), M.D., F.R.C.S.E.
The Medical Guide for Anglo-Indians. Being a Compendium of Advice to Europeans in India, relating to the Preservation and Regulation of Health. With a Supplement on the Management of Children in India. Second Edition. Crown 8vo. Limp cloth, price 3s. 6d.

MALDEN (H. E. and E. E.)
Princes and Princesses. Illustrated. Small crown 8vo. Cloth, price 2s. 6d.

MANNING (His Eminence Cardinal).
The True Story of the Vatican Council. Crown 8vo. Cloth, price 5s.

Marie Antoinette: a Drama. Small crown 8vo. Cloth, price 5s.

MARKHAM (Capt. Albert Hastings), R.N.
The Great Frozen Sea. A Personal Narrative of the Voyage of the "Alert" during the Arctic Expedition of 1875-6. With six full-page Illustrations, two Maps, and twenty-seven Woodcuts. Fourth and cheaper edition. Crown 8vo. Cloth, price 6s.

A Polar Reconnaissance: being the Voyage of the "Isbjorn" to Novaya Zemlya in 1879. With 10 Illustrations. Demy 8vo. Cloth, price 16s.

MARTINEAU (Gertrude).
Outline Lessons on Morals. Small crown 8vo. Cloth, price 3s. 6d.

Master Bobby: a Tale. By the Author of "Christina North." With Illustrations by E. H. Bell. Extra fcap. 8vo. Cloth, price 3s. 6d.

MASTERMAN (J.).
Half-a-dozen Daughters. With a Frontispiece. Crown 8vo. Cloth, price 3s. 6d.

McGRATH (Terence).
Pictures from Ireland. New and cheaper edition. Crown 8vo. Cloth, price 2s.

MEREDITH (George).
The Egoist. A Comedy in Narrative. 3 vols. Crown 8vo. Cloth.
*** Also a Cheaper Edition, with Frontispiece. Crown 8vo. Cloth, price 6s.

The Ordeal of Richard Feverel. A History of Father and Son. In one vol. with Frontispiece. Crown 8vo. Cloth, price 6s.

MERRITT (Henry).
Art - Criticism and Romance. With Recollections, and Twenty-three Illustrations in *eauforte*, by Anna Lea Merritt. Two vols. Large post 8vo. Cloth, 25s.

MIDDLETON (The Lady).
Ballads. Square 16mo. Cloth, price 3s. 6d.

MILLER (Edward).
The History and Doctrines of Irvingism; or, the so-called Catholic and Apostolic Church. 2 vols. Large post 8vo. Cloth, price 25s.

The Church in Relation to the State. Crown 8vo. Cloth, price 7s. 6d.

MILNE (James).
Tables of Exchange for the Conversion of Sterling Money into Indian and Ceylon Currency, at Rates from 1s. 8d. to 2s. 3d. per Rupee. Second Edition. Demy 8vo. Cloth, price £2 2s.

MINCHIN (J. G.).
Bulgaria since the War. Notes of a Tour in the Autumn of 1879. Small crown 8vo. Cloth, price 3s. 6d.

MOCKLER (E.).
A Grammar of the Baloochee Language, as it is spoken in Makran (Ancient Gedrosia), in the Persia-Arabic and Roman characters. Fcap. 8vo. Cloth, price 5s.

MOFFAT (Robert Scott).
The Economy of Consumption; an Omitted Chapter in Political Economy, with special reference to the Questions of Commercial Crises and the Policy of Trades Unions; and with Reviews of the Theories of Adam Smith, Ricardo, J. S. Mill, Fawcett, &c. Demy 8vo. Cloth, price 18s.

The Principles of a Time Policy: being an Exposition of a Method of Settling Disputes between Employers and Employed in regard to Time and Wages, by a simple Process of Mercantile Barter, without recourse to Strikes or Locks-out. Demy 8vo. Cloth, price 3s. 6d.

Monmouth: A Drama, of which the Outline is Historical. Dedicated by permission to Mr. Henry Irving. Small crown 8vo. Cloth, price 5s.

MOORE (Mrs. Bloomfield).
Gondaline's Lesson. The Warden's Tale, Stories for Children, and other Poems. Crown 8vo. Cloth, price 5s.

MORELL (J. R.).
Euclid Simplified in Method and Language. Being a Manual of Geometry. Compiled from the most important French Works, approved by the University of Paris and the Minister of Public Instruction. Fcap. 8vo. Cloth, price 2s. 6d.

MORICE (Rev. F. D.), M.A.
The Olympian and Pythian Odes of Pindar. A New Translation in English Verse. Crown 8vo. Cloth, price 7s. 6d.

MORSE (E. S.), Ph.D.
First Book of Zoology. With numerous Illustrations. New and cheaper edition. Crown 8vo. Cloth, price 2s. 6d.

MORSHEAD (E. D. A.)
The House of Atreus. Being the Agamemnon Libation-Bearers and Furies of Æschylus Translated into English Verse. Crown 8vo. Cloth, price 7s.

MORTERRA (Felix).
The Legend of Allandale, and other Poems. Small crown 8vo. Cloth, price 6s.

MUNRO (Major-Gen. Sir Thomas), K.C.B., Governor of Madras.
Selections from His Minutes, and other Official Writings. Edited, with an Introductory Memoir, by Sir Alexander Arbuthnot, K.C.S.I., C.I.E. Two vols. Demy 8vo. Cloth, price 30s.

NAAKE (J. T.).
Slavonic Fairy Tales. From Russian, Servian, Polish, and Bohemian Sources. With Four Illustrations. Crown 8vo. Cloth, price 5s.

NADEN (Constance W.).
Songs and Sonnets of Spring-Time. Small crown 8vo. Cloth, price 5s.

NEWMAN (J. H.), D.D.
Characteristics from the Writings of. Being Selections from his various Works. Arranged with the Author's personal approval. Third Edition. With Portrait. Crown 8vo. Cloth, price 6s.
⁎ A Portrait of the Rev. Dr. J. H. Newman, mounted for framing, can be had, price 2s. 6d.

NICHOLAS (Thomas), Ph.D., F.G.S.
The Pedigree of the English People: an Argument, Historical and Scientific, on the Formation and Growth of the Nation, tracing Race-admixture in Britain from the earliest times, with especial reference to the incorporation of the Celtic Aborigines. Fifth Edition. Demy 8vo. Cloth, price 16s.

NICHOLSON (Edward Byron).
The Christ Child, and other Poems. Crown 8vo. Cloth, price 4s. 6d.

The Rights of an Animal. Crown 8vo. Cloth, price 3s. 6d.

The Gospel according to the Hebrews. Its Fragments translated and annotated, with a critical Analysis of the External and Internal Evidence relating to it. Demy 8vo. Cloth, price 9s. 6d.

A New Commentary on the Gospel according to Matthew. Demy 8vo. Cloth, price 12s.

NICOLS (Arthur), F.G.S., F.R.G.S.
Chapters from the Physical History of the Earth. An Introduction to Geology and Palæontology, with numerous illustrations. Crown 8vo. Cloth, price 5s.

NOAKE (Major R. Compton).
The Bivouac; or, Martial Lyrist, with an Appendix—Advice to the Soldier. Fcap. 8vo. Price 5s. 6d.

NOEL (The Hon. Roden).
A Little Child's Monument. Small crown 8vo. Cloth, price 3s. 6d.

NORMAN PEOPLE (The).
The Norman People, and their Existing Descendants in the British Dominions and the United States of America. Demy 8vo. Cloth, price 21s.

NORRIS (Rev. Alfred).
The Inner and Outer Life Poems. Fcap. 8vo. Cloth, price 6s.

Notes on Cavalry Tactics, Organization, &c. By a Cavalry Officer. With Diagrams. Demy 8vo. Cloth, price 12s.

Nuces: Exercises on the Syntax of the Public School Latin Primer. New Edition in Three Parts. Crown 8vo. Each 1s.
⁎ The Three Parts can also be had bound together in cloth, price 3s.

OATES (Frank), F.R.G.S.
Matabele Land and the Victoria Falls: A Naturalist's Wanderings in the Interior of South Africa. Edited by C. G. Oates, B.A., with numerous illustrations and four maps. Demy 8vo. Cloth.

O'BRIEN (Charlotte G.).
Light and Shade. 2 vols. Crown 8vo. Cloth, gilt tops, price 12s.

Ode of Life (The). Third Edition. Fcap. 8vo. Cloth, price 5s.

OF THE IMITATION OF CHRIST. Four books. Demy 32mo. Limp cloth, price 1s.
⁎ Also in various bindings.

A List of

O'HAGAN (John).
The Song of Roland. Translated into English Verse. Large post 8vo. Parchment antique, price 10s. 6d.

O'MEARA (Kathleen).
Frederic Ozanam, Professor of the Sorbonne; His Life and Works. Second Edition. Crown 8vo. Cloth, price 7s. 6d.
Henri Perreyve and His Counsels to the Sick. Small crown 8vo. Cloth, price 5s.
Our Public Schools. Eton, Harrow, Winchester, Rugby, Westminster, Marlborough, The Charterhouse. Crown 8vo. Cloth, price 6s.

OWEN (F. M.).
John Keats. A Study. Crown 8vo. Cloth, price 6s.

OWEN (Rev. Robert), B.D.
Sanctorale Catholicum; or Book of Saints. With Notes, Critical, Exegetical, and Historical. Demy 8vo. Cloth, price 18s.
An Essay on the Communion of Saints. Including an Examination of the "Cultus Sanctorum." Price 2s.

PALGRAVE (W. Gifford).
Hermann Agha; An Eastern Narrative. Third and Cheaper Edition. Crown 8vo. Cloth, price 6s.

PANDURANG HARI;
Or, Memoirs of a Hindoo. With an Introductory Preface by Sir H. Bartle E. Frere, G.C.S.I., C.B. Crown 8vo. Price 6s.

PARCHMENT LIBRARY (The).
Choicely printed on hand-made paper, limp parchment antique, price 6s. each; vellum, price 7s. 6d. each.
Shakspere's Sonnets. Edited by Edward Dowden, Author of "Shakspere; his Mind and Art," &c. With a Frontispiece, etched by Leopold Lowenstam, after the Death Mask.
English Odes. Selected by Edmund W. Gosse, Author of "Studies in the Literature of Northern Europe." With Frontispiece on India paper by Hamo Thornycroft, A.R.A.

PARCHMENT LIBRARY (The)—*continued.*
Of the Imitation of Christ. By Thomas à Kempis. A revised Translation. With Frontispiece on India paper, from a Design by W. B. Richmond.
Tennyson's The Princess: a Medley. With a Miniature Frontispiece by H. M. Paget, and a Tailpiece in Outline by Gordon Browne.
Poems: Selected from Percy Bysshe Shelley. Dedicated to Lady Shelley. With Preface by Richard Garnet, and a Miniature Frontispiece.
Tennyson's "In Memoriam." With a Miniature Portrait in *eau forte* by Le Rat, after a Photograph by the late Mrs. Cameron.

PARKER (Joseph), D.D.
The Paraclete: An Essay on the Personality and Ministry of the Holy Ghost, with some reference to current discussions. Second Edition. Demy 8vo. Cloth, price 12s.

PARR (Capt. H. Hallam).
A Sketch of the Kafir and Zulu Wars: Guadana to Isandhlwana, with Maps. Small crown 8vo. Cloth, price 5s.
The Dress, Horses, and Equipment of Infantry and Staff Officers. Crown 8vo. Cloth, price 1s.

PARSLOE (Joseph).
Our Railways: Sketches, Historical and Descriptive. With Practical Information as to Fares, Rates, &c., and a Chapter on Railway Reform. Crown 8vo. Cloth, price 6s.

PATTISON (Mrs. Mark).
The Renaissance of Art in France. With Nineteen Steel Engravings. 2 vols. Demy 8vo. Cloth, price 32s.

PAUL (C. Kegan).
Mary Wollstonecraft. Letters to Imlay. With Prefatory Memoir by, and Two Portraits in *eau forte*, by Anna Lea Merritt. Crown 8vo. Cloth, price 6s.

PAUL (C. Kegan)—*continued*.
Goethe's Faust. A New Translation in Rime. Crown 8vo. Cloth, price 6s.

William Godwin: His Friends and Contemporaries. With Portraits and Facsimiles of the Handwriting of Godwin and his Wife. 2 vols. Square post 8vo. Cloth, price 28s.

The Genius of Christianity Unveiled. Being Essays by William Godwin never before published. Edited, with a Preface, by C. Kegan Paul. Crown 8vo. Cloth, price 7s. 6d.

PAUL (Margaret Agnes).
Gentle and Simple: A Story. 2 vols. Crown 8vo. Cloth, gilt tops, price 12s.
*** Also a Cheaper Edition in one vol. with Frontispiece. Crown 8vo. Cloth, price 6s.

PAYNE (John).
Songs of Life and Death. Crown 8vo. Cloth, price 5s.

PAYNE (Prof. J. F.).
Fröbel and the Kindergarten System. Second Edition.
A Visit to German Schools: Elementary Schools in Germany. Notes of a Professional Tour to inspect some of the Kindergartens, Primary Schools, Public Girls' Schools, and Schools for Technical Instruction in Hamburgh, Berlin, Dresden, Weimar, Gotha, Eisenach, in the autumn of 1874. With Critical Discussions of the General Principles and Practice of Kindergartens and other Schemes of Elementary Education. Crown 8vo. Cloth, price 4s. 6d.

PELLETAN (E.).
The Desert Pastor, Jean Jarousseau. Translated from the French. By Colonel E. P. De L'Hoste. With a Frontispiece. New Edition. Fcap. 8vo. Cloth, price 3s. 6d.

PENNELL (H. Cholmondeley).
Pegasus Resaddled. By the Author of "Puck on Pegasus," &c. &c. With Ten Full-page Illustrations by George Du Maurier. Second Edition. Fcap. 4to. Cloth elegant, price 12s. 6d.

PENRICE (Maj. J.), B.A.
A Dictionary and Glossary of the Ko-ran. With copious Grammatical References and Explanations of the Text. 4to. Cloth, price 21s.

PESCHEL (Dr. Oscar).
The Races of Man and their Geographical Distribution. Large crown 8vo. Cloth, price 9s.

PETERS (F. H.).
The Nicomachean Ethics of Aristotle. Translated by. Crown 8vo. Cloth, price 6s.

PFEIFFER (Emily).
Quarterman's Grace, and other Poems. Crown 8vo. Cloth, price 5s.

Glan Alarch: His Silence and Song. A Poem. Second Edition. Crown 8vo. price 6s.

Gerard's Monument, and other Poems. Second Edition. Crown 8vo. Cloth, price 6s.

Poems. Second Edition. Crown 8vo. Cloth, price 6s.

Sonnets and Songs. New Edition. 16mo, handsomely printed and bound in cloth, gilt edges, price 5s.

PIKE (Warburton).
The Inferno of Dante Alighieri. Demy 8vo. Cloth, price 5s.

PINCHES (Thomas), M.A.
Samuel Wilberforce: Faith—Service—Recompense. Three Sermons. With a Portrait of Bishop Wilberforce (after a Photograph by Charles Watkins). Crown 8vo. Cloth, price 4s. 6d.

PLAYFAIR (Lieut.-Col.), Her Britannic Majesty's Consul-General in Algiers.
Travels in the Footsteps of Bruce in Algeria and Tunis. Illustrated by facsimiles of Bruce's original Drawings, Photographs, Maps, &c. Royal 4to. Cloth, bevelled boards, gilt leaves, price £3 3s.

POLLOCK (Frederick).
Spinoza. His Life and Philosophy. Demy 8vo. Cloth, price 16s.

24 A List of

POLLOCK (W. H.).
Lectures on French Poets.
Delivered at the Royal Institution. Small crown 8vo. Cloth, price 5s.

POOR (Laura E.).
Sanskrit and its kindred Literatures. Studies in Comparative Mythology. Small crown 8vo. Cloth, price 5s.

POUSHKIN (A. S.).
Russian Romance. Translated from the Tales of Belkin, &c. By Mrs. J. Buchan Telfer (*née* Mouravieff). Crown 8vo. Cloth, price 3s. 6d.

PRESBYTER.
Unfoldings of Christian Hope. An Essay showing that the Doctrine contained in the Damnatory Clauses of the Creed commonly called Athanasian is unscriptural. Small crown 8vo. Cloth, price 4s. 6d.

PRICE (Prof. Bonamy).
Currency and Banking. Crown 8vo. Cloth, price 6s.

Chapters on Practical Political Economy. Being the Substance of Lectures delivered before the University of Oxford. Large post 8vo. Cloth, price 12s.

Proteus and Amadeus. A Correspondence. Edited by Aubrey De Vere. Crown 8vo. Cloth, price 5s.

PUBLIC SCHOOLBOY.
The Volunteer, the Militiaman, and the Regular Soldier. Crown 8vo. Cloth, price 5s.

PULPIT COMMENTARY (The). Edited by the Rev. J. S. EXELL and the Rev. Canon H. D. M. SPENCE.

Genesis. By Rev. T. Whitelaw, M.A.; with Homilies by the Very Rev. J. F. Montgomery, D.D., Rev. Prof. R. A. Redford, M.A., LL.B., Rev. F. Hastings, Rev. W. Roberts, M.A. An Introduction to the Study of the Old Testament by the Rev. Canon Farrar, D.D., F.R.S.; and Introductions to the Pentateuch by the Right Rev. H. Cotterill, D.D., and Rev. T. Whitelaw, M.A. Fourth Edition. Price 15s.

PULPIT COMMENTARY (The) —*continued.*

Numbers. By the Rev. R. Winterbotham, LL.B. With Homilies by the Rev. Prof. W. Binnie, D.D., Rev. E. S. Prout, M.A., Rev. D. Young, Rev. J. Waite, and an Introduction by the Rev. Thomas Whitelaw, M.A. Price 15s.

Joshua. By the Rev. J. J. Lias, M.A. With Homilies by the Rev. S. R. Aldridge, LL.B., Rev. R. Glover, Rev. E. de Pressensé, D.D., Rev. J. Waite, Rev. F. W. Adeney, and an Introduction by the Rev. A. Plummer, M.A. Second Edition. Price 12s. 6d.

Judges and Ruth. By Right Rev. Lord A. C. Hervey, D.D., and Rev. J. Morrison, D.D. With Homilies by Rev. A. F. Muir, M.A.; Rev. W. F. Adeney, M.A.; Rev. W. M. Statham; and Rev. Prof. J. R. Thomson, M.A. Second Edition. Cloth, price 15s.

1 Samuel. By the Very Rev. R. P. Smith, D.D. With Homilies by the Rev. Donald Fraser, D.D., Rev. Prof. Chapman, and Rev. B. Dale. Third Edition. Price 15s.

Ezra, Nehemiah, and Esther. By Rev. Canon G. Rawlinson, M.A.; with Homilies by Rev. Prof. J. R. Thomson, M.A., Rev. Prof. R. A. Redford, LL.B., M.A., Rev. W. S. Lewis, M.A., Rev. J. A. Macdonald, Rev. A. Mackennal, B.A., Rev. W. Clarkson, B.A., Rev. F. Hastings, Rev. W. Dinwiddie, LL.B., Rev. Prof. Rowlands, B.A., Rev. G. Wood, B.A., Rev. Prof. P. C. Barker, LL.B., M.A., and Rev. J. S. Exell. Fourth Edition. Price 12s. 6d.

Punjaub (The) and North Western Frontier of India. By an old Punjaubee. Crown 8vo. Cloth, price 5s.

Rabbi Jeshua. An Eastern Story. Crown 8vo. Cloth, price 3s. 6d.

RAVENSHAW (John Henry), B.C.S.
Gaur: Its Ruins and Inscriptions. Edited with consider-

RAVENSHAW (John Henry), B.C.S.—*continued.*
able additions and alterations by his Widow. With forty-four photographic illustrations and twenty-five fac-similes of Inscriptions. Super royal 4to. Cloth, 3*l*. 13*s*. 6*d*.

READ (Carveth).
On the Theory of Logic: An Essay. Crown 8vo. Cloth, price 6*s*.
Realities of the Future Life. Small crown 8vo. Cloth, price 1*s*. 6*d*.

REANEY (Mrs. G. S.).
Blessing and Blessed; a Sketch of Girl Life. New and cheaper Edition. With a frontispiece. Crown 8vo. Cloth, price 3*s*. 6*d*.
Waking and Working; or, from Girlhood to Womanhood. New and cheaper edition. With a Frontispiece. Crown 8vo. Cloth, price 3*s*. 6*d*.
Rose Gurney's Discovery. A Book for Girls, dedicated to their Mothers. Crown 8vo. Cloth, price 3*s*. 6*d*.
English Girls: their Place and Power. With a Preface by R. W. Dale, M.A., of Birmingham. Third Edition. Fcap. 8vo. Cloth, price 2*s*. 6*d*.
Just Anyone, and other Stories. Three Illustrations. Royal 16mo. Cloth, price 1*s*. 6*d*.
Sunshine Jenny and other Stories. Three Illustrations. Royal 16mo. Cloth, price 1*s*. 6*d*.
Sunbeam Willie, and other Stories. Three Illustrations. Royal 16mo. Cloth, price 1*s*. 6*d*.

RENDALL (J. M.).
Concise Handbook of the Island of Madeira. With plan of Funchal and map of the Island. Fcap. 8vo. Cloth, price 1*s*. 6*d*.

REYNOLDS (Rev. J. W.).
The Supernatural in Nature. A Verification by Free Use of Science. Second Edition, revised and enlarged. Demy 8vo. Cloth, price 14*s*.
Mystery of Miracles, The. By the Author of "The Supernatural in Nature." Crown 8vo. Cloth, price 6*s*.

RHOADES (James).
The Georgics of Virgil. Translated into English Verse. Small crown 8vo. Cloth, price 5*s*.

RIBOT (Prof. Th.).
English Psychology. Second Edition. A Revised and Corrected Translation from the latest French Edition. Large post 8vo. Cloth, price 9*s*.
Heredity: A Psychological Study on its Phenomena, its Laws, its Causes, and its Consequences. Large crown 8vo. Cloth, price 9*s*.

RINK (Chevalier Dr. Henry).
Greenland: Its People and its Products. By the Chevalier Dr. HENRY RINK, President of the Greenland Board of Trade. With sixteen Illustrations, drawn by the Eskimo, and a Map. Edited by Dr. ROBERT BROWN. Crown 8vo. Price 10*s*. 6*d*.

ROBERTSON (The Late Rev. F. W.), M.A., of Brighton.
The Human Race, and other Sermons preached at Cheltenham, Oxford, and Brighton. Second Edition. Large post 8vo. Cloth, price 7*s*. 6*d*.
Notes on Genesis. New and cheaper Edition. Crown 8vo., price 3*s*. 6*d*.
Sermons. Four Series. Small crown 8vo. Cloth, price 3*s*. 6*d*. each.
Expository Lectures on St. Paul's Epistles to the Corinthians. A New Edition. Small crown 8vo. Cloth, price 5*s*.
Lectures and Addresses, with other literary remains. A New Edition. Crown 8vo. Cloth, price 5*s*.
An Analysis of Mr. Tennyson's "In Memoriam." (Dedicated by Permission to the Poet-Laureate.) Fcap. 8vo. Cloth, price 2*s*.
The Education of the Human Race. Translated from the German of Gotthold Ephraim Lessing. Fcap. 8vo. Cloth, price 2*s*. 6*d*.
Life and Letters. Edited by the Rev. Stopford Brooke, M.A., Chaplain in Ordinary to the Queen. I. 2 vols., uniform with the Sermons. With Steel Portrait. Crown 8vo. Cloth, price 7*s*. 6*d*.

ROBERTSON (The Late Rev. F. W.), M.A., of Brighton—continued.
II. Library Edition, in Demy 8vo., with Portrait. Cloth, price 12s.
III. A Popular Edition, in one vol. Crown 8vo. Cloth, price 6s.
The above Works can also be had half-bound in morocco.
*** A Portrait of the late Rev. F. W. Robertson, mounted for framing, can be had, price 2s. 6d.

ROBINSON (A. Mary F.).
A Handful of Honeysuckle. Fcap. 8vo. Cloth, price 3s. 6d.
The Crowned Hippolytus. Translated from Euripides. With New Poems. Small crown 8vo. Cloth, price 5s.

RODWELL (G. F.), F.R.A.S., F.C.S.
Etna: a History of the Mountain and its Eruptions. With Maps and Illustrations. Square 8vo. Cloth, price 9s.

ROSS (Mrs. E.), ("Nelsie Brook").
Daddy's Pet. A Sketch from Humble Life. With Six Illustrations. Royal 16mo. Cloth, price 1s.

ROSS (Alexander), D.D.
Memoir of Alexander Ewing, Bishop of Argyll and the Isles. Second and Cheaper Edition. Demy 8vo. Cloth, price 10s. 6d.

SADLER (S. W.), R.N.
The African Cruiser. A Midshipman's Adventures on the West Coast. With Three Illustrations. Second Edition. Crown 8vo. Cloth, price 3s. 6d.

SALTS (Rev. Alfred), LL.D.
Godparents at Confirmation. With a Preface by the Bishop of Manchester. Small crown 8vo. Cloth, limp, price 2s.

SALVATOR (Archduke Ludwig).
Levkosia, the Capital of Cyprus. Crown 8vo. Cloth, price 10s. 6d.

SAMUEL (Sydney Montagu).
Jewish Life in the East. Small crown 8vo. Cloth, price 3s. 6d.

SAUNDERS (John).
Israel Mort, Overman: A Story of the Mine. Cr. 8vo. Price 6s.

SAUNDERS (John)—continued.
Hirell. With Frontispiece. Crown 8vo. Cloth, price 3s. 6d.
Abel Drake's Wife. With Frontispiece. Crown 8vo. Cloth, price 3s. 6d.

SAYCE (Rev. Archibald Henry).
Introduction to the Science of Language. Two vols., large post 8vo. Cloth, price 25s.

SCHELL (Maj. von).
The Operations of the First Army under Gen. von Goeben. Translated by Col. C. H. von Wright. Four Maps. Demy 8vo. Cloth, price 9s.
The Operations of the First Army under Gen. von Steinmetz. Translated by Captain E. O. Hollist. Demy 8vo. Cloth, price 10s. 6d.

SCHELLENDORF (Maj.-Gen. B. von).
The Duties of the General Staff. Translated from the German by Lieutenant Hare. Vol. I. Demy 8vo. Cloth, 10s. 6d.

SCHERFF (Maj. W. von).
Studies in the New Infantry Tactics. Parts I. and II. Translated from the German by Colonel Lumley Graham. Demy 8vo. Cloth, price 7s. 6d.

Scientific Layman. The New Truth and the Old Faith: are they Incompatible? Demy 8vo. Cloth, price 10s. 6d.

SCOONES (W. Baptiste).
Four Centuries of English Letters. A Selection of 350 Letters by 150 Writers from the period of the Paston Letters to the Present Time. Edited and arranged by. Second Edition. Large crown 8vo. Cloth, price 9s.

SCOTT (Leader).
A Nook in the Apennines: A Summer beneath the Chestnuts. With Frontispiece, and 27 Illustrations in the Text, chiefly from Original Sketches. Crown 8vo. Cloth, price 7s. 6d.

SCOTT (Robert H.).
Weather Charts and Storm Warnings. Illustrated. Second Edition. Crown 8vo. Cloth, price 3s. 6d.

Seeking his Fortune, and other Stories. With Four Illustrations. New and cheaper Edition. Crown 8vo. Cloth, price 2s. 6d.

SENIOR (N. W.).
Alexis De Tocqueville. Correspondence and Conversations with Nassau W. Senior, from 1833 to 1859. Edited by M. C. M. Simpson. 2 vols. Large post 8vo. Cloth, price 21s.

Seven Autumn Leaves from Fairyland. Illustrated with Nine Etchings. Square crown 8vo. Cloth, price 3s. 6d.

SHADWELL (Maj.-Gen.), C.B.
Mountain Warfare. Illustrated by the Campaign of 1799 in Switzerland. Being a Translation of the Swiss Narrative compiled from the Works of the Archduke Charles, Jomini, and others. Also of Notes by General H. Dufour on the Campaign of the Valtelline in 1635. With Appendix, Maps, and Introductory Remarks. Demy 8vo. Cloth, price 16s.

SHAKSPEARE (Charles).
Saint Paul at Athens: Spiritual Christianity in Relation to some Aspects of Modern Thought. Nine Sermons preached at St. Stephen's Church, Westbourne Park. With Preface by the Rev. Canon FARRAR. Crown 8vo. Cloth, price 5s.

SHAW (Major Wilkinson).
The Elements of Modern Tactics. Practically applied to English Formations. With Twenty-five Plates and Maps. S cond and cheaper Edition. Small crown 8vo. Cloth, price 9s.
** The Second Volume of "Military Handbooks for Officers and Non-commissioned Officers." Edited by Lieut.-Col. C. B. Brackenbury, R.A., A.A.G.

SHAW (Flora L.).
Castle Blair: a Story of Youthful Lives. 2 vols. Crown 8vo. Cloth, gilt tops, price 12s. Also, an edition in one vol. Crown 8vo. 6s.

SHELLEY (Lady).
Shelley Memorials from Authentic Sources. With (now first printed) an Essay on Christianity by Percy Bysshe Shelley. With Portrait. Third Edition. Crown 8vo. Cloth, price 5s.

SHERMAN (Gen. W. T.).
Memoirs of General W. T. Sherman, Commander of the Federal Forces in the American Civil War. By Himself. 2 vols. With Map. Demy 8vo Cloth, price 24s. *Copyright English Edition.*

SHILLITO (Rev. Joseph).
Womanhood: its Duties, Temptations, and Privileges. A Book for Young Women. Second Edition. Crown 8vo. Price 3s. 6d.

SHIPLEY (Rev. Orby), M.A.
Principles of the Faith in Relation to Sin. Topics for Thought in Times of Retreat. Eleven Addresses. With an Introduction on the neglect of Dogmatic Theology in the Church of England, and a Postscript on his leaving the Church of England. Demy 8vo. Cloth, price 12s.

Church Tracts, or Studies in Modern Problems. By various Writers. 2 vols. Crown 8vo. Cloth, price 5s. each.

Sister Augustine, Superior of the Sisters of Charity at the St. Johannis Hospital at Bonn. Authorized Translation by Hans Tharau from the German Memorials of Amalie von Lasaulx. Second edition. Large crown 8vo. Cloth, price 7s. 6d.

SKINNER (James).
Cœlestia: the Manual of St. Augustine. The Latin Text side by side with an English Interpretation, in 36 Odes, with Notes, *and* a plea *for the* Study *of* Mystic Theology. Large crown 8vo. Cloth, price 6s.

SMITH (Edward), M.D., LL.B., F.R.S.
Health and Disease, as Influenced by the Daily, Seasonal, and other Cyclical Changes in the Human System. A New Edition. Post 8vo. Cloth, price 7s. 6d.

Practical Dietary for Families, Schools, and the Labouring Classes. A New Edition. Post 8vo. Cloth, price 3s. 6d.

Tubercular Consumption in its Early and Remediable Stages. Second Edition. Crown 8vo. Cloth, price 6s.

Songs of Two Worlds. By the Author of "The Epic of Hades." Sixth Edition. Complete in one Volume, with Portrait. Fcap. 8vo. Cloth, price 7s. 6d.

Songs for Music. By Four Friends. Square crown 8vo. Cloth, price 5s. Containing songs by Reginald A. Gatty, Stephen H. Gatty, Greville J. Chester, and Juliana Ewing.

SPEDDING (James).
Reviews and Discussions, Literary, Political, and Historical, not relating to Bacon. Demy 8vo. Cloth, price 12s. 6d.

STAPFER (Paul).
Shakspeare and Classical Antiquity: Greek and Latin Antiquity as presented in Shakspeare's Plays. Translated by Emily J. Carey. Large post 8vo. Cloth, price 12s.

St. Bernard on the Love of God. Translated by Marianne Caroline and Coventry Patmore. Cloth extra, gilt top, price 4s. 6d.

STEDMAN (Edmund Clarence).
Lyrics and Idylls. With other Poems. Crown 8vo. Cloth, price 7s. 6d.

STEPHENS (Archibald John), LL.D.
The Folkestone Ritual Case. The Substance of the Argument delivered before the Judicial Committee of the Privy Council. On behalf of the Respondents. Demy 8vo. Cloth, price 6s.

STEVENS (William).
The Truce of God, and other Poems. Small crown 8vo. Cloth, price 3s. 6d.

STEVENSON (Robert Louis).
Virginibus, Puerisque, and other Papers. Crown 8vo. Cloth, price 6s.

STEVENSON (Rev. W. F.).
Hymns for the Church and Home. Selected and Edited by the Rev. W. Fleming Stevenson.
The most complete Hymn Book published.

STEVENSON (Rev. W. F.)—*continued.*
The Hymn Book consists of Three Parts :—I. For Public Worship.—II. For Family and Private Worship.—III. For Children.
*** *Published in various forms and prices, the latter ranging from* 8d. *to* 6s. *Lists and full particulars will be furnished on application to the Publishers.*

STOCKTON (Frank R.).
A Jolly Fellowship. With 20 Illustrations. Crown 8vo. Cloth, price 5s.

STORR (Francis), and TURNER Hawes).
Canterbury Chimes; or, Chaucer Tales retold to Children. With Illustrations from the Ellesmere MS. Extra Fcap. 8vo. Cloth, price 3s. 6d.

STRETTON (Hesba).
David Lloyd's Last Will. With Four Illustrations. Royal 16mo., price 2s. 6d.

The Wonderful Life. Thirteenth Thousand. Fcap. 8vo. Cloth, price 2s. 6d.

Through a Needle's Eye: a Story. Crown 8vo. Cloth, price 6s.

STUBBS (Lieut.-Colonel F. W.)
The Regiment of Bengal Artillery. The History of its Organization, Equipment, and War Services. Compiled from Published Works, Official Records, and various Private Sources. With numerous Maps and Illustrations. 2 vols. Demy 8vo. Cloth, price 32s.

STUMM (Lieut. Hugo), German Military Attaché to the Khivan Expedition.
Russia's advance Eastward. Based on the Official Reports of. Translated by Capt. C. E. H. VINCENT. With Map. Crown 8vo. Cloth, price 6s.

SULLY (James), M.A.
Sensation and Intuition. Demy 8vo. Second Edition. Cloth, price 10s. 6d.

Pessimism: a History and a Criticism. Demy 8vo. Price 14s.

Sunnyland Stories.
By the Author of "Aunt Mary's Bran Pie." Illustrated. Small 8vo. Cloth, price 3s. 6d.

Sweet Silvery Sayings of Shakespeare. Crown 8vo. Cloth gilt, price 7s. 6d.

SYME (David).
Outlines of an Industrial Science. Second Edition. Crown 8vo. Cloth, price 6s.

Tales from Ariosto. Retold for Children, by a Lady. With three illustrations. Crown 8vo. Cloth, price 4s. 6d.

TAYLOR (Algernon).
Guienne. Notes of an Autumn Tour. Crown 8vo. Cloth, price 4s. 6d.

TAYLOR (Sir H.).
Works Complete. Author's Edition, in 5 vols. Crown 8vo. Cloth, price 6s. each.
Vols. I. to III. containing the Poetical Works, Vols. IV. and V. the Prose Works.

TAYLOR (Col. Meadows), C.S.I., M.R.I.A.
A Noble Queen : a Romance (Indian History. New Edition. With Frontispiece. Crown 8vo. oth. Price 6s.

Seeta. New Edition with frontispiece. Crown 8vo. Cloth, price 6s.

Tippoo Sultaun: a Tale of the Mysore War. New Edition with Frontispiece. Crown 8vo. Cloth, price 6s.

Ralph Darnell. New Edition. With Frontispiece. Crown 8vo. Cloth, price 6s.

The Confessions of a Thug. New Edition. With Frontispiece. Crown 8vo. Cloth, price 6s.

Tara : a Mahratta Tale. New Edition. With Frontispiece. Crown 8vo. Cloth, price 6s.

TENNYSON (Alfred).
The Imperial Library Edition. Complete in 7 vols. Demy 8vo. Cloth, price £3 13s. 6d. ; in Roxburgh binding, £4 7s. 6d.

TENNYSON (Alfred)—*continued.*
Author's Edition. Complete in 6 Volumes. Post 8vo. Cloth gilt ; or half-morocco, Roxburgh style :—

VOL. I. **Early Poems, and English Idylls.** Price 6s. ; Roxburgh, 7s. 6d.

VOL. II. **Locksley Hall, Lucretius, and other Poems.** Price 6s. ; Roxburgh, 7s. 6d.

VOL. III. **The Idylls of the King** (*Complete*). Price 7s. 6d.; Roxburgh, 9s.

VOL. IV. **The Princess, and Maud.** Price 6s.; Roxburgh, 7s. 6d.

VOL. V. **Enoch Arden, and In Memoriam.** Price 6s. ; Roxburgh, 7s. 6d.

VOL. VI. **Dramas.** Price 7s.; Roxburgh, 8s. 6d.

Cabinet Edition. 12 vols. Each with Frontispiece. Fcap. 8vo. Cloth, price 2s. 6d. each.

CABINET EDITION. 12 vols. Complete in handsome Ornamental Case. 32s.

The Royal Edition. With 25 Illustrations and Portrait. Cloth extra, bevelled boards, gilt leaves. Price 21s.

The Guinea Edition. Complete in 12 vols., neatly bound and enclosed in box. Cloth, price 21s. French morocco or parchment, price 31s. 6d.

The Shilling Edition of the Poetical and Dramatic Works, in 12 vols., pocket size. Price 1s. each.

The Crown Edition. Complete in one vol., strongly bound in cloth, price 6s. Cloth, extra gilt leaves, price 7s. 6d. Roxburgh, half morocco, price 8s. 6d.

** Can also be had in a variety of other bindings.

TENNYSON (Alfred)—*continued.*

Original Editions:

Ballads and other Poems. Fcap. 8vo. Cloth, price 5s.

The Lover's Tale. (Now for the first time published.) Fcap. 8vo. Cloth, 3s. 6d.

Poems. Small 8vo. Cloth, price 6s.

Maud, and other Poems. Small 8vo. Cloth, price 3s. 6d.

The Princess. Small 8vo. Cloth, price 3s. 6d.

Idylls of the King. Small 8vo. Cloth, price 5s.

Idylls of the King. Complete. Small 8vo. Cloth, price 6s.

The Holy Grail, and other Poems. Small 8vo. Cloth, price 4s. 6d.

Gareth and Lynette. Small 8vo. Cloth, price 3s.

Enoch Arden, &c. Small 8vo. Cloth, price 3s. 6d.

In Memoriam. Small 8vo. Cloth, price 4s.

Queen Mary. A Drama. New Edition. Crown 8vo. Cloth, price 6s.

Harold. A Drama. Crown 8vo. Cloth, price 6s.

Selections from Tennyson's Works. Super royal 16mo. Cloth, price 3s. 6d. Cloth gilt extra, price 4s.

Songs from Tennyson's Works. Super royal 16mo. Cloth extra, price 3s. 6d.

Also a cheap edition. 16mo. Cloth, price 2s. 6d.

Idylls of the King, and other Poems. Illustrated by Julia Margaret Cameron. 2 vols. Folio. Half-bound morocco, cloth sides, price £6 6s. each.

Tennyson for the Young and for Recitation. Specially arranged. Fcap. 8vo. Price 1s. 6d.

Tennyson Birthday Book. Edited by Emily Shakespear. 32mo. Cloth limp, 2s.; cloth extra, 3s.

** A superior edition, printed in red and black, on antique paper, specially prepared. Small crown 8vo. Cloth extra, gilt leaves, price 5s.; and in various calf and morocco bindings.

Songs Set to Music, by various Composers. Edited by W. G. Cusins. Dedicated by express permission to Her Majesty the Queen. Royal 4to. Cloth extra, gilt leaves, price 21s., or in half-morocco, price 25s.

An Index to "In Memoriam." Price 2s.

THOMAS (Moy).
A Fight for Life. With Frontispiece. Crown 8vo. Cloth, price 3s. 6d.

THOMPSON (Alice C.).
Preludes. A Volume of Poems. Illustrated by Elizabeth Thompson (Painter of "The Roll Call"). 8vo. Cloth, price 7s. 6d.

THOMSON (J. Turnbull).
Social Problems; or, an Inquiry into the Law of Influences. With Diagrams. Demy 8vo. Cloth, price 10s. 6d.

THRING (Rev. Godfrey), B.A.
Hymns and Sacred Lyrics. Fcap. 8vo. Cloth, price 3s. 6d.

TODHUNTER (Dr. J.)
A Study of Shelley. Crown 8vo. Cloth, price 7s.

Alcestis: A Dramatic Poem. Extra fcap. 8vo. Cloth, price 5s.

Laurella; and other Poems. Crown 8vo. Cloth, price 6s. 6d.

Translations from Dante, Petrarch, Michael Angelo, and Vittoria Colonna. Fcap. 8vo. Cloth, price 7s. 6d.

TURNER (Rev. C. Tennyson).
Sonnets, Lyrics, and Translations. Crown 8vo. Cloth, price 4s. 6d.

TURNER (Rev. C. Tennyson)— *continued.*

Collected Sonnets, Old and New. With Prefatory Poem by Alfred Tennyson; also some Marginal Notes by S. T. Coleridge, and a Critical Essay by James Spedding. Fcap. 8vo. Cloth, price 7s. 6d.

TWINING (Louisa).
Recollections of Workhouse Visiting and Management during twenty-five years. Small crown 8vo. Cloth, price 3s. 6d.

UPTON (Major R. D.).
Gleanings from the Desert of Arabia. Large post 8vo. Cloth, price 10s. 6d.

VAUGHAN (H. Halford), sometime Regius Professor of Modern History in Oxford University.
New Readings and Renderings of Shakespeare's Tragedies. 2 vols. Demy 8vo. Cloth, price 25s.

VILLARI (Prof.).
Niccolo Machiavelli and His Times. Translated by Linda Villari. 2 vols. Large post 8vo. Cloth, price 24s.

VINCENT (Capt. C. E. H.).
Elementary Military Geography, Reconnoitring, and Sketching. Compiled for Non-Commissioned Officers and Soldiers of all Arms. Square crown 8vo. Cloth, price 2s. 6d.

VYNER (Lady Mary).
Every day a Portion. Adapted from the Bible and the Prayer Book, for the Private Devotions of those living in Widowhood. Collected and edited by Lady Mary Vyner. Square crown 8vo. Cloth extra, price 5s.

WALDSTEIN (Charles), Ph. D.
The Balance of Emotion and Intellect: An Essay Introductory to the Study of Philosophy. Crown 8vo. Cloth, price 6s.

WALLER (Rev. C. B.)
The Apocalypse, Reviewed under the Light of the Doctrine of the Unfolding Ages and the Restitution of all Things. Demy 8vo. Cloth, price 12s.

WALTERS (Sophia Lydia).
The Brook: A Poem. Small crown 8vo. Cloth, price 3s. 6d.

A Dreamer's Sketch Book. With Twenty-one Illustrations by Percival Skelton, R. P. Leitch, W. H. J. Boot, and T. R. Pritchett. Engraved by J. D. Cooper. Fcap. 4to. Cloth, price 12s. 6d.

WATERFIELD, W.
Hymns for Holy Days and Seasons. 32mo. Cloth, price 1s. 6d.

WATSON (William).
The Prince's Quest and other Poems. Crown 8vo. Cloth, price 5s.

WATSON (Sir Thomas), Bart., M.D.
The Abolition of Zymotic Diseases, and of other similar enemies of Mankind. Small crown 8vo. Cloth, price 3s. 6d.

WAY (A.), M.A.
The Odes of Horace Literally Translated in Metre. Fcap. 8vo. Cloth, price 2s.

WEBSTER (Augusta).
Disguises. A Drama. Small crown 8vo. Cloth, price 5s.

WEDMORE (Frederick).
The Masters of Genre Painting. With sixteen illustrations. Large crown 8vo. Cloth, price 7s. 6d.

Wet Days, by a Farmer. Small crown 8vo. Cloth, price 6s.

WHEWELL (William), D.D.
His Life and Selections from his Correspondence. By Mrs. Stair Douglas. With Portrait from a Painting by Samuel Laurence. Demy 8vo. Cloth, price 21s.

WHITAKER (Florence).
Christy's Inheritance. A London Story. Illustrated. Royal 16mo. Cloth, price 1s. 6d.

WHITE (A. D.), LL.D.
Warfare of Science. With Prefatory Note by Professor Tyndall. Second Edition. Crown 8vo. Cloth, price 3s. 6d.

32 A List of C. Kegan Paul & Co.'s Publications.

WHITNEY (Prof. W. D.)
Essentials of English Grammar for the Use of Schools. Crown 8vo. Cloth, price 3s. 6d.

WICKSTEED (P. H.).
Dante: Six Sermons. Crown 8vo. Cloth, price 5s.

WILKINS (William).
Songs of Study. Crown 8vo. Cloth, price 6s.

WILLIAMS (Rowland), D.D.
Stray Thoughts from the Note-Books of the Late Rowland Williams, D.D. Edited by his Widow. Crown 8vo. Cloth, price 3s. 6d.

Psalms, Litanies, Counsels and Collects for Devout Persons. Edited by his Widow. New and Popular Edition. Crown 8vo. Cloth, price 3s. 6d.

WILLIS (R.), M.D.
Servetus and Calvin: a Study of an Important Epoch in the Early History of the Reformation. 8vo. Cloth, price 16s.

William Harvey. A History of the Discovery of the Circulation of the Blood. With a Portrait of Harvey, after Faithorne. Demy 8vo. Cloth, price 14s.

WILLOUGHBY (The Hon. Mrs.).
On the North Wind—Thistledown. A Volume of Poems. Elegantly bound. Small crown 8vo. Cloth, price 7s. 6d.

WILSON (Erasmus).
Egypt of the Past. With Chromo-lithographs and numerous Illustrations in the Text. Crown 8vo. Cloth.

WILSON (H. Schütz).
The Tower and Scaffold. A Miniature Monograph. Large fcap. 8vo. Price 1s.

Within Sound of the Sea. By the Author of "Blue Roses," "Vera," &c. Third Edition. 2 vols. Crown 8vo. Cloth, gilt tops, price 12s.
** Also a cheaper edition in one vol. with frontispiece. Price 6s.

WOLLSTONECRAFT (Mary).
Letters to Imlay. With a Preparatory Memoir by C. Kegan Paul, and two Portraits in *eau forte* by Anna Lea Merritt. Crown 8vo. Cloth, price 6s.

WOLTMANN (Dr. Alfred), and WOERMANN (Dr. Karl).
History of Painting in Antiquity and the Middle Ages. Edited by Sidney Colvin. With numerous illustrations. Medium 8vo. Cloth, price 28s.; cloth, bevelled boards, gilt leaves, price 30s.

WOOD (Major-General J. Creighton).
Doubling the Consonant. Small crown 8vo. Cloth, price 1s. 6d.

WOODS (James Chapman).
A Child of the People, and other poems. Small crown 8vo. Cloth, price 5s.

Word was made Flesh. Short Family Readings on the Epistles for each Sunday of the Christian Year. Demy 8vo. Cloth, price 10s. 6d.

WRIGHT (Rev. David), M.A.
Waiting for the Light, and other Sermons. Crown 8vo. Cloth, price 6s.

YOUMANS (Eliza A.).
An Essay on the Culture of the Observing Powers of Children, especially in connection with the Study of Botany. Edited, with Notes and a Supplement, by Joseph Payne, F.C.P., Author of "Lectures on the Science and Art of Education," &c. Crown 8vo. Cloth, price 2s. 6d.

First Book of Botany. Designed to Cultivate the Observing Powers of Children. With 300 Engravings. New and Cheaper Edition. Crown 8vo. Cloth, price 2s. 6d.

YOUMANS (Edward L.), M.D.
A Class Book of Chemistry, on the Basis of the New System. With 200 Illustrations. Crown 8vo. Cloth, price 5s.

YOUNG (William).
Gottlob, etcetera. Small crown 8vo. Cloth, price 3s. 6d.

LONDON:—C. KEGAN PAUL & CO., 1, PATERNOSTER SQUARE.

www.ingramcontent.com/pod-product-compliance
Lightning Source LLC
Chambersburg PA
CBHW032034220426
43664CB00006B/466